Quilted All Day

The Prairie Journals of Ida Chambers Melugin
(1867–1955)

May angels twine for thee.
A wreath of immortality.
Your friend,
Lizzie Elliott
Iowa Falls, Iowa
Holland Dec 15 1881

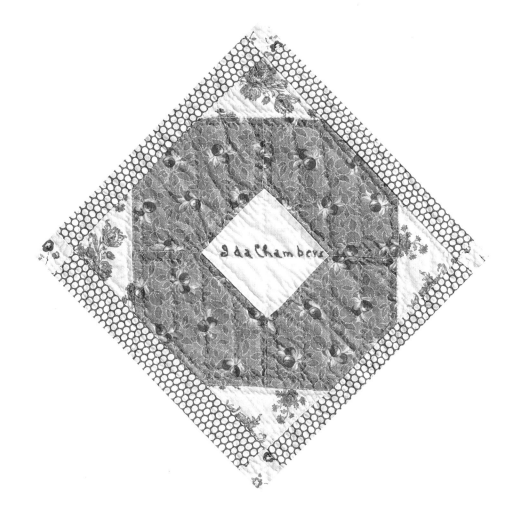

Quilted All Day

The Prairie Journals of Ida Chambers Melugin
(1867–1955)

By Carolyn O'Bagy Davis

SANPETE PUBLICATIONS
Tucson, Arizona

Ida C. Melugin, 1899.
Photo courtesy of Audry Gaunt.

Second Printing 1997
Library of Congress Catalog Card Number 92-62536
ISBN 0-9635092-0-9

Sanpete Publications
Post Office Box 85216
Tucson, Arizona 85754-5216

Fourth and State streets looking north. This is approximately the same view Ida had as she sat at her quilting frame each day in front of her parlor window. Photo courtesy of Rawlins County Historical Society.

Contents

Author's Notes

Many people have asked where I found the diaries of Ida Chambers Melugin, whose story is told in these pages. When I wrote to the Rawlins County Historical Society in Atwood, Kansas, in 1987, inquiring about a particular historic quilt, Inez Minney Walters, volunteer museum director at that time, replied that she did not have the particular item I had asked about, but if I liked quilts perhaps I would enjoy reading the quilting diaries that were in the house she had inherited from her mother, Lulu Lambach Minney.

After my immediate reply, Inez began sending one diary at a time, which I typed or photocopied and then returned to Kansas. After two years of correspondence, Inez wrote that she would allow me to borrow all of the Chambers' diaries and papers if I would go to Atwood to meet her. I quickly planned a trip and managed to convince my husband to drive across the state of Kansas in a winter snowstorm to spend one night with Jim and Inez Walters. That first meeting cemented our telephone- and letter-based friendship, and through the following years Inez has continued to share information, her home, and her knowledge of local history. This book could not have been written without her help and constant encouragement. As an inadequate acknowledgment, I would like to dedicate Ida's story to Inez Walters, who saved the diaries.

A few comments about the diaries will aid the reader in understanding them as well as Ida's life. Ida Chambers Melugin's earliest surviving diary begins in 1916, just months after the death of her husband, John. I do not believe that this was a coincidence or that widowhood suddenly inspired Ida to begin the daily discipline of journal writing at the age of forty-nine. A number of references in the diaries of Mary Chambers (Ida's mother), as well as comments made in interviews with Ida's family and with women who quilted with her, all indicate that Ida always kept a journal, and, indeed, from 1916 until her death in 1955, there are journals for nearly every year of the following four decades of her life.

There are two probable explanations for the loss of the diaries from the early years of her life. On the day that John died, Ida moved to her mother's home and never returned to live in the house she had shared with her husband for twenty-two years. Perhaps those diaries were lost or overlooked during that move or when Ida subsequently rented her old home. The other explanation, which is likely closer to the truth, is that Ida destroyed some of the early diaries herself. As every person does, Ida lived through times of trouble and loss, and there were events and tragedies in her life that in those times could not be righted and that she simply endured. I believe those early diaries held references to those troubles, which she never wanted revealed to others.

Fortunately, there are wonderful resources, including documents, photographs, letters, and Mary Chambers' diaries, which all contribute to piecing together the story

Jim and Inez Walters

of the early years of Ida's life. Among the collection of diaries are the surviving journals of Mary Chambers, which cover the years 1902 through 1919. Mary's daily entries are one or two pages each and detail the enormous amounts of domestic work she and her daughters were required to do each day. On Mondays, when they washed, Mary started the fire in the kitchen stove in the predawn darkness and carried in buckets of water pumped from the well behind the house to fill the wash-tubs. While the water was heating, she cooked breakfast and got her family fed and off to school and work. After breakfast was cleaned up and the dishes washed, the clothes were sorted, soaked, and rubbed. Then the actual washing could begin, all by hand. White clothes were boiled, then everything was rinsed in clean water, wrung out, and carried outside to be hung on the line to dry. In the event of a dust storm everything had to be washed again, and if it rained, clothes had to be brought in the house and spread about on chairs and tables to dry. During the winter, clothes froze into solid, flat sheets and had to be brought inside to thaw. Washing clothes took all day, and it was a good day if the women finished, emptied the tubs, mopped the floors, and got the dry clothes in before suppertime. Tuesday began with heating the "flats" to commence the day-long process of ironing. One interesting aspect of Mary's diaries is the detailing of the incredible amount of strenuous physical work completed each day by those hardy plains women.

Mary's diaries would make a fascinating study in themselves, not only for their wonderful detail, but also because her own sturdy character is revealed. She was intensely devoted to her family, and her love and concern for them is a constant theme. She brags about Rodney's high marks in school and frets when a girl gets a higher grade–he could have done better, of course, if only he had "applied himself." She is in anguish when one son becomes angry and won't talk with her for a few months. Her worry for the health and safety of her family mirrors every mother's timeless concerns.

Mary's writing is neat and legible, except when she is obviously upset or ill. She uses several delightful original spellings, such as "moped" for mopped and "couldent" for couldn't. Her early diaries use the then common "fs" for "ss." For a long time I thought her young boarder's name was Mifs Anderson. Only later did I realize that it was Miss Anderson she was referring to, and I never did learn her first name.

Throughout this book I have kept, as much as possible, the original form and spellings of the journals and letters. This has largely been possible because the Chambers family seems to have been quite well educated, and their writings are generally very legible. There are many abbreviations, such as M. E. Church for Methodist-Episcopal Church and Cong Church for Congregational Church. SS is Sunday School, WCTU is the Women's Christian Temperance Union, and OK is o'clock. None of the writings contain much punctuation, such as commas or periods, and few capital letters are used. An attempt has been made with spacing to indicate sentence breaks, but this was done sparingly because introducing spacing sometimes can change subtle meanings. The diaries and letters may take a bit longer to read and interpret without punctuation and spelling corrections, but it has been my observation that in reading the original diaries, the little bursts of understanding build a connection between the reader and the diarist's mood and intent at the time she sat writing in the book.

Nicknames were common in the Chambers family. Antoinette was always "Nette" (Nettee), and Mary's sister, Celestia Rose, was "Aunt Let." Mira's name, incidentally, was pronounced Myra. In all of Ida's early journals, her niece Doris is called "Toodles." Ida's brother, William

Henry, was known as "Henry", brother Charlie's wife, Minerva, was "Nerve," and Jesse's wife, Leona, was "Ona." John and Mary Chambers were known to their family and most people of Atwood as Pa and Ma.

Five of Nette's diaries exist today. They cover the years from 1902 through 1941. Nette, however, was not a faithful daily writer. Her entries are sporadic, sometimes with gaps of several years between writings. Some entries are brief, consisting of just a sentence or two, while at other times she writes quite intensively for a time. Her last diary, begun in 1937, is the longest and contains the most consistent entries. Of course, Nette's diaries tend to reflect her wonderful, outgoing personality. Nette's journals contain recipes, pressed flowers, poetry, lists of books she read, movies she attended, and all of the clubs, church and musical events, socials, and meetings that she loved so much.

In contrast, Ida's nine surviving diaries reflect her home-centered interests. Covering the years 1916 through 1955, Ida's daily writings reveal a woman devoted to her home and family. She cleaned and cooked and gardened; she attended a few town musical and social events and many church and temperance meetings, but Ida's constant and nearly daily theme was quilting. Quilting was interwoven with every association Ida joined. Quilting for others provided a tiny income, and quilting for her family was a common occurrence. Ida's diaries are an absolute treasure of quilting lore and reflect the intense love and lifelong devotion some women hold for the craft.

When Ida "worked with pieces" she was marking, cutting, and hand stitching the various squares and triangles that made up a quilt block. If she got "batten" or "lining" at the general store, she had purchased the cotton batting or filler for a quilt, and the lining was stitched together for the back of the quilt. The lining and top were then stitched onto muslin strips tacked onto the wooden quilt frames; she "sewed the lining into the frames." Quilting,

Hazel Gaunt

Audry Gaunt

Doris Gaunt Shaeffer

7

of course, is the hand stitching in long, running stitches that held the pieced top, batting, and lining together.

After the quilting was finished, the quilt was taken off the frames, and the raw edges were covered with a binding sewn around the edges. The last step, and a favorite of most quilters, including Ida, was a visit to a neighbor to show off the newly finished quilt.

Ida's diaries are very much like her own character–brief, tidy, legible, to the point, and practical. With her long, brown hair always pulled back into a neat bun, her clean house and crisp white apron, soft-spoken Ida was ordinary, organized, devoted and dependable–a dear, lovable, and caring lady, very much like many of our own beloved aunts and grandmothers. In reading her plain words, an intense awareness of Ida's enduring presence envelopes the reader. In her soft and unassuming way, she reaches across the years and allows you into her home and her life. It is easy to visualize her sitting across the quilt frame, sharing quiet hours of talk and stitching.

I would like to thank the many people who shared their time and information. Without their assistance this book could not have been written. Thank you to the wonderful people of Atwood, Kansas, and especially everyone at the Atwood Public Library and Natalie Mickey, director of the Rawlins County Historical Society. Also, thanks to Wilbur Leebrick, who answered many questions about Ida's homestead, and Lance Leebrick, who didn't mind my unannounced visit to his barn one summer afternoon and who graciously showed me about the claim and the site where Ida's sod house once stood. Thank you also to the many people who shared stories and memories about Ida and her family, answered questions, and sent information in response to my many requests.

Ida's family deserves a special mention. For many years, Pat Chambers Thomas has corresponded and shared diaries, photos, genealogy, and her wonderful quilts. Jean Gillette Gilbert in Texas also provided information and much support to this research. And although she is not a family member, Evelyn Hartman, a former neighbor of Ida's in Atwood, shared her beautiful Friendship quilt, which Ida made in the 1930s. And to Mira's family, Audry Gaunt, Hazel Gaunt, and Doris Gaunt Shaeffer, I owe a tremendous debt of gratitude. In addition to providing invaluable information and family stories, they shared their most valuable family heirlooms: century-old letters, photographs, and of course, the quilts. Audry allowed me to borrow a bundle of Chambers' family letters, more than two dozen old and irreplaceable photographs, and Ida's delightful 1881 autograph book. Many times I held it in my hands and pictured her as a young girl getting ready to set off for a new home in western Kansas. To Audry: I especially value your great trust.

Hazel and Doris are also warm and generous ladies, and the loan of their quilts made Ida's story come vigorously alive. I did sense a moment of worry in their eyes when I drove off to the photography studio in Denver, the back of my car packed to the roof with their quilts. I was, after all, a stranger, known to them only through the telephone and letters. But again, their trust and support were invaluable gifts and a responsibility much treasured.

I would like to thank my quilting friend, Helen Young Frost, author, teacher and lecturer. Her advice and comments are always valued, and her quilt drawings and patterns are a beautiful addition to the book. Helen's instructions will give many of us the pleasure of stitching Ida's lovely quilts.

The last thank you goes to my own dear family. My husband and children are all proud and supportive and have grown quite used to the cold dinners and an untidy house spread with books and boxes of research material when I am in the last stages of a project. So a much overdue thank you goes to Travis, Paul, Laura, Leah, and John Henry. And to my husband, John, who traveled nearly 6,000 miles on research trips, gave support, criticisms, and wonderful advice and sometimes even cooked our dinners, I give the dearest thank you of all.

Foreword

The writings of the women in the Chambers family are a wonderful find. From my perspective as a quilt historian, I see them as a remarkable description of quilting's role in women's lives. In research with the board of the Kansas Quilt Project, we were thrilled to come across the writings of Mary Schenck Ellison, who recorded thirty instances of quiltmaking in a six-month diary. At the time we considered hers to be an unusually extensive record. Imagine my delight to read Carolyn Davis's account of Ida Chambers Melugin's far more prodigious writings on the topic.

The completeness of Ida's references is valuable because it gives us insight into aspects of quiltmaking that we cannot uncover in reading the published patterns or in examining the surviving quilts. Her "pie quilts," with the words "cherry" or "apple" above each block, are an excellent example of a trend that was not recorded in print. Were pie quilts a national design that was passed around hand to hand in the 1930s rather than through the newspapers and magazines? Or were they a local fad in Atwood? Such glimpses into a previously unrecorded past generate questions that may be answered by the growing numbers of quilt historians, like Carolyn Davis. What is a "comforter protector?" (At first I thought it might be the strip on the end that protects the top of the comforter, but then it seemed Ida meant a top to be made into a comforter.) Mary's reference to quilting at a 1902 meeting of the Women's Christian Temperence Union is a find. What kinds of quilts did the WCTU make? Did they quilt Drunkard's Paths, Capital T's and Temperance Trees, or just plain nine-patch quilts?

The completeness of the Chambers family's records also give us insight by what they omitted. Like Carolyn, I am curious about the sparseness of specific quilt pattern names. Most diarists refer to their quilts by names such as the pink quilt or Aunt Nancy's quilt, rather than as the Log Cabin or the Dove in the Window. I have always suspected that this omission was evidence that the quilter of a hundred years ago had little knowledge of the colorful names we take so for granted today. But Ida's consistent use of a more generic name for the quilt she is sewing indicates that women use generic names because that is the way they think about their own quilts, whether or not they know a more poetic name. Ida worked in the 1930s when hundreds of newspapers printed patterns with names like Trip Around the World, Anvil and Turkey Tracks. She must have been familiar with such names, yet she, like nineteenth-century diarists, rarely mentioned the romantic names. Readers who are both quilters and diarists might check their own writing to see how often they mention specific pattern names. Or do they write about the blue quilt, the star quilt or Jenny's quilt?

The Chambers papers also give us an appreciation of the social network that quiltmaking offered. The women quilted with friends and family and in women's organizations. Ida's limited social life (limited as compared to sister Nette's) revolved around the Methodist-Episcopal Church and its sewing groups. Quilters may note that things have not changed too much. Ida's devotion to the creative process of quiltmaking and to the quiltmaking community is much like the lives of today's dedicated quilters. We need only substitute words like "Quilters Guild" and "Workshop" for "Ladies Aid" and "Sunday School" and Ida's life parallels ours.

Best of all, the papers reveal to us the intimate lives of Mary Chambers, Nette Chambers, and Ida Melugin. We sense the connectedness of women living in a group and see an alternative to the usual historical perspective of women as wives and mothers only. These single women and widows relied on each other as friends, sisters, and companions. They looked to women's organizations, such as the Eastern Star and the Ladies Aid, for their social lives. And they added to their extended family with high school boarders and orphaned children. Grief over death, illness, poverty, and betrayal were all cushioned with family love. The warmth of a large, loving family in a small town shines through in every entry in these diaries.

Barbara Brackman
Lawrence, Kansas

Barbara Brackman, a Kansas resident, is a widely known quilt historian, teacher, author, and lecturer. She is a regular contributor to *Quilter's Newsletter Magazine*, the American Quilt Study Group's *Uncoverings*, *Quilt Digest*, *Americana*, and *Fiberarts*. She is the author of *Encyclopedia of Pieced Quilt Patterns* and *Clues in the Calico: A Guide to Identifying and Dating Antique Quilts*. Brackman also serves as a consultant to state quilt projects, is a member of the board of the Kansas Quilt Project, and has curated quilt exhibits for museums and galleries.

Wheatfield near Chardon Corners, Rawlins County, Kansas.

Homestead Years

At seventeen years of age, John Henry Chambers left his home in Pendleton County, Kentucky, to go out on his own. He eventually journeyed to Illinois, where he made good friends and worked for farmers plowing and harvesting. In the fall of 1859, John hired out to work for Demus Grippen for one year. His pay was eleven dollars per month. While working for Mr. Grippen, John met Grippen's fifteen-year-old niece, Mary Angeline Thorne. They were married two years later at her uncle's home; Mary was seventeen and John was just a week short of his twentieth birthday. John later wrote: "My girl looked lovely in her linsy wolsy dress and they gave us a fine party afterwards." The union proved to be a long and loving marriage, lasting more than half a century and producing a closely bonded family of four girls and five boys.

The year of their marriage also saw the beginning of a great civil war. John was a staunch believer in the causes of the North and a firm backer of President Lincoln. He also knew that it was just a matter of time until he would be drafted into the Union army, so in the summer following his marriage, John enlisted in the 74th Regiment of the Illinois Voluntary Infantry. His absence from home lasted nearly three years except for one or two brief visits.

During the hard years that John was away at war, Mary lived on their rented farm on the Tras Bridge and Rockford Road. Charlie Thorne was born in the winter of 1863, seven months after John had joined the army. Fortunately, with her uncle living nearby, along with her cousin, Nancy Herring and her husband, John, Mary did have some family help and support. A second son, William Henry, was born two years later, just a few weeks after John's discharge from the army.

Returning to farming in the fall of 1865, the family moved to Winnebago, Illinois, where John rented a farm and supported his growing family by farming on shares and renting out his team. Ida Bell was born on January 28, 1867, followed a year later by Angeline Celestia and Marie Antoinette in 1870. Now supporting a family of seven, John looked to the west, where he could acquire his own farm. In the summer of 1870 he went to Grundy County, Iowa, where he worked for a Mr. Wilson breaking prairie. In October he sent for Mary to come out and bring their five children, ranging from Charlie, who was sixteen, to Marie Antoinette, or Nette as she was always known, who was just three weeks old. The family spent that winter on Mr. Jake Whilbeck's place. John later wrote that it was one of the coldest winters he recalled: "We saw the hardest time that winter we had ever seen." He credits "Ma's good courage" with getting them through that time.

In the spring the family bought a small farm of their own. At forty acres it was too small for their needs, but it was the only place available. John later rented additional acreage for raising various crops. The Chambers family spent the next fifteen years at Holland, Iowa, and the family grew with the birth of Jesse Sherwood, born in 1875, John Garfield, born in 1878, and Mira Ethlyn in 1880, totaling eight children. The following is a letter from Mary Chambers to her mother, with a note added from eleven-year-old Ida:

Holland Grundy Co. Iowa
January 20th 1878
Sunday evening

Dear ma Leet [Mary's sister, Celestia Rose]
and Charlie
How do you do we are all usualy well Jesse has a very bad cold but it dont seem to make him sick but he coughs so nights we cant any of us sleep. I got your letter Thursday 1 oclock. so you see we can hear from each other often if we only write you wanted to know how I got along on the road. I went to Freeport all right got my trunk checked and bought my ticket (I paid $5.95 to Hartford) just as the train come up got on all right but when the conductor come on for tickets he wanted half fare for both girls I told him I hadent got it he said you no buisness to get on the train then. I asked him how much it would be he said $3 to Dubuque I only had a dollar and a half. I gave him that and he said no more and when I changed cars at Dubuque the conductor wanted half fare for one of them but I dident have it he was pretty mad but that was all the good it done him I was mad to I dident enjoy my ride home a bit. they were the same conductors I had when I went down I guess they dident feel very good. I was awful tired when I got to Hartford and then I had to ride 6 miles in a lumber wagon over the roughest roads you ever see, and it was real cold to I was most froze when we got to Charlies and I received a very cool welcom there but I staid all night and Charlie hitched our frisky team in the morning and was a going to take me over to Aunt Sallys and when he turned around they both jumped in to a run they got away from him and run till they got ready to stop they first throwed off the bar broke the reach and they run with fore wheels till the neck yoke come down then the tongue run about three feet in to the ground and broke it off I tell you they scattered things pretty well but they soon got things togather again I got over to Aunt Sallys about ten and she made me a cup of tea the first thing she was glad to see me I went there Thursday and stayed there until the next Tuesday only

Mary Angeline Thorne Chambers and Charlie Thorne Chambers, 1864. Photo courtesy of Atwood Public Library.

one day and night I stayed with Mira she has moved to the Falls now I ought to tell you Charlie was not in the wagon he was walking by the side of the wagon and they jerked the lines right out of his hands I was afraid John would blame him but he dident he said he couldent hold them himself

Dear Grandma I thought I would finish up ma's letter she has gone up to Mrs Smith today to help her wash she told me to finish it up I will tell you what I got christmas I got a nice Slipper all cuverd with shell it cost 25 cts and some candy besides tell mable I think lots of that little churn and the little tin pail and little box and that motto that aunt let gave me and that other one tell mable and mary I think of them lots of times tell aunt mattie I think lots of them pieces [presumably fabric scraps for quiltmaking] write soon love to you all kiss mable and mary for me goodby

An 1883 letter written by Grandmother Thorne to her daughter Mary Chambers has also survived the years:

To: Mrs. Mary A. Chambers
         Holland, Grundy Co. Iowa
         Fairmont May 27: 1883
Dear children
    Ange thinks it has ben a long time sence I

In the fall of 1864 John H. Chambers was twenty-three years old. He was a tall (6'2"), handsome man with blue eyes and light hair. He had just grown a beard, which he liked so much that he wore one for the rest of his life. He had his photo taken while on leave from his service in the Union army to send to his wife, Mary, back at the farm in Illinois.

John Henry Chambers

John Henry Chambers was a great admirer of Abraham Lincoln and in July 1862, when the president called for 600,000 men to fight in the war against slavery, John and his cousin "left the women folks home to dig the potatoes and husk the corn" and traveled to Durand, Illinois, where they enrolled in Captain Rufus D. Pettit's "H" Company, 74th Regiment of the Illinois Voluntary Infantry. John had been married to Mary Angeline Thorne for only nine months, and except for a couple of brief visits, his leaving began a separation that lasted nearly three years. In John's handwritten memoirs he described his years in the war. In the Battle of Perryville, "we laid on the battlefield the next day and I saw for the first time dead

soldiers lying over the field. it was quiet, terribly quiet. We could even hear some birds singing. Tangles of bodies, in blue and grey, and abandoned equipment were everywhere." That day was John's twenty-first birthday. Later came the Battle of Stones River and other clashes and long marches. John was eventually hospitalized with a severe illness and after a long recuperation was transferred to the Veterans Reserve Corps on August 1, 1863. He was stationed in Albany, New York, and his duties included guarding Confederate prisoners.

On April 9, 1865, General Lee surrendered to General Grant at the Appomattox Courthouse. The war had ended and all the soldiers in Company "F" were looking forward to receiving their discharges and

returning to their homes. With a few days off duty, John and a friend decided to go to the city of Washington and "look around for the last time." The two soldiers arrived in town on the morning of April 14, 1865, and bought tickets to see Miss Laura Keene in the play *"Our American Cousin."* They walked the city streets, toured the capitol building, and climbed to the top of the dome. Later they had dinner at the Willard Hotel and arrived early at Ford's Theater.

There was great excitement because the President and Mrs. Lincoln were expected shortly. Their box was decorated with American flags, and when they entered the theater the entire house stood up, clapping and cheering. To John, the president looked "tired and sad." He bowed once and then sat down. The play commenced and proceeded until the third act, when there was a lot of commotion and confusion. Then a woman screamed and someone shouted, "He shot the President." There was panic in the audience and outside on the streets a pushing and shoving mob gathered. John and his friend, both in uniform, helped guards clear a path through the crowd for the tragic procession leaving the theater: five soldiers carried the president, followed by two doctors, Mrs. Lincoln, Laura Keene, and another lady. The president was carried to a house across the street, where he died in the early morning hours of April fifteen.

John and some other members of his company were given permission to pay their last respects to their "late beloved president." They stood in line for hours to pass Lincoln's body lying in state in the Capitol building. John wrote: "It was a parade of sorrowUnder that gigantic dome, nothing was…heard but unashamed sobbing and the shuffling of feet. We had only a moment to see his face. He looked so calm and peaceful…With an intense devotion to the cause he was serving, he had guided this nation through a terrible war to victory, and now he was promoted to greatness and was perhaps the last soldier to give his life on the battlefield that was the Civil War."

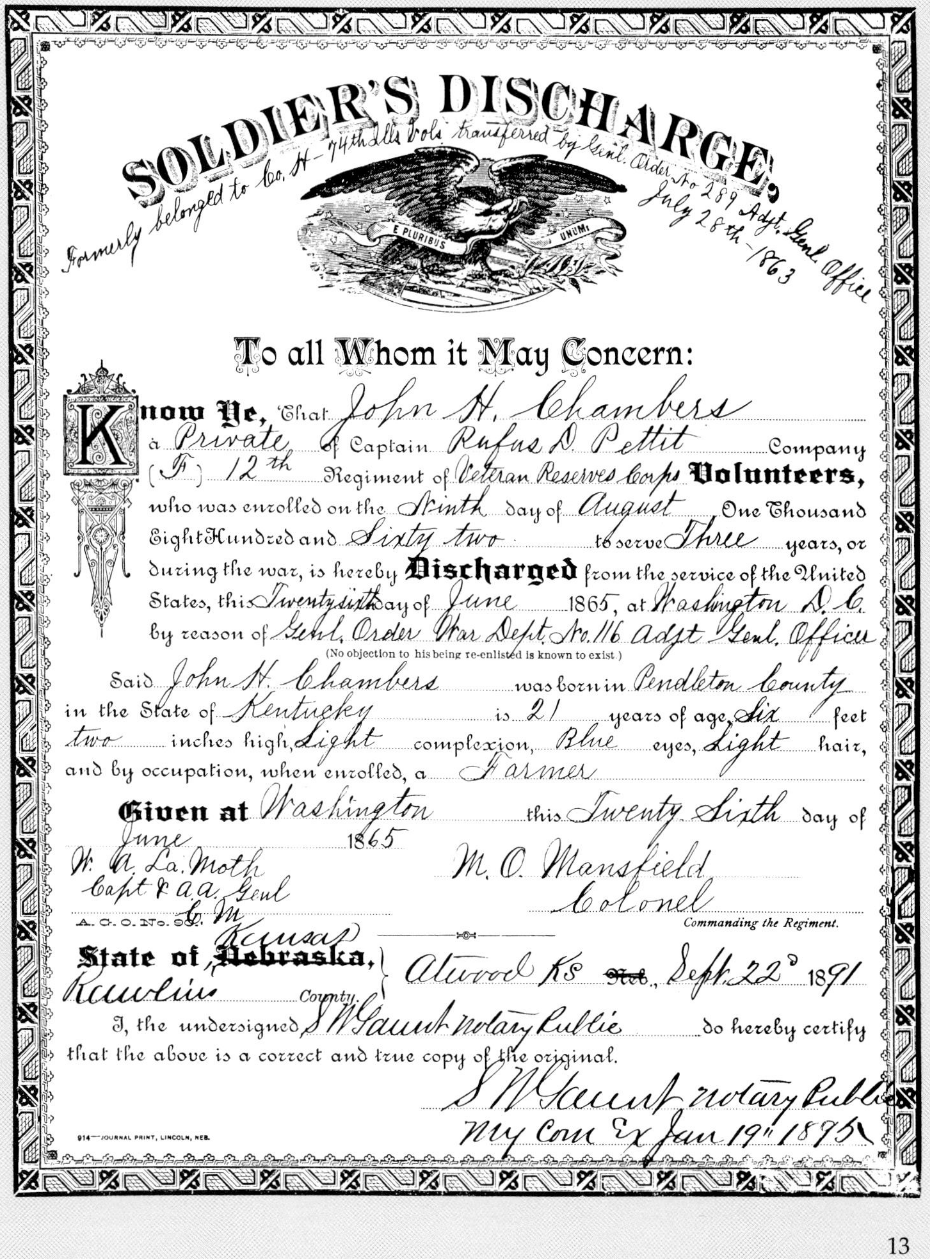

SOLDIER'S DISCHARGE.

Formerly belonged to Co. H 94th Ills Vols transferred by Genl Order No 289 July 28th 1863 Adjt Genl Office

To all Whom it May Concern:

Know Ye, That John H. Chambers a Private of Captain Rufus D. Pettit Company (F.) 12th Regiment of Veteran Reserves Corps Volunteers, who was enrolled on the Ninth day of August One Thousand Eight Hundred and Sixty two to serve Three years, or during the war, is hereby Discharged from the service of the United States, this Twenty sixth day of June 1865, at Washington D. C. by reason of Genl. Order War Dept. No. 116 Adjt Genl. Office

(No objection to his being re-enlisted is known to exist.)

Said John H. Chambers was born in Pendleton County in the State of Kentucky is 21 years of age, Six feet two inches high, Light complexion, Blue eyes, Light hair, and by occupation, when enrolled, a Farmer

Given at Washington this Twenty Sixth day of June 1865

W. A. La. Moth
Capt & a.a. Genl
A. G. O. No. 99.

M. O. Mansfield
Colonel
Commanding the Regiment.

State of Nebraska, Kansas, Atwood KS ret. Sept. 22° 1891
Rawlins County.

I, the undersigned S W Gaunt Notary Public do hereby certify that the above is a correct and true copy of the original.

S W Gaunt Notary Public
My Com Ex Jan 19" 1875

814—JOURNAL PRINT, LINCOLN, NEB.

It is likely that the tiny red- and silver-stamped souvenir book was a gift on the occasion of Ida's fourteenth birthday. The inscription inside reads "Ida Chambers Jan. 28, 1881," and entries are dated 1881 through 1883. Ida packed the book in her trunk and carried it with her on the move from Holland, Iowa, to the family's new homestead in western Kansas.

well Anges school is most out and she is awfull glad she hasent seemed to like her school atall I dont know as it is a going to do her much good to go I have got most discouredy we all went to memorial servis today at the methodist church had a splendid sermon, Wednesday is decoration day they will decorate the graves here in the morning then they all go to Geneva and have a big day thare was about 75 soldiers here today all dressed in uniform marched in to church and was seated in the body pews John dont you wish you was here I do crops are looking just splendid here all but corn that is rather backward but warm weather will soon fetch it along

I had a letter from Arte and Matt last weak he has commenced buylding on my place he is very busy now love to all write as often as you can

from Ma Thorne

I cant get Lette to write any one isent she mean

wrote to you but it realy seemes as if I had more to hender me from writing than ever I am more nervous than ever and thare is so much confusion I cant write but thare is no one els that will do it so I will have to try well I got so far and Charley drove up with a double carage for us all to go riding we drove over to Lellys and they ware all gone so we had to come back again I wish I had stayed at home and done my writing well we had Billy Patten and family here all day yesterday and it seamed as if I could go crazy he is looking for a location he has sold out his hard ware store in Winnebago

John and Mary eventually bought a lot in the town of Holland and built a house while John continued to rent land for farming. It was a difficult living, however, and when Mr. Moffet sold his farm after renting it to John for several years, the Chambers family decided to move west again and take up some of the free government land. From his army service John received a pension of two dollars per month and $448 back pension. This money gave the Chambers family the financial means to relocate, and in the spring of 1885, they loaded their belongings onto a railroad car and went west to search for a claim. John rented a home in Indianola, Nebraska, for a month, as that is the area where the family initially planned to settle. He then set out to search for an

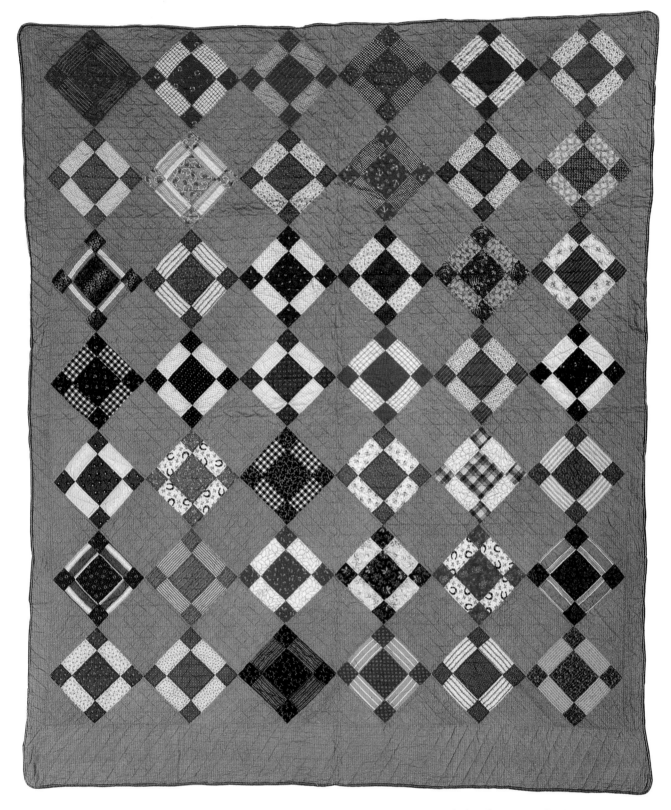

Puss in the Corner quilt, 70½" x 82½", c. 1890s. Ida's earliest surviving quilt is the lovely Puss in the Corner pattern. The forty-two hand-pieced blocks are set on the point and each pieced block alternates with a solid block. In a corner on the back of the quilt Ida embroidered her name. Quilt courtesy of Hazel Gaunt. Photography by Brian S. Birlauf, Birlauf and Steen Photo, Denver, Colorado.

unclaimed homestead.

John and Mary's oldest daughter, Ida, who was eighteen in 1885, found it difficult to part with her many dear friends in Iowa, where she had spent most of her growing up years. Her younger sister, Angie, was staying behind with relatives. Angie wanted to get a teaching certificate, a goal that would not be immediately obtainable in the new territory to which the family was moving. She stayed on in Holland for two more years until her studies were completed before rejoining her family. Ida, however, chose to go west in spite of her sorrow at parting with her Iowa friends. On February 7, 1885, a girlhood friend wrote in her autograph book: "Friend Ida; When far away in Nebraska, remember the Carpet rag sewing, at Your friend's, Carrie E. Maubry." Maggie Bowersock wrote, "May the hinges of our Friendship never rust."

But as much as Ida hated leaving her friends, it would have been more difficult for her to be separated from her family. If Angie was the scholar of the clan, Ida was the homebody. At 5' 4", with hazel eyes and light brown hair, Ida had a quiet beauty that complemented her soft-spoken manner. And even in a time when strong family ties were perhaps more commonplace than in today's mobile society, Ida's devotion to her parents and siblings was exceptional and lifelong.

As she packed her small trunk in preparation for her last move west, she included her photograph album, which was inscribed inside with her name: "Ida Chambers Dec 2 1881 Holland Iowa" She later wrote: "Pa give me this before we come to Kans." Ida also slipped into the trunk a small souvenir book containing the autographs and remembrances of her friends. The tiny 2"-by-4" volume contained entries dated from 1881 through 1883 and the carefree thoughts of young girls, such as:

> "Remember me and bare in mind that pretty
>   boy's are hard to find
> but when you find one handsome and gay,
> hang on to his coattail night and day."
>   Lizzie

On October 25, 1883 Eva Nought wrote:

> As sure as comes your wedding day,
>   A broom to you I'll send;
> In sunshine, use the brushy part
>   In storms, the other end.

And in an entry that was prophetic of the lifelong love and caring between the sisters, Nette penned the following lines:

> Round is the ring that has no end
> so is my love for you my Friend
>   Your sister
>   NC

Jan 19 1883   Holland

On a more serious note, Ida's aunt made the following somber inscription:

> Dear Ida-
>   Remember me, till death shall close
> These eyelids in their last repose.
> The evening breeze shall gently wave
> The flowers that bloom
>   on Aunt Lett's grave.
>   July 12, 1882

With the help of Jack Mikesell, John filed on a 160-acre claim in Mikesell Township, Township 4, Range 34, Section 27, located about twelve miles southwest of Atwood, Kansas. Twenty-two-year-old Charlie took a section to the southwest, and the father and son also filed for timber claims. In the belief that increased trees and vegetation would boost annual rainfall and improve conditions for agriculture in the midwest ("rain follows the plow" was a popular slogan of the time), the legislature created the Timber Culture Act of 1873, which allowed a homesteader an additional 160 acres provided that one-fourth of the land was planted in trees within four years. John immediately built a 20'-by-36' sod house consisting of three rooms with four doors, five windows, and a board roof. On the twelfth day of May, he and Mary and seven children moved in, with their furniture listed on their homestead application as consisting of:

1 stove. 3 Bed stids & Beding. 2 cupboards. 1 Beaurow. 1 sewing machine. 12 chairs. 3 Tables.

That first summer the dirt-floored house was left unplastered while John, Charlie, and Henry broke about twenty acres of sod and raised three hundred bushels of corn, some potatoes, and watermelons. The following winter of 1885–86 was especially cold with a great deal of snow. In one terrible blizzard in January 1886, so much snow fell that fences and even trees were completely covered. In the absence of trees and wood for fuel, the Chambers, like all prairie families, gathered a good supply of buffalo and cow chips, or "cow wood," and saved corncobs and stalks to burn for heat and cooking through the long winter.

Ma was especially dependent on Ida's help that first year in the sod house because she was expecting their ninth child, Artemus Royal, who was born on October 4, 1885. Because the Chambers lived out on the prairie far from a doctor or neighbors, it is likely that eighteen-year-old Ida assisted her mother during the delivery, as she did in later years with her sister's children. Perhaps it was the harsh climate and the exceptionally brutal coming winter, but Artemus was the only one of John and Mary's children who failed to grow to adulthood. Little Artemus died the following summer at nine months of age.

A sod schoolhouse was built for the homesteaders'

Ida's Sod House

Left to right: Minerva and Charlie Chambers, Ida Bell Chambers, Mr. Mallory and Henry Chambers, 1888. Photo courtesy of Audry Gaunt.

A sod house with two doors on the same sidewall was quite unusual on the midwestern frontier, but not for brother and sister Charlie and Ida Chambers, who homesteaded adjoining sections of land in Rawlins County, Kansas, near Chardon Corners. Their sod house straddled the boundary of their claims and with the two doorways each could enter the house from their own land. The sod building blocks were cut from the dense buffalo grass and after the walls were up the sides were shaved or trimmed smooth. The house has no visible ridgepoles or beams on the gabled roof, but there was a board roof, probably topped with tar paper and then a layer of sod on top with a second layer of sod blocks on the ridge top and down along the sides of the roof.

The eight pane, double frame window is rounded off and plastered to seal off cracks and admit more light. The doors are recessed to leave an alcove-type entryway, and the openings are also plastered. The board threshold indicated that it was likely that there was a board floor. There is also a rock stepping stone visible in front of the left entryway. One stove pipe can be seen in the center of the roof ridge, indicating that rather than a fireplace, Ida and Charlie had a stove set in the center of their shared home.

In the photo Charlie and his wife Minerva are standing to the left next to a horse drawn mower which was used to cut the wild prairie grasses. These grasses grew to a height of several feet and were mowed, raked and stacked for winter feed. Interestingly, their pet dog was included in this photograph as well as their two teams of horses, one hitched to a wagon and the other to a plow.

Today nothing remains of Ida and Charlie's sod home but a round, mounded area that is never planted in crops, plowing over the area always turns up bits of tin and purple glass. And the last remnants of their presence are the ruts of a wagon trail that stretches across the prairie paralleling an old fence line.

Sod house information courtesy of Barbara Oringderff, author of *True Sod*. Special thanks to Wilbur and Lance Leebrick, owners of the Chambers' homesteads.

children about four miles west of the Chambers' claim. Ida's schooling was complete, but the four younger children walked the eight-mile round trip to school every day the following spring. A church was also organized in 1886, and construction was begun on the lovely Stevens Chapel, or the Stone Church. The children walked to Sunday School at Jake Becker's sod house, and because the chapel was not completed for several years, church services were held at the home of the preacher, "Uncle" Dick Stevens, for whom the church was named.

The years on the claim were hard but not without progress. As John and the older boys broke more sod, they fenced more acreage and planted corn, rye, oats, millet, and potatoes. John plastered the house and laid a board floor. They built a sod stable measuring 18' by 36', a 12'-by-14' chicken house, and a hog shed, and they dug a well and a cave for food storage. The family planted twenty fruit trees and four hundred forest trees, and their livestock numbered three horses, three cows, and five hogs.

Undoubtedly, John's back pension pay contributed heavily to the Chambers family's relative prosperity. The daughter of another settler remembered that when her family started out on the western journey their total cash assets amounted to only nine dollars, while the Chambers had the princely sum of $448.[1] Even John Chambers' $2.00 monthly pension would have been a significant benefit. In western Kansas in the 1880s money was scarce and a dollar was hard to come by for the sod house settlers. Most often a man had to leave his family for weeks or months to look for employment. Then, if he was lucky, he might get work that would pay as little as $1.50 per week. Most sod homes of the time had a sod roof and dirt floor. The Chambers home had a board roof, a true luxury in a land with no trees, and a real blessing as it kept mud, snakes, and bugs from dropping onto the tables and beds of the inhabitants below. The eventual addition of the board floor must have been a joy for Mary Chambers. Even with the board roof the house was very damp during rains. A grandson, Jesse Gaunt, later wrote: "Whenever it rained they would sleep with umbrellas over them to keep dry, after it had rained a while the pictures would begin to fall down because the stakes had been washed out."

Angie, who had stayed behind in Iowa to attend school, wrote the following letter to her family in Kansas:

> Holland, Ia.
> Feb. 6th 1886
>
> Dear brother Charley
>   I rec. your kind and welcome letter yesterday and you may guess I was glad to hear from you and that you were all well. we have had some awful cold weather here but it is warmer now it was awful nice to day I had a sleigh ride to day It seems so nice to take a sleigh ride without freezing half to death
>   All the ladies in town were here this afternoon sewing for Harmes. We have told you I suppose that Mrs Harmes has had two strokes of the parylises She cant speak now. They are on the town now. Oh! Charley what do you think we have a brass band in Holland what do you think of that. Thank you for your kind invitation but please dont look for us for I fear you will be disapointed. Well our dance

The high, rolling prairie of Ida's claim is bisected by the north branch of Sappa Creek.

Stevens Chapel, the Stone Church.

did not come off but they had one out to Hoover's the night before we intended to have our and the[n] we had the worst blizzard of the season that night and had to stay all night and then in the morning Mrs S and I walked home. Well Charley as I want to write to the girls I will close hoping to hear from you soon I remain your ever loving sister. Angie

Dear Sister Nettie

how do you do this fine evening. we are all well but Wess is awful tierd well Nett I hope you have lots of fun down in Kansas we havn't had very many dances here this winter and what we did have were very good. I seen Bob and told him and he seemed pleased to think you thought of him and Clarence said to tell you Hello for him we had examination yesterday We are almost through our physoligy and to the second year of the Civil war. We have two new scholars two Miller boys' both young men so you see we have quite a large school. Well Nett where has Eddie gone You dont say any thing about him any more Well this paper is nearly full and I am tired. Oh yes we are going to have new neighbors Jim Krugers on our left Treeches house and Charley Badgies across the street in Treniles they are moving down over the store and Treniles are going back to the farm you must have the

babys picture taken [Artemus was four months old] and tell the little and Mira Angie would like to see them awful well but she sends them and all the rest of you a kiss now write soon from your loving sister Angie

During these country farming years, Ida emerged as the family seamstress, a valuable talent then and also in later years when she sewed for her many nieces and nephews as the next generation of children came along. Clothing construction in the 1800s was heavily dependent on the skill and imagination of each housewife. Patterns were printed in miniature in ladies' magazines and had to be enlarged by hand. Complete instructions did not appear with the patterns until 1910.[2] In western Kansas it is likely that Ida did as most frontier women of the time: a crude paper pattern was drawn by laying it over sections of an existing piece of clothing and tracing each shape, or by carefully unpicking the seams of a garment, working backward from the order of construction to trace each piece. Because a dress generally required ten yards of fabric, most women then made a muslin pattern that could be basted together for the final fitting. At ten cents a yard on the Kansas frontier, even common cotton calico would have been too expensive for the prairie seamstress to waste the smallest piece.

The daughter of a neighboring homesteader, Ivy Morton Yoos, whose family settled in Achilles Township in the early 1890s, recalled that the calicoes available at that time were mostly drab colors, except for the bright,

Ida Bell Chambers, c. 1893. Photo courtesy of Audry Gaunt.

colorfast turkey red. There was a heavier fabric available known as "dutch blue." It was dark blue with a small white figure. There were also ginghams, outing flannels, muslin, chambray shirting, and a semisheer fabric called "India-linon," although there was no linen in it. By the 1890s calico sold for 4 to 6 cents per yard, but it came only in twenty-four-inch widths. Ivy Roos recalled that it took many yards to make a typical dress with long sleeves and very full, long skirts. One "oversized" woman in the area always bought sixteen yards for a dress.[3]

When all the seam adjustments were made, the dressmaker could then begin to cut into the dress fabric. A pattern often served for several dresses or for every female member of the household, and cutting and stitching clothing for a large family was a tedious and time-consuming task even for a woman fortunate enough to own a sewing maching. Obviously, with all this work to stitch a dress or a shirt, only a woman with a great deal of skill and a genuine love of needlework would continue to sew for herself and her extended family, as Ida did for most of her life, even after store-bought garments were more easily obtainable in later years.

Mary Chambers never developed a love of stitching. She rarely quilted or worked on fancy needlework as did most women of her time. Her sewing was generally confined to patching and darning and keeping serviceable the assorted clothing required for her large family. All of her daughters, however, acquired a talent for and appreciation of needlework and were proficient with a needle

as were most women of that time out of necessity. Ida often worked on the practical quilts and garments, but her younger sister, Nette, loved most the delicate and less utilitarian pieces of handwork. Where Ida tied a heavy wool comforter, Nette pieced a Grandmother's Flower Garden or Double Wedding Ring quilt. And when Ida sewed pants and shirts for the family, Nette made beautiful cutwork bureau scarves. The youngest sister, Mira, was as versatile in her sewing talents as Ida, and as she matured she learned to stitch a dress or coat or a quilt with equal ability.

Ida's earliest surviving quilt comes from the first years after the family moved off the farm and into town. It is a Puss in the Corner quilt, with hand-pieced blocks set on the point, alternating with a solid block of red. It was made about 1890, and on the back of the quilt in a corner is embroidered the name "Ida." A few years later, Mira made a similar quilt, perhaps using Ida's original pattern pieces. This Puss in the Corner quilt has a slightly different look, because Mira set the blocks in straight rows rather than on the diagonal and used light borders and blue sashing blocks. Ida's earliest quilt, made when she lived in Iowa, has not survived, but in later years when she left a list of "quilts I have pieced and helped quilt," she recorded: "one for myself that pieced before we left Iowa dont know the name." Another quilt was listed as a "nine patch for myself."

It has always been a necessary practice of quiltmakers to use cutaways, or scraps left after a garment has been cut from a new piece of fabric, and pieces from worn clothing in piecing a quilt. Ida was no exception; in her quilt list she noted a quilt made of "just pieces of my things" and another of the family things. For using up assorted fabric scraps, a perfect quilt would be: "a charm quilt gave it to Mira." Charm quilts were traditionally made of hundreds of different scraps of fabric. When a quilter had collected a large enough variety of materials she pieced the Charm quilt without ever repeating a fabric, if possible. But an especially treasured quilt must have been the quilt "pieced of Grandma Thorne's dress and mine."

When families lived apart on the frontier, communication by letter was slow and sometimes unreliable. For women the separations were especially difficult because they often lived out on a claim, far from town and neighbors, and they had even less opportunity than men to socialize. It was natural to turn to their domestic talents to lessen that sense of isolation. Friendship quilts were frequent gifts to girls or women when their families left for the West, and when they arrived at a new home, women made more quilts using treasured scraps of fabric brought by wagon or sent in a letter from a friend or loved one. Stitching a bit of fabric, scraps cut from a piece of a mother's or an old friend's dress, brought dear memories of old times and sometimes relieved the burden of distance. Angie's sisters, Ida and Nette, would have treasured the pieces of lawn and gingham that she sent to them in the following letter:

Holland Ia May 25 [1886]

Dear Sisters

Here this is Tuesday evening and I am just agoing to ans your letter I rec. it Saturday and I tell you I was glad to hear that ma and the baby [Artemus] were better but you dont know how funny I felt when I read that Grandma was dead. [Grandma Thorne had been visiting her daughter, Mary Chambers, in Atwood, Kansas, when she passed away.] I just can't believe that it is so I can't think of it at all or I have the funniest feeling come over me and it seem as if I couldn't stand it. Will you send me all the particulars when you write again. I feel so glad to think that the baby and ma are getting well again. Now Ida I want you to get the babies picture taken and send it to me for I want to see what he looks like anyway. They are going to do some thing over to the Center Decoration day but I dont know what it is. The Holland band have got so they play a few pieces very nicly. I started to school again Monday. We are over in Partial Payments Wess is getting better slowly She can't stand it to do very much at a time Tell pa I will send him some Soft Maple seed. Asa say he wants to plant them just about as deep as corn one seed in a place and plant them as soon as you get them while they are damp they wont grow after they get dry. I guess there will be enough so they can plant some on all three of your claims. Wess went to the Centre and got me the prettiest lawn dress I will send you piece of it when we make it I forgot to put in a piece of my ghingham the last time I wrote. I will send one in this if I dont forget it. My Ida you are getting poor arnt you. you weighed 148 over to the Centre that day. I dont know how much I weigh I havn't been weighed for a long time. Mattie said she got a letter from Nettie the other day. I dont know what Bob preserved his kiss in I did ask him. Oh! girls I cant think of any thing to write so I will close and let Wess tell the news kiss all the little one for me and give my love to all I remain your true and loving
Sister Angie
P.S. Tell Charley and Henry hello.

For the settlers scattered across the prairie, gathering with their neighbors served as an important social outlet that today's urban dwellers can only begin to imagine. The Chambers family was always deeply religious, but on the western plains, church functions were often regarded with a great deal of anticipation for their social as well as religious aspects.

In the early years of the twentieth century, Ida's younger brother Jesse wrote a delightful letter to his parents reminiscing fondly of those early times, "my balmy days"; of walking four miles to the sod Sunday school and then strolling home with his sweetheart. He requested that his mother tell Ida that he hoped they could soon rehearse the "Singing School songs we learnt in the little sod school house out by the Stone chapel."

For Ida there were other social events: dances and parties to husk corn, sew carpet rags, and of course, to quilt. There were many young people scattered among the farms, and Ida made lifelong friendships during her early years on the Kansas homestead. Ida began a second autograph book in the mid 1880s that contains verses and thoughts from many of her friends living out in the country:

On a homestead
Rawlins Co. Kan. Oct 18/85
Buffalo grass, buffalo pumpkins, buffalo peas,
Think of me when taking your ease
E.M. Duensing

A December 16, 1887, entry reads:

Friend Ida
Roses may wither,
Flowers may die.
Friends may forsake thee
But never shall I.
Ever Your Friend
Blanche Angell

On March 9, 1888, Harry Gaskill simply wrote:
Sweet Kan. air.

Ida's father also wrote some affectionate words in his daughter's autograph book:

Oct 10-85
My Dear daughter Ida
When in this book you look and see my name
remember that I wrote it on my forty forth
birthday
may you live long and be happy is your
father wish
John H. Chambers

On February 13, 1888, one month after she became twenty-one, Ida homesteaded the section of land directly to the south of her parents and east of Charlie's place. The claim is located on high rolling prairie, bisected in the middle from west to east by the north branch of Sappa Creek. Her Homestead Affidavit states that in November 1885 (when she was only eighteen), she had "commenced settlement" on her land and the improvements consisted of "a House and 5 acres of Breaking" valued at $100. ("Breaking" refers to the plowing under

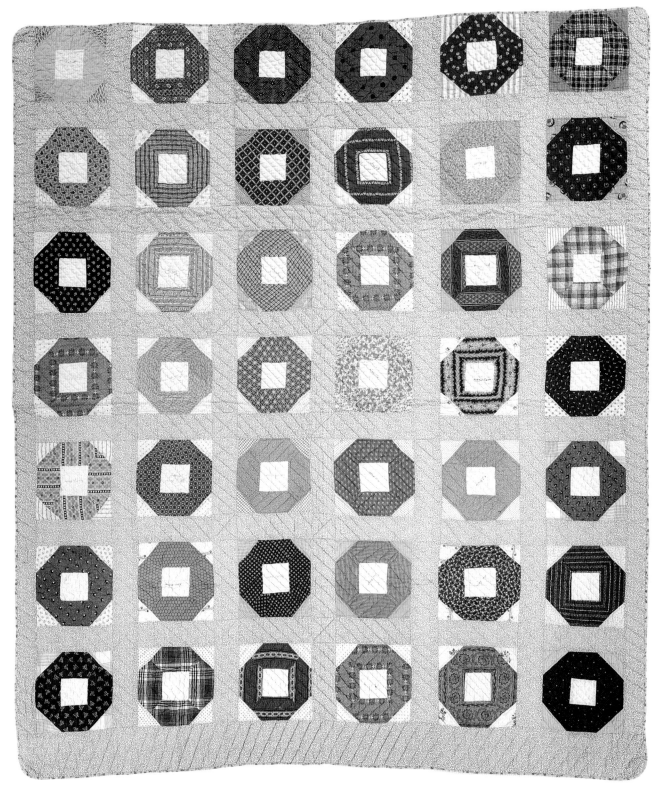

Friendship quilt, 71" x 81", c. 1890s. Ida's Friendship quilt is hand pieced with forty-two blocks. The center squares of nearly every block contain inked or stamped names of family members. Photography by Brian S. Birlauf, Birlauf and Steen Photo, Denver, Colorado.

*Ida's autograph book, 1885-1888.
Courtesy of Atwood Public Library.*

of the tough layer of buffalo grass in preparing the land for planting.)

Because Charlie was Ida's neighbor to the west, the brother and sister built a sod house that straddled the boundary of their two claims. The house had two front doors so they each could enter the house from their own land. Five years later when Ida "proved up" on her claim, the improvements were listed as "sod house, cave, 90 acres fenced, post and wire, value $200." The following notice was posted for thirty days in the *Republican Citizen:*

> Notice of final proof, No. 24,412.–Land Office at Oberlin, Kansas, July 31, 1893. Notice is hereby given that the following-named settler has filed notice of her intention to make final proof in support of her claim and that said proof will be made before the Clerk of District Court, at Atwood, Kansas, on September 19th, 1893. viz: Ida B. Chambers, H.E.No. 12,760, for the northeast quarter of section 34, township

4 south, range 34 west She names the following witnesses to prove her continuous residence upon and cultivation of, said land, viz: R.S. Larrabee, W.A. Roberts, S.C. Martin and W.H. Granlee, all of Atwood, Kansas.

Cyrus Anderson, Register.

Family records do not indicate what amount of work Ida physically contributed to her homestead claim. It was likely that her father and brothers built the sod house, broke the prairie, and planted and fenced her land. Ida never seemed to be one for outside work, although she loved flowers and gardening and often recorded in her journals the hours that she worked in her garden, the plants she set out, and which flowers were blooming. But Ida loved her land and held onto it for years, even on through her marriage, renting it to Charlie and other farmers for crops and grazing, until she finally sold the land in 1910 to C. S. McDougal for $1,000.

The Chambers family, 1896. Front row: John, Mira, and Mary. Back row: Angie, John, Nette, Jesse, and Ida. Note that the three older girls are wearing dresses cut from the same pattern with variations on collars and embellishments. Photo courtesy of Audry Gaunt.

Ida and the Doctor

About the time that Ida filed on her land, her parents and younger brothers and sisters moved twelve miles north into the eight-year-old town of Atwood, Kansas. The previous fall, John had been elected registrar of deeds and was later made justice of the peace, an office he held for more than twenty years. The family built a house on the corner of Sixth and State streets and moved in during the month of July 1888. This house stayed in the Chambers family for the next sixty-seven years. Ida divided her time between her claim in Mikesell Township and her parent's house in town. But she moved into town permanently shortly after she

proved up on her section in 1893, as there was a stronger attraction in town in the form of the handsome young doctor, John N. Melugin.

Like Ida, John was born in Illinois, although they did not know each other until they met years later in Kansas. Born in 1854, John was thirteen years older than Ida. During his twenties he went to western Kansas to try his hand at the adventurous career of cowboying. He worked on the range for a few seasons but then went to Keokuk, Iowa, to study medicine. After a two-year period during which John completed courses in the principles and practices of medicine and diseases of children, as well as in physiology, microscopic anatomy, and diseases of the nervous system, he returned to Atwood in 1888 and commenced practicing medicine.

Wedding Announcement Apr. 27, 1894

Dr. John N. Melugin and Miss Ida B. Chambers were united in marriage at the home of the bride's parents in this city Wednesday evening by Rev. W. K. Loffburrow in the presence of a few relatives and immediate friends. We understand Mr. and Mrs. Melugin will shortly remove to Western Illinois where the Doctor has been offered a large practice built up by a brother whose ill-health has now incapacitated him from hard work.

We shall be sorry to lose Dr. Melugin and his estimable bride. By faithful attention and study he has attained no inconsiderable success in his profession and Mrs. Melugin will be missed in the social life where she has been so popular and in the church circles where she has labored so earnestly. May happiness and prosperity attend them, will be the heartfelt wish of their many friends.

John and Ida were married in her parents' home on April 27, 1894. One of the wedding gifts the couple received was a moonlit snow scene painted by Ida's sister Angie. An inscription on the back of the painting reads: "A wedding present to Dr and I from sister Angie-this her own work April 25th 1894 for Hazel Gaunt." The initial plan was for the newlyweds to move to Illinois, where John would join his brother in his large medical practice. But they never did leave Kansas. No reason was ever recorded, but people who knew Ida indicated that she couldn't bear to leave her family. Ida and the doctor bought a house a block south of her parents' home and lived there for the next twenty-two years.

Ida was always active in the Methodist Episcopal Church. She taught Sunday School and joined the Ladies' Aid Society, where she worked on quilts for charity and fund-raising every Tuesday afternoon. With her mother she was also a member of the Women's Relief Corps. Formed after the Civil War to aid widows, orphans, and veterans, WRC members also made many quilts and worked on civic and service projects. In later years their duties included maintaining graves of war veterans.

Notice from an undated and unidentified newspaper clipping in the Chambers family files:

Atwood W.R.C. No. 175

This splendid order was organized in Atwood on April 25, 1888, with twenty five charter members, and at present has a membership of thirty-three in good standing. Since the organization there has been 126 members initiated.

The object of the organization is to care for old soldiers and their widows and orphans and teach patriotism. During the past eighteen years they have materially assisted many worthy persons. Each quarter they give a bean dinner at Fraternal hall free to all old soldiers and their families.

The National W.R.C. was organized in Denver in 1883, and at present has a working organization in every state in the Union. Kansas has over 6,000 members. It was through this worthy organization that the stars and stripes were placed over every public school while in session.

At a meeting of Atwood Lodge No. 175 on Saturday, January 12, the following officers were installed:
President-Fannie Boyer
Senior Vice-president-Ida Mulugen
Junior Vice-president-Julia A. Hemming.
Treasurer-Nettie Chambers.
Chaplain-Mary Gaunt.
Conductress-Bosa Randall.
Guard-Eva Lamback.
Assistant Cond.-Mattie Tindall.
Assistant Guard-Mary Holcomb.

Several of Ida's surviving quilts come from the early years of her married life. Ida quilted at church, with her women's clubs, and at home with her mother and sisters. All of her quilts are hand pieced, although she often machine stitched the large pieces of the quilt linings. She continued to be the family seamstress, sewing waists, skirts, aprons, shirts, pants, and caps, but as ready-to-wear clothing became more affordable and was purchased, she increasingly turned her time to quilting.

Of course, Ida did other forms of needlework, such as embroidery, and she especially enjoyed crocheting. In one of Ida's diaries, she mentions, in addition to quilting, crocheting table mats and pot holders, hemming tea towels and dish towels, mending, embroidering pillow slips, and sewing caps, aprons, an "outing gown for Nette" and sleeves for Nette's dress. "Ida was down a while she was makeing lace." (2-20-15 Ma)

While Ida often stitched a quilt or a cap to celebrate the birth of a child, there was on occasion the necessity to use her needle for a more somber purpose. Ma recorded such a time in a 1903 journal:

Sunday 9 [August 9, 1903] Ida come down and got breakfast and Dr and Louise come when they got up I washed up all the dishes and then she went home and got ready for SS I got Rodney ready and then I finished up the work and got dinner Ida come home from SS

Ida Bell Chambers' calling card. Courtesy of Atwood Public Library.

dident stay to Church they eat dinner here and she washed the dishes and then she went home thought she would write some letters but Mrs Preder sent for her to help make a little dress for her Bro little girl that died that morning I went to bed a while and Mrs Washington come up and then after a while Mrs Gaunt come she stayed till I started to get supper and then she went down to Mrs Lee's it got real cloudy and thundered quite bad but pa went to Church any way it rained a little but not very bad the Elder come home with pa stayed all night

Quite possibly that Sunday in August of 1903 is the only time that Ida sewed on the Sabbath day. It is very apparent from five decades of journal entries that the Chambers women viewed Sundays as a day of rest. There might be cooking and kitchen chores, but other than necessary work the family attended church, visited, read, walked, and wrote letters, but sewing and quilting are never mentioned as Sunday activities.

Ida dearly loved the doctor and found her married life very fulfilling. Her only lament was the long hours that John spent away at his practice. Often he was called out to the country and returned late at night or wasn't able to return at all until the next morning. It was a blessing to have her family close. Ida washed on Mondays with her mother and often returned on Tuesday to join her sisters in the ironing, and most evenings she sat at her parents' home with her piecing. The doctor knew to call at the Chambers first to bring Ida home when he got in from working. Ida would have loved a child, but as the years went by without that joy she found pleasure in helping care for the extended family at Ma and Pa Chambers' home.

In Ma's early diaries there is a young girl named Louise who is mentioned frequently. She apparently lived with Ida and the doctor for several years and she often played with Ida's nephew Rodney Gillette, who was six years old in 1902 when Ma first writes of Louise. "Ida come down and we had a little visit but had to talk to the children most of the time." (9-8-02) They must have been a rowdy pair because Ma often complains of the noise Louise and Rodney made. Ma also wrote: "Ida quilted a little yesterday she said she would quilt some every day if it wasent for the children."

The young girl who lived with Ida for several years was Louise York, granddaughter of their neighbor, Loretta Corrells. Mrs. Corrells' oldest son, Denney, was left with five children to raise when his wife abandoned the family. Louise lived with Ida and the doctor for several years but later went away to school. She eventually went to medical school in Nebraska and became one of the first female doctors in the midwest, a rarity in the early years of this century. Another granddaughter of Mrs. Corrells, Patrice Nichols Lilley, said that it was Dr. Melugin who inspired Louise to study medicine. Louise had originally talked of being a nurse, but the doctor encouraged and convinced her to become a physician.

For several years Louise's name appears in Ma's journals, but after 1910 there is no mention of her for nearly a decade. Ida occasionally noted a letter she had written to Louise and when she came back to Atwood for a visit in 1920, Ida wrote of a quilt she made for her. After that time their lives went in separate directions and Louise's name disappears from Ida's journals.

But there were other children in the immediate family for Ida to share her love and talents with. In September 1892, Mary Chambers' sister Celestia Rose (Aunt Lett) died as a result of burns. At a Fourth of July celebration, firecrackers landed under her skirts and her dress instantly caught fire. Mary went to Nebraska to care for her dying sister for several months, and when she returned to Atwood in September she brought with her Paul Treadwell, Celestia's five-year-old son, who spent the rest of his growing-up years in John and Mary Chambers' home.

Another orphan became a member of the household six years later. After Angie completed her schooling, she joined the family in Atwood and taught school in Rawlins County for five years. She married Burt Gillette in 1895 and had one son, Rodney. Three years later she died, at the age of 29, after a long illness. John and Mary went to Raton, New Mexico, to be with Angie during her last days, and once again, Mary returned to Atwood with a child to raise, her two-year-old grandson, Rodney. In later years Rodney always thought of the Chambers as his family and always remembered Ida and Nette on Mother's Day with a card or visit.

When Rodney was almost eleven years old he wrote the following delightful letter to his two "dear girls," Ida and Nette, who were visiting family in Nebraska:

Atwood, Kans.
Feb. 23, 1907.

Dear girls:
    I thought I would write you a few lines today. How are you getting along? We are all

well so far. Dr. [Melugin] had to go out to Butler's old place today. I don't know who was sick. When are you coming home? I do the chores every night. My book from the library is "Wild Animals I have known." I couldn't get "Bob Hampton of placer." Today has been a nice day. Rollin Mc Skimming, Glen Tobias, and I went down to the creek. The Larkin goods came yesterday. Mr. Innes brought it up. Mabel brought 2 lbs. of butter yesterday. Mabel, Grandma Lyons, & Nerve was up here yesterday. The other day G. [Grandma] Pinegar came over and washed the breakfast dishes, swept the kitchen, and pealed the potatoes. The entertainment of the Unity was real good. The house are pretty near full. I got 100% every day last week in spelling. Grandma says, "It beats the dutch, the way she can fly around and do things." Some days she feels fine and others not so good. Marshall sent me a nice Valentine. Well I must close
Your nephew.
   Rodney.
P.S. Paul [Treadwell] went to take Alice out to her school. Nette, get me a good base ball and I will pay for it when you get here.

John Chambers added the following note on the back of Rodney's letter:

I just read Rodneys letter he wrote nice letter. he told you all the news. Nerv wanted to take some of the clothes home to wash for Ma but she would not let her, she feels quite well

some days, but the moneys a good deal. it would be better for her if she would not fuss so much. nothing new to write about. Dr is feeling well.
   Yours in love
   JHC

Years later when Rodney was a young man, Ida copied the following lines from a Mother's Day card into her journal:

Monday May 14th 1923 night letter from Rodney for Mothers Day.
"Today I join with those who greet their Mother's and send you words of love, away from you and the old home, my heart goes back to you today as the years pass my love for you grows deeper and my debt to you more plain, love to all Rodney."

Entry from Ma's 1902 journal:

Monday Sept. 1 I got up at 5:30 made a fire got on wash water and then got breakfast, baby and Ona [Jesse's wife Leona and their daughter, Myrle, born on August 17, 1902] slept late this morning and Ida was late so we dident get the washing done as early as we ought to Ida and Dr were here for dinner after dinner I cleaned the coal house and swept the kitchen and put down the carpets and Ona and Mira went down town I took care of babe Mrs Carter was here thought our babe was nice the quartette practiced here this afternoon, and Mrs Ive and Grandma

An 1894 embroidered quilt identifies Ida Chambers as president of the Ladies' Aid Society and a Sunday School teacher for the Methodist Church. Other blocks depict local businesses, clubs, and churches.

Quilt courtesy of Rawlins County Historical Society.

Chambers Home in Atwood, Kansas, 1888. L. to R.: Claude Arbuckle, John, Mira, Jesse, Angie, Nette, Mary, and John Chambers. Photo courtesy of Audry Gaunt.

Pinegar were here quite awhile grandma is so nice we had our supper and washed dishes Charley Low was here to day cutting down weeds around the house it looks a good deal better Ona just got a letter from Jesse he wants them to come home Saturday instead of Monday I hate to have them go for I dont think Ona and baby are well enough to go but Ona is very anxious to get home babe and Ona slept good we were all a bed early

Tuesday Sept. 2 got up at 5 OK this morning made the fire and then took baby up and fixed her a bed in the rocking chair she slept till 9 OK she is just as good as she can be Ida come down and washed and dressed her. Nette made cake for social Mira ironed I helped a little Nette cooked all the ice cream for eight gallons all they have got to night they dident seem to be any one that could help much today I am afraid Nette will be sick for she is not very well Ona is making Myrle a little bonnet to wear home it is just as cute as it can be they have all gone to the social now but the baby and I Ona expects to go home Saturday and Mira is a going with

her I hate to have her go but guess she can go a while Jesse is dispatcher now and will have more responsibility Myrle is fast asleep and I am awful sleepy Ona went down to the social a little while and babe stayed with me we dident get to bed till late.

Wed Sep 3 I got up at 5.30 this morning made a fire mixed my bread and then had to rest a while I made pancakes for breakfast after breakfast the girls washed the dishes and then they went down where they had the social to help clean up they were gone till 11 OK I cleaned up the kitchen while they were gone then they got dinner after noon I washed out some things Nette went to Club Mira and Ida went down town and done some tradeing and then they went to prayer meeting then Nette tried to develop some pictures they were no good the Kodak was out of whack we were up quite late

Thursday Sep 4 got up at 5.30. made a fire started breakfast and then made me a cup of tea and eat something before the rest were up after we had our breakfast the girls washed the dishes I fed the pig and chickens and made my bed. Nette cooked up the plumbs she worked with them till after 5 OK Ona finished baby's little bonnet to day and her quilt. Mira and Ruby had their pictures taken to day and Mira called on grand ma Pinegar I tried to help but dident do much but stand around the girls went to League this evening Ida come down a little while but Ona went to bed right away so she dident stay very long when the rest were all abed Ona got up and got a piece to eat and we dried the baby and then went to bed babe slept till 4 OK

Friday Sep 5 got up at 6 OK had an awful head ache but I mixed my bread and got breakfast we done quite a washing for baby and Ona then we cleaned up and got dinner after dinner we done the ironing Mrs Walts and her girls come to see the baby and Mrs Flinn come a while the girls went to the WCTU meeting in the evening I wanted to go real bad but had to stay with Ona and baby I drefsed [Ma often used the traditional method of writing a double "s" in a word as "fs," a practice that had generally died away by the late nineteenth century.] a chicken to have for lunch for Jesse and the girls when they were going from Cedar Bluffs to McCook Jessie Alcott was here a while in the evening and Cady stayed here while the boys went to the Church

Saturday Sep 6 got up early to get breakfast and get things ready for the girls to go we were all ready on time Mr Hacker come and got the trunks and then come with the buss and took the girls and my dear little baby we miss them so much pa had to go away of course, so Nette had to stay in the store and Rodney and I were alone in the fore noon but had plenty of company in the afternoon Ida was putting up plumbs so she had to stay home all day Eva was here a while little Ida stayed here while Eva went to Corps Cady and her boys were here a little while. Nette come up early and we had our supper and pa dident come till almost sundown I got supper for him and then I went and done my chores. Ida come down a while but she dident stay long the children wont give us a minutes peace Nette went to Choir practice dident get home very early I went to bed early and slept awful hard Mira and Ona went away.

Near the end of his life, John Chambers began to write his life story. It is not a long document, and the bulk of the papers describe his Civil War experiences.

Regrettably, he deals with the decades of his life after the war in just a page or two. Mary Chambers, however, was a lifelong journal keeper, and she passed along this wonderful discipline to at least two of her daughters, Ida and Nette. Mary's earliest surviving diary begins on Wednesday, August 20, 1902. Her son Jesse's only child, Myrle, is just 16 days old. John's wife, Leona or "Ona," has come to her mother-in-law's home for the birth of her child. Dr. Melugin brought Myrle into the world, and Ona had the doting presence of her mother-in-law and three sisters-in-law to help care for the baby. The "girls" sewed bonnets, clothing, and quilts for their new niece.

Mary Chambers' journals continue until the last years of her life, with occasional gaps where a book has been lost. Mary recorded her days faithfully, making corrections if she got a fact wrong or confused the time of an event or bit of work. She rarely left her house, except to go to Ida's or a close neighbor's home, since it seemed to exhaust her, but she was by no means a recluse. Mary enjoyed a wide circle of friends and loved to have her large family return to her home. Young people such as Lulu Lambach, whose parents were farmers, stayed with the Chambers to attend high school in town, returning home to their families during vacations. Mary's journals record a parade of guests and others who stayed for dinner or the night. People came into town from their farms in the country and stayed a night or two with the Chambers family. Once, a lady passing through Atwood collapsed. She and her daughter were brought to Mary's home, where they stayed several days until she had recovered her strength and could go on with her journey. Mary never recorded her name, but each day she wrote of "the lady" or "the lady's daughter" and the recovery she was making. People in town also called on the Chambers family. Mary's friends came every day, often stayed all afternoon and for meals. Mary didn't need to leave her home; the small world of western Kansas seemed to come to her.

Mary and John were known by their family, friends, and most of Rawlins County as Ma and Pa Chambers. Similarly, John Melugin is always referred to as Doctor, and even in friendship quilts made by Ida and Mira in later years, the names embroidered on the blocks are "Dr" and "Ma and Pa Chambers."

Because Mary's sphere was literally bounded by the walls of her home, that is the world she recorded in her diaries. And it is interesting to note that even though she was a deeply religious woman who vigorously supported her church and often entertained and boarded the Episcopal preachers, she rarely went to church herself. Sunday after Sunday she got her family dressed and ready for church and then stayed at home alone cooking the big meal to have it ready when they all returned from the services. Each daily entry begins with the time she got up and then proceeds with the round of her work.

Sun Oct 19. [1902] they all went to SS and Church but me I stayed home and got dinner and I write and read some in afternoon and

Streak of Lightning quilt, c. 1890. While the maker of the Streak of Lightning quilt is not definitely known, it is a Chambers family quilt that was packed in a trunk when Thorne Chambers, son of Henry and Minnie Chambers, moved his family to California in 1936. Ida is the person likely to have stitched the quilt four decades earlier. The Streak of Lightning quilt, also known as Zigzag, is hand pieced with three fabrics—a pink and white stripe, a purple print, and a solid pink—and is quilted in parallel rows stretching diagonally across the quilt. Quilt courtesy of Pat Chambers Thomas. Photograph by Jack Mathieson.

we all went to Church in the evening Mrs Edmonds died in the night

Mon Oct 20 we washed and Mira finished her drefs her blue Mother Hubbard Mrs. Edmonds was burried in the afternoon funeral at the Christian Church Nette went to help sing

Tuesday Oct 21 we done our ironing Mira was cutting out pieces for her necktie quilt it was a very nice day we got a letter from John and Cora in the evening the girls and Ruby [Ruby was Loretta Corrells' daughter and a cousin of Louise York] went to Lodge

Wednesday Oct 22 the girls cleaned the front rooms Nette made cake the Club met here and we served cake and Coffee I went up to Idas and stayed with Louise and Rodney

thought they could have a better time with out the children Nette and Mira went to prayer meeting in the evening

Thursday Oct 23 the girls cleaned the kitchen Nette made cookies in the afternoon the girls all went to society pieced on a quilt and the girls went to the Cong Church to prayer meeting in the evening I dont know what I done

Friday Oct 24 the girls went to call on Mrs Leanning they think she is very pleasant they like her ever so much then they went down town Mira got her some buttons she has been wanting so long and then she went to see Linnie and her baby she has such a nice baby they are such a happy couple Mira got a letter from Elmer [her future husband, James Elmer Gaunt] and answered it and they all went to choir practice when I say all I mean Ruby

Saturday Oct 25 Mira riped up the shirt she is going to color to make her a waist of then she fixed up her doll and made her some new blue stockings Ruby went to a party at Mr Hemmings our girls were not invited Nette went to Royal Neighbors. I stayed at home with my boy

Sunday Oct 26 the folks all went to SS and Church I stayed at home and got dinner as usual I wrote some in afternoon we sent a letter to Jesse and Ona. Mira went over to Ruby's a while

National events and politics were not a part of Mary's world, so she rarely mentioned them. Similarly, these were not journals to record her private thoughts and emotions, but that makes her occasional personal observations all the more striking. Like all mothers she worried and fretted over her children. When one of them was far away she often noted how deeply she missed them. Raising Rodney was both a pleasure and a heartache for Mary. She occasionally noted how he reminded her of her dear Angie. His presence in her home was a bittersweet joy.

Tuesday Sept 16 [1902] I got up early made a fire and mixed my bread and got breakfast and then we done up the work and went to ironing we both ironed until Nette had to take her music lesson I finished the ironing put the bread in loves and started dinner after dinner Lulu and I washed the dishes and we had our work all done up early but pa come up and brought us a letter from Bert

[George Burton Gillette, Angie's husband and Rodney's father] and he said he was going to be married and it made me so nervous I couldent do any thing all the afternoon I think it is all right. but it made me think so much about Angie the dear girl I mifs her so much yet but I know it is best for Bert to get married I dont think he will want Rodney as long as pa and I live

The following spring of 1903, Mary made another poignant observation:

May 20 Nette went up and washed for Lulu Mira and I done up the work and then she made cookies and I finished the ironing then we got dinner Nette come home a little after dinner and she hadent been home but a few minutes when Allie and Merrill come and they stayed here most of the afternoon Merrill and Rodney had a good time and we had a nice visit with Allie It seems funny to have the little ones play togather for their mothers were always such good friends but Rodneys mama has gone and his papa has another companion so goes the world

Mary seemed to be an uncomplaining, steady woman who found a great deal of purpose in keeping a home for her family and friends. One of her rare recorded complaints is one that every married woman can at some-time in her life empathize with. Every morning, Mary got up before the rest of her household in the freezing darkness to start the fires to warm the house. And since she was up anyway, she might as well start that day's work. By the time John customarily arose at 8 or 9, several hours after Mary's day had begun, the house was warm, the boiler was on for washing (with water pumped and hauled into the house by the bucket), the bread raising, and the coffee and breakfast was made. That was the daily routine, but only once, on a particularly cold morning did Mary complain: "pa and Rodney got up and had their breakfast and went away. Rodney to school and pa to his office they dont never think about what there is to do in the house" (March 27, 1911).

The early years after the turn of the century were happy ones for the busy Chambers family. Pa's coal and feed store was prospering and he was also active in local politics, serving as treasurer for the school district and justice of the peace. The four boys were all married, and Charlie moved into town to help in his father's store. Mary and her girls were all active and close, working together and enjoying each other's company daily.

Sunday May 24 [1903] I got up and made the fire and the girls got up and got breakfast and done up the work I felt so weak I couldent do much but they all went to SS and then went to

In 1885 the Chambers family moved to a homestead in Rawlins County, Kansas. Eighteen-year-old Ida packed her quilts and personal belongings into her green- and gold-trimmed trunk for the family's last westward move. Courtesy of Hazel Gaunt.

the Cong Church to Memorial services then we all slept and rested till supper time then they all went to our Church but Rodney and I but we went to bed early

Monday May 25 I got up and made the fire got the boiler on dident feel very stout I got things ready for breakfast the girls done the washing I couldent help much we got all done before dinner after dinner I helped some about the dishes and cleaning up out side Mira moped the floor and I went into Mrs. Corrells [a neighbor] a few minutes and the girls come a running over to tell us Corvina had a little girl baby born the 25 and she was married the 26 of Nov. and every body thought she was all right and just think how it has turned out

Tuesday May 26 I helped do up the work and then Nette went to ironing and Mira begun Nettes red waist I went to Cadys a while come home and helped get dinner after

Ladies Band of Atwood, Kansas, 1892. Angie and Nette Chambers joined a small band formed by a Mr. Wilson in 1889. Atwood historian Ruth Kelley Hayden wrote that musical groups were very popular in the western prairie country, and "bands were formed almost as soon as the towns were settled."

Back row L. to R.: Delia Gaunt, Belle Spear, Angie Chambers, Maggie Cochran, Nette Chambers, Lulu Hotchkiss, Sophia Cochran. Front row L. to R.: Frank Spear, Ida Dudley, Truman Price, Helty Belford, Gertie Greason. Photo courtesy of Audry Gaunt.

dinner we done up the work the girls sewed a while and then they went over to Selma's Mira took the waist to work on and Nette crocheted I done a little mending the girls were going to the graveyard after supper but it rained so they couldent go

Wednesday May 27 we done up the morning work and then the girls looked over the things in the bookcase and cleaned and moved it into the front room I was over to Mrs Corrells a few minutes after dinner Central called and said Ludell wanted to talk to me had a talk with John he got there last night I am so glad he is so near home Mira was trimming her hats to day after dinner Mira and Cady Ruby and Nette with the Junior League went to the graveyard and fixed up some of the graves. after supper At [Atwood Cochran] took Nette down to Ludell to see John he was all right Cora will come as soon as she gets her pass

Thursday May 28 '03 I helped some with the work Mira finished Nette's waist and her blue drefs and done some Mending and sewed lace on Nette's white shirt and then in the PM she went to the Church to quilt after supper Nette and Mira went to the graveyard and set out some rose bushes on Artie and grandma's graves
Friday May 29. it was rainy in the morning the girls done some bakeing Nette made cake and pies and Mira made cookies it just rained most all day Mira went over to Rubys and

made some paper flowers to put on Arties grave the girls were both invited over to Mungers in the evening they had a party it rained so they dident near all go but the girls thought they had a good time they got home about 11 OK

Saturday May 30 we got up pretty good season it was cloudy and damp not a very good day for Decoration but we got our work done as soon as we could and then fixed the flowers Mrs Ginger and Bonnie sent flowers for Lambachs and they sent Nette and Lulu a nice Boquet they brought their dinner and eat with us they dident go to the graveyard till afternoon after the speaking there was a big crowd in town

John is well here it is July 23 1903 I have neglected my book most two months we have had some very warm weather and we have had some nice rains we have had nice weather for all crops they are harvesting now the farmers have hard work to get help the wheat is nearly all ripe now pa has sold a number of harvesters and headers our hollyhocks are very pretty this year and the sweet peas our blue grass has got a real nice start now

Angie and Nette Chambers, 1892. Photo courtesy of Audry Gaunt.

IDA'S SOAP "RECEIPT"
Dissolve one can Lewis Lye in 1 qt hot water.
let cool have 2 qts melted tallow or lard. pour
slowly into Lye. stirring untill mixed
½ tablespoon borax in ½ cup hot water, ½
cup Ammonia

On Mondays Ida brought up her washing and combined it with the family's, and Mary and her three daughters shared the work of scrubbing and hanging the clothes. Tuesdays were for ironing, and the first thing Ma did after she built up the fire in the kitchen stove was put the flats on to heat. The Chambers family kept a cow, so there was churning to be done several times a week. Ma and Ida each kept chickens, and Ma often noted in her journals the occasions when her hens laid more eggs than Ida's. In a 1914 letter written to Mira, Ma mentioned her chickens and the impressive number of eggs they had produced that month: "O I wanted to tell you how many eggs we git and use pretty near all of them in the month of March we got 303 we always set it down on the Calender when we bring them in I have 18 hens but two have been setting over a week." Ma enjoyed animals, so there was often a dog about, and she also raised small songbirds in cages in her house, a practice that Ida continued for some years, sometimes noting when she sold a bird:

There was a barn and an orchard behind the house with a variety of fruit trees that kept the family busy with picking and canning and jelly making. There were a number of cherry trees, and when the fruit was ready, all the family and their friends gathered in the mornings to pick fruit; the excess produce was sold.

Nette is picking apricots I guess she has
picked nearly a bushel this morning and

When Angie Chambers taught school in the early 1890s, it is likely that her sod schoolhouse was similar to the one used by Gladys Mahoney, another Atwood teacher, 1900. Photo courtesy of Irene Parr.

Ida's plate. Courtesy of Doris Gaunt Shaeffer.

those two crabapple trees in the orchard are as full as they can be or pretty near and we have sold two bushels off of them now they are real nice Emma says they jell so easy and are such a pretty color. (Letter from Ma to Mira, August 10, 1915)

In July 1917, Ida noted "Cherries sold" in her journal:

Mrs Swartwood	25qts.	$2.15
Mr Brown Joe	10qts.	1.00
Mrs Morrison	10qts.	1.00
Millie	10qts.	1.00
Aunt Mollie	13qts.	1.25
Mrs Mather	6qts.	.60
May Eicher	15qts.	1.50
Mrs Burton	15qts.	1.50

Fred Bodin's folks picked on the shares July 6th Henry Martin's folks picked on the shares July 9th we canned July 9th and 10th 35 quarts.

The days were a busy round of work and visiting and companionable stitching together in the afternoons after the day's work was done. Except for a special occasion when Ma or Nette hosted the society at their house with a quilting and luncheon, quilts were generally put on and quilted at Ida's. Time after time, Ma recorded that the girls had gone up to Ida's to quilt. For everyday bed-covers the girls could "tie off a comfortor" in just a few hours and have it off the frame by early afternoon. Ma seldom quilted, although she was always patching and darning clothes for her family. But she would often finish

the quilts and comforters, stitching on the binding at home, and she sometimes mentions going up to Ida's to sew carpet rags.

Because most women learned quilting from their mothers, it is tempting to speculate where Ida learned the skills and love of quiltmaking. Mary could very likely have been a fine quilter herself, but she never seemed to develop an appreciation of the craft, and in all of her diaries she mentions quilting only once or twice at a quilting bee; more often she was enlisted to put on the binding. On February 19, 1904, Ma wrote, "Then I went up to Ida's and quilted a little stayed about an hour and a half it is the first I have quilted and it is almost out." Mary was possibly referring to that particular quilt, but given the scarcity of quilting references in her journals, she could have meant literally that it was the first time she had quilted. Ma did write of doing an impressive amount of mending and darning, but there are some hints that she may have been an unusual nineteenth-century woman in that she may not have known how to sew. In a 1914 letter to Mira, she wrote: "I wished I could sew I would make something for Jesse & John."

Perhaps it was back in Iowa that Ida learned quilting from her Grandmother Thorne. There is a mention in her "life quilt list" of the quilt she had made while the family still lived in Iowa, and there is the quilt made of clothes that had belonged to her and Grandma Thorne. Because of those references and the pieces of fabric that Angie sent in letters to Ida, it is very likely that Ida's great passion for quilting was in place very early in her life. From Ma's diaries:

Monday Sept 15 [1902] I got up at 6 OK this morning made a fire and put on the wash water and then got things ready for breakfast Lulu [Lulu Lambach boarded with the Chambers and also with Ida and the doctor while she attended normal school in Atwood, her father was a cousin of John Melugin] baked the pancakes Ida come right away and we begun to wash got all done by noon Lulu washed breakfast dishes and was home in time to get dinner and wash dishes again we were looking for a letter to night but dident get one I patched two or three pair of stockings in the afternoon Nette was down town a while in the evening Ida was here with me but we couldent visit much the children were so noisy Ida quilted some for Mrs Correll in the afternoon

Friday Oct 10 [1902] we done up our work Nette made a cake and raspberrie pies and fixed our chickens to bake. I got the potatoes ready and we had dinner very near ready when school was out Lulu helped Nette take up dinner and I went in the frontroom with company Mr and Mrs Butler and Walter Mr and Mrs Hambly and three boys were here it was pa's birthday he was 61 Nette went to Choir practice in the evening she gave pa a bill book and Ida gave him a picture of McKinley framed I gave him a pair of socks Eva [Eva Lambach, Lulu's mother] come in after Lulu she wont go to school any more this year they threw her grade out she feels awful bad about it but they couldent afford to hire another teacher and that was all they could do

Monday Nov 10 it was cloudy and misty I got up at 6:30 and put the boiler on and got the water hot. but the girls thought it was to stormy to wash so I washed out a few pieces for carpet rags, but they dident dry all day was wetter at night then when I hung them up we are trying to fix a few carpet rags to help make carpet for the parsonage I tried to mend some in the afternoon and the girls finished their skirts that they put purple ruffles on they look real nice they both stayed home in the evening

Tuesday Nov 11 it was raining when I got up so dident get ready to wash Mira colored the skirt she is going to make a waist of and I colored a few carpet rags Nette went up to Mrs Tommy Bones and got the Ritual Mira and Ruby were out soliciting for their fair Ida come down a little while and Mrs Noble come here and got some patterns of Ida I think little Hugh is so cute. Mrs Lyon was here a while and we had a real nice visit pa was here for supper before she went home I dont do much in the evening lately I cant see by lamp light

Wednesday Nov12 it was cloudy and cold but it dident rain so I got the wash water on and we done a big washing Ida come down late but we got done before dinner we done up the dinner work and I moped the kitchen and cleaned up the coal house and porch the clothes dident dry very good but we folded them and they were all right to iron in the morn Mira dident feel very well in the afternoon but she went and stayed with Mrs Lanning in the evening she was sick and Mr L had to work this is Court week Nette started for prayer meeting went as far as Lovejoys and we had a little shower so she come back home and fixed some of her letters ready to mail Ida dident come down that night Mira dident get home till we were all a bed

Thursday Nov 13 we done up the work

Mira wasent able to do much Nette done some bakeing pa expected Mr Greason to come to dinner with him but he couldent come that day. I ironed what I could and we left the rest till the next day Mira felt better and she and Ida went to Society in the afternoon Nette went out to Franks to take Bonnie home and to tell them Frank was on the Jury and could not go home Nette stayed until the next afternoon she helped Lulu and Eva do the chores

Friday Nov 14 Mira got up as early as usual and helped do all the work we finished the ironing and got dinner after dinner I took the carpet rags that we had torn and went up to Ida's and Mrs Lanning was there we sewed all the afternoon Mrs L took some home to sew and I took the rest expected Ida to come down and sew some in the evening but Louise was to sick to come so I took the rags and went back up there and we sewed quite a ball Nette got home a bout 3 OK Lulu brought her Mifs Reid stoped when school was out and stayed all night she is helping Mira with a jacket (Angies old plush coat) Nette went to Choir practice with Ruby I come home at 9:30 found them all up but Rodney.

Saturday Nov 15 got up about 6:30 got breakfast. had buckwheat pancakes Mifs Reid and Mira worked on her jacket all morning Nette done up the work I helped what I could but I always have so much fussing to

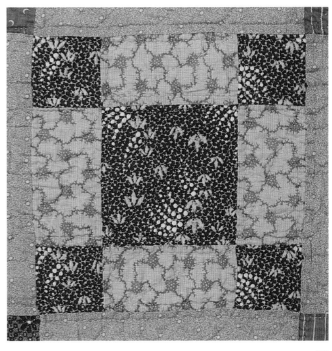

Ida (center, back row) posed with friends for an 1893 Fourth of July photograph. The flags pinned to the young ladies' bodices offer a whimsical but patriotic note to their somber expressions.

Fourth of July

The Fourth of July was always an occasion for great celebration on the frontier, as it is today, especially in rural communities. Each town held sporting events and games; there were speeches, races, parades, picnics, a band concert, and in the evening a dance and fireworks. All of the Chambers women noted at some time in their journals the events held on that holiday.

In 1912, Mary Chambers made the following entries in the first days of July:

Tuesday July 2 I got up about 5:30 got the breakfast done the work Ida come down and made cookies and I made two cherrie pies Ida canned the last of the early cherries just a pint then she come down in PM and arranged blocks for quilt big four patch to be joined with pink Mrs Yates is going to join it for her

Mrs Nickols come in and stayed quite a while had a real nice visit

wed July 3 real warm rained a nice shower in PM Ida ironed some and baked bread and was down home a while in AM I just done my every day work I have to churn almost every day Ida went by Nerves [Charlie's wife, Minerva] when she went home and got her a mess of peas she got some onions and some pie plant [rhubarb] for Mrs Pilnacek then Mrs Scott wanted her to come down there and get a mess of greens so she went down and got them and put them on to cook Ida sent pa some of the peas in the PM she come down here and she went over to Mrs Corrells and went with Mrs Harper and took the quilt over to the Church they dident stay very long for there was a storm comeing up and there dident any one come to quilt so they come home and they had to run all the way and got wet some then we had a nice shower Mrs H stayed here till about 5 OK we had a nice visit. Rodney come home from Curtain's

Thursday July 4. I got up early it was cool and pleasant but in just a little while it began to get cloudy Rodney was going out to Woofters Grove to the picnic he and Warren Harper were going with Bernard Briney but Warren couldent go had to go back to Beardsley so Rodney and Bernard went it began to rain before they got out of town and rained all the way out there but they thought they had a good time Ida come down here and stayed all day she went and took Mrs Yates some milk then she come down here and we had dinner togather Dr come and eat with us after we had our dinner we visited a while and then done a little mending Ida got supper down here Dr had to go to country it was awful stormy looking in the evening and did rain a little Mrs Ida Davis died at 5 OK it is a very sad death so many little ones with out a mother she suffered terrible I am so sorry for the family

Friday July 5 it was pleasant Ida done a little ironing and then she got ready and went over to the Church to help fix up the things for the funeral Brother Rice phoned for Rodney to be there to ring the bells I done up my work and got dinner had it ready when the funeral was over Ida come in and eat dinner then went home and rested a while then she come back down here Mrs Thomas come and she and Ida went over to Mrs Pinegars to see her a while Mrs Doty and her mother called on Ida dident find her at home so they come on down here and Ida see them come so she come back home we had a real nice visit we went out in the back yard to see the cherries

Sat July 6 got breakfast and done my every day work Ida come down and helped do the work she will come down here and work and let her own work go I wish she wouldent do that way she went home and got dinner and finished up her work then she rested a while and come down here again and looked over some wild currants Eva come up here a little while Ida come down a little while in evening I churned to day

Fifteen years later Nette made the following brief entries:

June-28-1927 Picked and canned cherries. quilted in P.M. Had my hair shampooed & fingerwave.

June-29- picked & canned cherries. Lulu and Inez was here in P.M. we quilted.

June-30- went to church. Letter from Carl. Paul & Alice here in P.M. I went to church Hot wind.

July-1- washed. finished quilt in P.M. Letter from Alice T. Helped Mary pit cherries.

July -2- Picked cherries. Ironed Mary took Elmira to Hospital. Took care of baby.

July-2- went to see Sophia in evening.

July-3- picked cherries. made cake. Hot winds

July -4- Legion Boys put on big celebration. It was estimated about 15,000 here. Nice day. cloudy most of the day. Jesse & Ona come over for lunch. went with them to see fireworks and with Lulu & Frank to the dances.

Ida's Fourth of July entry nine years later is a delightful comment that will touch the heart of every quilter:

July 1 1936 Another warm day. we ironed some for Mrs Kelley. Mrs Doty come, we quilted in P.M. in evening had a neighborhood picnic. had nice time. Mr Hayden's were here.

July 2 Warm. Mrs Doty come in A.M. we quilted some in A.M. and P.M. Nette and I went to see Mrs Reeves in evening. Mrs. Doty went with us.

July 3 Still warm. Mrs Doty come, we quilted in A.M. and P.M.

July 4 Warm. We cleaned up the house in A.M. was busy all forenoon. Cady was here. in P.M. we quilted a while. that the way we celebrated. Nette went to the show in evening. I stayed home

Friendship quilt, 70½" x 83½", c. 1945. Mira Chambers Gaunt pieced a Friendship quilt that is very similar to two Friendship quilts that Ida made. Mira may have sent small squares of fabric to friends from Atwood, Ellsworth, Nebraska, and Colorado, requesting them to sign their names on the fabric, which she then embroidered over. The name blocks have different styles of handwriting, indicating that each person or family may have signed personally. This could also be a memory quilt, because several people whose names are on the blocks, such as "Docter Melugin," Ma and Pa Chambers, and Nerve and Charlie Chambers, had already passed away when the quilt was made in the mid 1940s. The 8¾" blocks are hand-pieced, while the blocks and sashings are stitched together by machine. The backing is green fabric turned to the front and stitched down with heavy, red cotton thread. The top is quilted with green thread.

Quilt courtesy of Hazel Gaunt.
Photography by Brian S. Birlauf, Birlauf and Steen Photo, Denver, Colorado.

do after dinner the girls took a notion to go to Court so I cleaned up the front room fixed the fires and had the dishes most washed when Eva and Lulu come they left Ida [Ida Lambach] here and they went to Court I finished up my work and then tried to patch some but dident do much but fuss with the children Ida and Louise come down a while and Mrs Ellison come in a little while this was the first week of Court they have tried Dulls case and convicted him of murder in the second degree. Jury come in about midnight I am so sorry for Dull's wife

Sunday Nov 16 got up most seven got breakfast. girls washed the dishes I made my bed and then got Rodney ready for SS I had dinner ready when they come home Ida and Dr eat dinner here to day Mira and Ida washed the dishes Nette went to ride with her young man [Atwood Cochran] she had a bad headache when she come home I made mush and we just had mush and milk for supper, and then we all went to Church Brother Hansel preached a temperance sermon and then we had sacrement we come home from Church and all had a lunch. and the rest have all gone to bed and asleep it is 10:30 and I must go to bed it has been clear and cool to day

Monday Nov 17 I got up at 5:30 this morning made the fires got on the wash water and then got breakfast. we got along pretty well with the washing it was all done before dinner Mrs Davis come in just before dinner and of course we had to visit some after dinner she sung and played some for us and then Nette sung some of her songs then we done up our work and cleaned up I was busy most of the afternoon. Nette went to Mrs Butlers a while this afternoon we sent our carpet rags to the weaver this morning we are going to make a carpet for the parsonage they are telling awful stories on our preacher just hope they are all false it was real cold this morning but was a pleasant day

Tuesday Nov 18 got up at 6:30 made a fire and started breakfast when the folks were ready we had breakfast and then done up the work the girls went to ironing and I ironed some Nette made a cake to take to Lodge to night they are going to initiate Mrs Walker after dinner I tried to do some patching Nette and Mira went down town Mira went to Mrs Pinegars they were home at suppertime got supper and done up the work and then they all went to Lodge after Lodge and lunch pa come home but Nette and Mira went to the Church to a Junior League Social. Linnie was

here this afternoon to see Mira got a card
from Jesse said they had moved to Denver
went today Nov 18 has a regular trick now.
our folks come home from social about 11 OK
went to bed awful tired

Friday Nov 28 we got up late they are all so
tired being up so late nights we done up our
work and I guess Mira had time to sew some
before dinner and after dinner Ida Mira Nette
and Lulu went over to the Church and put in
the red and white quilt the[y] got it in and
quilted quite a lot. they are going to have it in
the fair. when the girls come home we had to
get supper and do our chores as quick as we
could to get ready to go to the lecture. he read
Who killed Joe's baby and showed the pictures it was very nice they sung three songs
ilistrated by pictures

Sat Nov 29 we got up about 8 OK I had the
house warm and breakfast ready when the
rest got up I made bread and Nette moped
the kitchen Mira cleaned up the front room
Lulu helped afternoon Nette and Lulu went
down town Nette come back after a litle and
Ida was here they [Ida and Nette] went down
to see Cady and the baby Franks folks come
in in the afternoon but I did not see them
they dident stay long Lulu went home with
them after supper Ida come down a while
Dr called in and see Mira she was haveing a
bad time with her stomach when the Dr
come back he brought her some medicin and
he brought some oysters Ida cooked them
and we all had a nice dish of oyster soup
then Ida and Dr went home I bathed Rodney
and got him to bed and then I read a little and
I went to bed

Sunday Nov 30 last day of the month got up
at 7 OK got breakfast I blacked Rodneys
shoes girls helped do up the work after
breakfast and they got ready for SS and
Church I got Rodney ready the Baptist had
our Church today it was half past 12 when
they got home I had dinner waiting it is 4
OK Nette went out to Franks this afternoon
Mira is over to Rubys pa is a bed. I want to
write some letters and then go to Church this
evening Sunday evening just got home from
Church went to hear the Baptist minister
liked him real well Nette dident go but a little
ways this afternoon it was to cold Ida come
and went to Church with us she had to go
home alone dont know where the Dr was.
well I must go to bed and get up early to
wash.

*Detail of Mira Gaunt's Friendship quilt. It is interesting to
note that even in a quilt, John Melugin was known to the family as doctor. That is the way he was referred to in letters,
diaries, and interviews. Perhaps that is because there was a
John in every generation of the Chambers family, but more
likely it was a term of respect and recognition of John's educa-
tion and skills.*

Monday Dec 1 got up at 6 have breakfast
started and the boiler on I have a bad
headache but hope it will get better my head
did get better we got our washing all done
before dinner had to wash dishes and clean
up the kitchen after dinner Granny come and
talked a while with the girls I brought in the
clothes and took down the line Ida Mira and
Nette have gone over to Mrs Butlers to help
tie a comforter for the society they are going
to quilt at the Church tomorrow and it is
Mothers meeting to I have sprinkled the
clothes to have them ready to iron tomorrow

Tuesday Dec 2 I got up early but the rest
dident get up till 8 OK we done up the work
and then the girls done the ironing I dident
help much to day but done all I could they
got through before dinner after dinner we
went to the WCTU [Women's Christian
Temperance Union] meeting I enjoyed it ever
so much and we had a nice little visit after
the meeting was out some of the ladies stayed
and quilted a while. Mira went out to stay on
her claim to night [When Mira was twenty-

Ida Chambers Melugin, wedding photo, 1894. Photo courtesy of Audry Gaunt.

one she had filed on a claim just north of Atwood over the Nebraska line.] Mr and Mrs Gaunt come in after her they brought us some butter the wind come up toward evening and it is blowing like everything now and it is 8 30. Nette and pa have gone to Rebekah Lodge they want to practice instalation so they can have it public I am affraid we are going to have some winter now

Wednesday Dec 3 I got up a little after 6 this morning it was real cold and it was snowing and blowing like everything we dident all have our breakfast till 9 OK then we done up the work and it was about dinner time Nette made a mince pie for dinner after dinner Ida and Nette went to Club at Sister Hambly's Louise stayed here and I tell you I dident get lonesome it is clear but real cold to night. dident get any mail from Colby to day

Thursday Dec 4 we was up a little earlyer than comon had breakfast by eight OK. we

done up our work and then Nette went down town and got things to make a fruit cake for Christmas we thought Mira would be home to day but she dident come guess she will be here in the morning Ida went down to quilt this afternoon took Louise with her Nette was home all day went to Cong prayer meeting in the evening and Ida went to the parsonage to quilt and Nette went around that way after her Louise stayed here and they [Rodney and Louise] made me awful tired and nervous

Wed Dec 24 got up this morn at 6 30 made the fires and then mixed my bread and then started breakfast Nette made the mince meat and let it cook a while and after she washed the dishes she made a cake I dident bake my bread till after dinner the girls helped wash dishes and then they went down to the Church and helped fix the Church and tree and they dident hardly have time to eat their supper I made the pies in the afternoon just as we were through supper Frank and Lulu come they were cold some got warm and then went to the Christmas tree. they all went but me they brought me some presents we kept Frank and Lulu all night it was so cold and the roads so bad I fixed Frank a bed on the cot we fixed the fire so it kept.

Thursday Dec 25 I got up at 6 OK made the fire in the kitchen and got breakfast when it was 7 30 I called Frank and told him the coffee was boiled enough when he was ready for breakfast we baked pancakes for him and pa and then we had our breakfast and then we all went to work Nette got the Turkey in to bake the first thing and then washed the dishes and Lulu wiped them Mira swept and dusted the front rooms. it was awful cold but Franks folks come about 11 OK Mr and Mrs Lanning come and so did Ruby but Lon was not at home we had a very pleasant time they all seemed to enjoy themselves. we had some music after dinner the men went down town Ida and Eva went to do some tradeing Nette washed the dishes Mrs Lanning wiped them Mira and Lulu cleared up the dishes and put them away after they were washed so it dident take them long when it was all done we visited a while and at 4 OK Frank's folks started home and Frank and Lulu went to but Mr and Mrs Lanning stayed quite a while longer. Ruby had to go as soon as she eat her dinner her mother had to go to some star doings Sam Gaunt came up a while he eat supper with us Ida and Louise stayed to

supper after supper Mira Nette and At went
up to Mr Lannings and spent the evening
they thought they had a very pleasant time
they come home about 10:30 Ida dident feel
very well and went home early and went to
bed it was an awful cold night we all got lots
of presants

Nette copied down the following fruit cake recipe in
her journal:

ENGLISH FRUIT CAKE
2 cups butter.
2 cups granulated sugar
8 eggs
$\frac{1}{2}$ lb of raisins
$\frac{1}{2}$ lb currants
$\frac{1}{2}$ lb figs
$\frac{1}{2}$ lb dried apricots
$\frac{1}{2}$ lb shelled almonds or walnuts
$\frac{1}{2}$ citron. Juice 1 lemon.
1 cup sour milk
1 cup grape juice
$\frac{1}{4}$ cup molasses
2 teaspon Baking Powder
2 teaspoon cinnamon. nutmeg
1 teaspoon cloves.
6 cups flour.
Cream butter add sugar Add beaten egg
yolks & molasses
Sift dry ingredients together & combine alter-
nately. first sour milk. then with fruit juices
Have chopped nuts & fruits thoroughly
floured & add gradually to mixture. Last fold
in egg whites beaten stiff
This recipe makes about four two lb. cakes

After Christmas was over the Chambers women went
back to their quiltmaking:

Wed Dec 31 I got up at 6 OK made the fires
and mixed my bread and have the breakfast
as near ready as I can till they get up well we
had our breakfast and done up the work and
then the girls went up to Ida's and got the
quilt frames and they put on a comforter and
they tied it off by 2 OK it is for Cora and John
I done up the work in the kitchen and tended
to my bread and I made three pies I got the
dinner and then done up the work so the girls
dident have to stop only to eat their dinner
they went to Mrs Jacobs to Club this afternoon and I sewed the quilt around the edge
Louise stayed with us.

The following week the girls put Mira's Log Cabin
quilt on the frame in the evening after supper. Ida came
down to help and they tied enough to "roll twice" even

Dr. John Nelson Melugin, July 2, 1899. Photo courtesy of Audry Gaunt.

though Ida had to leave early when the doctor came for
her. The next day was the dinner for the Women's Relief
Corps, and though they had to bake beans and a pork
roast, a cake and some pies to take to the luncheon,
when they came home they still finished the quilt and
got it off the frames. Entries from Nette's journals also
briefly describe their days:

January 5 1903 Ma and I washed today, Mira
was not well. It was fine day to wash. I went
to town this eve to get outing for Mira's quilt.

Jan 8 1903 Cant think what we did that day.
Put Mira's Log Cabin on and tied some
Jan 9 1903 Baked cake and pies this
forenoon. finished tying off Mira's quilt, went
to practice with Royal Neighbors.

When she was just a young girl of thirteen, Nette
wrote the following prophetic lines in Ida's autograph
book:

February 20,1883

Dear friend
   Roses bloom
   Lillies fade.

*Ida's crystal pitcher.
Courtesy of Inez Minney
Walters.*

But Never Never
Be an old made.
    Your sister
      N

Where Ida was like her mother in that she was generally content to stay at home and work at her quilting and domestic chores, Marie Antoinette, or "Nette," was a very different spirit. A tall, slender girl, Nette had a dramatic beauty, musical and singing talent, and a natural attraction to people and activity. At another time and place she could have been a business executive or an urban dweller following a frantic social life. In Atwood, Kansas, Nette was a member of every club that was formed, an attendant at every church activity and a lifelong, avid movie-goer. Where Mary Chambers' journals reveal that she often went days without leaving her house, and Ida's visits were to her mother or a neighbor's home and church events, Nette was in and out throughout the day. While her father and Charlie had the feed store she helped in the office in the mornings, and afternoons were taken up with visiting or clubs. At various times through her life she belonged to the Unity Club, Cosmopolitan Club, Bethany Bible Class, Farm Bureau, Ladies' Aid, WCTU, Jr. Aid, Delta Deck, the Pinochle Club, the Women's Society of Christian Service, and the Home and Fireside Club. Having been a charter member of the Rebekah Lodge, she was an active member for fifty-eight years. She also belonged to the Radiant Chapter of the Order of the Eastern Star for thirty-five years. Nette avidly played bingo, bridge, pitch, pinochle, and mah-jongg. She belonged to the Methodist Church for sixty-five years, taught Sunday School, sang soprano in the choir, and was often requested to sing at funerals and other religious services. Nette was a member of the first Atwood City Ladies Band. She attended almost every sports meet, high school play, concert, lecture, and 4-H event that came to Atwood.

There is a sense that where Ida was satisfied with her life in western Kansas, Nette had an energy and zest that pushed against the borders of her existence. Nette never married, but she had a great love, a relationship that endured for more than thirty years. Atwood Cochran was named for the town because he was the first child born there in 1882. By the time he was twenty years old in 1902, he was keeping company with Nette, escorting her to church, movies, and social events. With a difference of twelve years in their ages (Nette was in her early thirties at that time), their relationship was looked on with great disapproval by their families. In a 1914 letter to Mira, Ma lamented: "Nette has gone to the show that fellow is still around just as he has been the last 12 years O dear I do get so disgusted I dont know what to do" Perhaps another reason that Ma was disaproving of the relationship is that when At, as he was called, was in his teens his brother was involved in a tragic murder-suicide. That sad event may have prejudiced Ma against the family, but in later years Ida and Nette had several dear friends among the Cochran family.

Consequently, Nette and Atwood never married, but they did continue "keeping company" until the mid 1930s; it was a relationship that endured for three and a half decades. As the years went by, in addition to escorting Nette to church and the movies, At became a great help to the Chambers women with the work around the house. He took time away from his job as a plasterer to come by early on Mondays to pump water and carry the heavy buckets for washing, often staying on through the morning to help with the rubbing and to carry the big laundry tubs. He could also be counted on to help with

Triangle quilt, 72" x 80", c. 1900. This lovely quilt is hand-pieced with 629 triangles and is attributed to Mira Chambers Gaunt. Each piece is outline quilted ¼" in from the seam lines. The quilt backing is muslin and the binding is a soft purple, cut on the straight and hand applied. There is a wonderful variety of nineteenth-century fabrics in this quilt. Quilt courtesy of Doris Gaunt Shaeffer. Photography by Brian S. Birlauf, Birlauf and Steen Photo, Denver, Colorado.

other heavy domestic work such as setting up the stove for winter or clearing ground for the annual garden behind the house.

From Mary's journal:

Monday March 27, 1911 Nette got up made the fire and got on the wash water and then got her breakfast pa and Rodney got up and had their breakfast and went away Rodney to school and pa to his office they dont never think about what there is to do in the house Charlie and Steen sent their washing and Ona brought her clothes and we had a pretty big washing all togather made a big washing I dont know what she would have done if At hadent come to help her he done all the rubing on the machine and brought in and carried out all the water. I dident do a thing but make my bed I dident set up all the time Nette wouldent let me do any work any way she worked hard all day dident get her washing all done and cleaned till 4 OK and then the wind got to blowing real hard and she

had to get the clothes in and begin to do night chores and get supper it always hurts me to see some body else work so hard and I cant do any thing but I just thought I would try and be careful and see if I would get stronger Nette put the boiler on again in the evening for the washing next day

Tuesday March 28: Nette got up and made the fire and got the breakfast washed dishes and cleaned out the Base Burner and done all the work and started Mrs C washing At come again and done the rubing and he brought in the rinse water then he went home to help Sophia [his sister] do their washing Nette got her's all out before dinner it begun to blow after dinner and was just terrible dusty she brought some of them in and dried them by the fire.

Perhaps Nette and Atwood chose to be just close friends for all of those years, although some have said that Nette would have gone ahead and married in spite of the family's disapproval if At had agreed. The only clues Nette left that may reveal her private feelings are a collection of wistful poems she copied in the back of her journal:

If we had parted when the first chance word
 was spoken,
When the first gay smile was given,
Before the deeper founts of life were stirred,
Before the veil that wrapped our eyes were
 riven,
Love locked light dropped no meaning in that
 touch,
We might have parted then with fond regret,
And my poor heart have never ached so
 much
As now it aches this still September day–
To feel that thou art vanished from my sight,
No more to see thee on thy lonely way,
No more to wait thy coming morn or night.
If we had parted ere we come to know love's
Lesson learned a little year ago
If we had parted while our lips were free
 from
Sweet close kisses which have altered life for
 me too surely,
and I think for thee,
How calm had been the parting now so rife
 with tears,
With vain heart-burnings and despair,
Yet, shall I chide fate, that close linked us in
 so fond,
 so fair, so brief a union and does now
  divide?
I think not so,

John H. Chambers, 1898.
The Chambers store sold
flour, feed, and coal.
Photo courtesy of Rawlins
County Historical Society.

I keep my sorrow free from chiding, though I
   say farewell today to the last glimpse of
   youth, of love, of thee,
And I turn my face toward a darkened way.
Ah, had it never known love's magic touch,
I think my poor heart would not ache so much.
                 Author Unknown

Nette's diaries have a very different feel from Ma's,
who seldom left the house and meticulously recorded
her unending round of work through the day. ("Friday
Feb 5 1915.....I begun to do the work in my bedroom
there is always so many things to pick up and put away
empty slop clean spitoons and lots of things you cant
mention") Nette would mention helping with the ironing or that she "did up the work," but the rest of the
daily entry would be filled with her activities, clubs and
musical events, and the names of the many friends she
called on. Nette enjoyed cooking and baking and often
included a recipe in her journal. She also listed her
favorite authors and the books she read. Nette recorded
birthday and Christmas gifts and notations of her cash
expenses, a practice also seen in Ida's diaries. It is interesting to note the prices on some of the sewing supplies
Nette bought:
Oct -09 [there is no indication if that was the ninth of
October or the year 1909]
     Pins .25
     Special pins .10
     Silver Thimble No.11   .40
     Scissors .75
     Collar & Cuff-Buttons .50

Being a single woman all her life, Nette was also
called on to be the family nurse. Many of John and
Mary's brothers and sisters had moved to Fairmont,
Nebraska. John's youngest sister, Nancy, lived there with
her husband, Ike. She was never in good health, and
early as 1902, Ma recorded that they had sent for Nette
to come and help out, since it appeared that Nancy was
dying and possibly would not last until John and Nette
could make the trip east. Nancy recovered but continued
to have bouts of sickness, sending for Nette each time,
who dutifully went and cared for her aunt and took on
all the household work for weeks and months at a time.
This continued for decades until Nancy's death almost
forty years later. Nette also traveled to Colorado and
California to care for her brothers and their families
when they needed her. While she was away, she and Ma
and Ida kept a constant stream of letters going back and
forth, writing almost daily. The following entries are
from Nette's earliest surviving diary:

Jan 15. 1903 Left home this morning about
7K. arrived in Oxford about 6K Ethel met me
at the train. Left this Friday morn about 8.
arrived in Fairmont at 12 noon. Uncle Ike met
me. found Aunt N. some better. Got dinner.

Jan 17. 1903. I did up the work and rested a
little. Uncle I. went to town. when he came
home I got supper. Mollie was up and gave
Aunt a bath. Mr Homing & son came out a
few minutes.

Jan 18 1903 Sun- I did up the work swept the front room. combed Aunt's and Fannies hair. Mr & Mrs Lashbrook came up. Mrs Hall was here a while. Fannie's father Mr Cassone came out few minutes.

Jan 19 1903. Monday When the Dr came out this morning he brought Mrs Frasier with him. Mollie came to give Aunt her bath but could not as they were here. Uncle Ike and I washed. Mrs Albro came down and we gave Aunt her bath. my first experience in that line. I am learning a little every day. I wrote a letter to Virginia Chambers this eve for Aunt.

Jan 20 1903. Did up the mornings work. Mrs Lashbrook came and give Aunt her bath. We had soup for dinner. I rec'd a letter & paper from Rastus. Mr & Mrs McCashlin were over. Mr Horning was out a few minutes. Dr came out to see Fannie. I did the ironing after dinner. Uncle Ike went to bed and I am going to sleep in the room with Fannie.

January 21 1903. Mrs Perkins and Badger came over to do the washing but it was done. They washed the dishes for me. Mrs Chas Perkins came over in P.M.

Jan 22 1903. Uncle Ike went to town today. I did not get the Breakfast dishes washed untill about one. Got a letter from the folks at home. I slept on the couch untill two. Aunt got up then and slept in the Chair. Mrs Badger brought some buter milk and left a lb of butter.

Jan 23 1903. The same thing over again today. Mrs Albro came up a few minutes this P.M. All about the same.

Jan 24 1903. Uncle Ike went to town this A.M. brought me a letter from home. I moped after dinner and made a fruit cake. The folks are about the same. This has been a fine summer day.

2-21 [no year indicated] 44 this morning. Sure fine out. windy today. Cleaned & dusted, bedrooms & front room. finished my tenth block. Ida finished quilt Thundered and rained.

Nette continued to care for her family in times of sickness for all of her life. Nearly ten years later she nursed her older brother Henry back to health from a near fatal illness. With Nette away Ida stepped in to care for her parents, now in their seventies. Thinking that Henry would soon die, John wrote an exceptionally caring and

Ida and John Melugin's home, Atwood, Kansas, 1896. Photo courtesy of Rawlins County Historical Society.

poignant letter that reveals the depth of his wisdom and love for his family.

Atwood Kans 9/24-12

Dear Mira & all

Just a line to let you know how Henry is Dr Melugin has binn to See him and got home yesterday he told Ma Henry was a very sick man and could not last long unless he changed for the better soon, he had quite a talk with the Dr that is waiting on Henry and they changed the medisin for him, and it may help him. but by the way he talked to Ma he has but little hopes for him and Henry wants if he dies to be burried at Atwood & Minn says anything Henry wants will be don. So, we can prepair for the worse. one year ago we wer all at home an happy and little did we realize that Henry would be the 1st to go oh Mira how nisisary it is to be ready when the good Lord cals for us, Ma is holding up bravely, she has said all the time Henry would not get well Nettie is at henrys and will stay as long as it is nisisary. Ma and I are getting along all right Ida helps all she can Love to all
    JH Chambers

By the following month Ma wrote to Mira that Henry was regaining his health, possibly with the assistance of Nette's good care:

Atwood Kans
Oct 11 1912

State Birds and Flowers quilt, 75½" x 90", c. 1943. In the late 1930s Hazel Gaunt embroidered forty-eight blocks depicting the birds and flowers of each state. A few years later her aunt Ida Melugin set the blocks together with a solid purple fabric and quilted the top for Hazel. On the back Ida embroidered the date of the quilt's completion: "Oct 1943." Quilt courtesy of Hazel Gaunt. Photography by Brian S. Birlauf, Birlauf and Steen Photo, Denver, Colorado.

11.30 OK

Dear Mira I got your letter last night and I wanted to write but I am so tired every evening I cant do anything it rained yesterday and most all night and has rained all the morning and it is cold pa has to set in the corn[er] in the kitchen we must get the stove up in dineing room but you know we have to let fire out in the range to put the pipe on and we will have to move the cupboard Ida is working so hard I am afraid she will be sick she is putting up pears today had a half bushel I must put my potatoes on now I have not swept or made beds yet bakeing bread and churning but I will get around by bed time

pa and Rodney will be here in a few minutes pa is not as well as usual dont eat enough to keep a flea alive yesterday was his birthday 71 years old I cooked a chicken fried some of it for Rodney and boiled some for pa he eat a little broth nothing with it but a very little of the boiled chicken he dont like potatoes or bread wont eat a bit so what can you get him sometimes he will eat a little toast but he dont seem to feel very bad just weak well. Rodney come and has had his dinner pa has not come yet. I got a letter from Nette yesterday they seem to think Henry is improveing his Dr says he is doing just fine the worst is he gets nervous and cant sleep good at night Nette and Minnie take turns setting with him sometimes they can both sleep I think Nette is getting anxious to come home I want her to stay with Henry as long as he wants her I can get a long some how if I feel as well as I have and I have felt awful bad some times but I dont care for Henry wants her and they need her I dont know as she will stay till Henry can come but I want her to if she thinks she can (I suppos At is getting anxious) well. pa has come and had his dinner he eat a litle bit of rice and cream and drank a glass of milk he said he had been reading a book Charlie gave him for his birthday now Mira let me know if you get this tomorrow I will try and write more when I possibly can I ought to write to John and Jess. Mira I am so glad you are getting where you can find a little time to sew Ida dont have much time to sew now she has a star boarder she dont do near as much work as she makes do you need more stuff to make Jesse pants what are you going to make him waists of

kiss them for me love from ma bushels of love from grandma it is now 1 OK and I have not eat any dinner write when you can write to Nette anyway

Nowhere is the difference between Ida and Nette more apparent than in the style of needlework they did. Where Ida sewed clothing for the family and generally gave her time to her first love of quiltmaking, Nette was more often making lovely, but less practical, needlework items such as bureau scarves and tablecloths. She was very skilled at hardanger, pulled thread, and cut work and embroidery, and the surviving pieces of her needle-work show a highly developed skill at these precise crafts. "Nette got our supper and then she worked a lit-tle bit on her hard anger. then At come and they went to the picture show." (3-33-19 Ma) Many journal entries describe neighbor women and friends who came to Nette for assistance with their fancywork.

The youngest Chambers daughter, Mira, was also a great seamstress and quilter and many of her lovely quilts have survived as treasured heirlooms of her descendants. Mary Chambers noted that "Mira finished her drefs her blue Mother Hubbard" and that she was cutting out pieces for her necktie quilt. (10-21-02) Just days later Mira "riped up the skirt she is going to color to make her a waist of." On a practical but mournful note, Mira worked on a jacket for herself, made from her late sister Angie's old plush coat.

In 1901 when Mira was twenty-one, she filed on a homestead north of Atwood and just over the state line near McCook, Nebraska. Perhaps the sandhill country to the north was the only land available and that would account for Mira taking a claim so far from her home. It is also the area where the Gaunt family filed, and three years later, Mira married James Elmer Gaunt. Mira's time away proving up her claim was the beginning of a lifelong separation from her family that Ma and "the girls" always lamented.

But in the times when Mira was at home in Atwood

One of John's red Physician's Memorandum books contains the entries of Ida's earliest surviving diary. The first page begins: "Monday June 19th 1916. picked enough cherries in Ma's south lots for two pies." This journal was begun just four months after John's death.

she was busy quilting with Ida and Nette. There was a Log Cabin quilt that Mira pieced and the girls tied with an outing flannel backing, and they quilted her Necktie quilt. In the fall the girls and their friend Lulu Lambach pieced and quilted a "red and white quilt" that was donated to be sold at the Methodist Church fair.

> 1-8-03 after supper the girls put on Mira's quilt and they rolled twice Ida come down a little while but the Dr come and they went home early the girls left the quilt and went to bed

> 2-24-03 got up at 6 Ok had a hard time to get the fires to go it was so still it was snowing and had snowed quite a bit before I got up I started breakfast and Mira and Rodney were soon ready to eat. pa eat his breakfast about 8 and had to hurry down to weigh a load of coal and then come back and done the chores we done up our work and got on the flats to heat then Mira went over to see how Mrs C was found her a good deal better she come

home and we begun to iron and we had to hurry to get all done before dinner but we got it done and had dinner ready when school was out we hung the clothes on the line in the front room to let them dry and air and took them down toward night Mira washed her hair I combed it out for her and then she set by the stove and pieced while her hair was drying I did not do much this afternoon. I was to tired to work I wrote some and Ida was here a while and I was looking over pieces Mira had to do the out door chores again to night it was so wet under foot after we had our supper and done up the work Mira and Ruby went to Rebekah Lodge pa went to so Rodney and I were alone only the boby brought the milk and stayed a little while pa and Mira come home about 9.30. we had a little visit and I made my sponge and pancake and then went to bed.

As Mira's wedding approached in the fall of 1904, the quilting activity increased and there are numerous journal references to putting on quilts to tie or quilt. "Mira went up [to Ida's] and put in another quilt this after noon." (8-3-04 Ma) "Mira went up to Ida's and quilted in the fore noon." (8-4-04 Ma) After the September wedding, Mira and Elmer moved 210 miles north of Atwood to Ellsworth, Nebraska, a two-week trip by wagon, where they raised cattle on their sand hills ranch. Farming was nearly impossible in the sandy soil, and the vegetation was barely adequate to support cattle. It was a hard and lonely life for Mira living out on the prairie with her growing family. Her parents and sisters worried about her welfare and whether there was adequate food and clothing for the children who soon came along. They often urged her in their letters to bring the children down to Atwood, where they could attend school and where Ida could help Mira in sewing clothes for the children.

There is no evidence that Mira ever kept a diary except for the brief fragment reprinted here, which consists of half a dozen pages written the year following her marriage to Elmer. It is understandable, given the large family of six children that Mira eventually had, that she simply didn't have time to write daily entries. However, Ma had more children and she was a faithful diarist, so it must have been more of a personal inclination that kept Mira from writing.

Nov-1 1905 We came into Grandma Powell's house Nov 18-Cora came Elmer and I went down to see her, she stayed with me all day Sunday I was sick Nov 20 I took her to train then I stoped at store got 3 yds of calico for cupboard 2 yds of ribbon 4 yds of white goods. Then went to Ona's stayed until about five. During week I worked two aprons finished pillow cases finished drawn work across one end of scarf. Nov 26-Elmer did not have to work so we went to Johns and spent day. had awful nice time. Nov 27- Raining. Dec 22 Went over home with Jesse folks had an awful nice time I got some nice presents.

Came home Saturday. Dec. 30. Jan 1-Was cloudy all day did not seem much like New Years. Jan-2 Was snowing when got up and kept it up nearly all day Received letter from Father G. and Luella. Jan 3-Still snowing After Xmas made piece of drawn work Then commenced to work on Ona's Pattern-Feb 15 finished it Feb. 26-Feb 27 commenced Baby pillow finished it Mar-5 Then finished up center piece Hazel had commenced. Mar-6-Made front and collor of drawnwork. Commenced pillow Mar 15-Put fringe on scarf and made 5 blocks to my quilt.

A 1912 letter from John to his daughter Mira reveals the love and concern that existed among the family members. They wrote two or three times a week and always sent food or clothes and gifts for Mira's children.

Atwood Kans 6/5-1912

Dear Mira & Elmer Jesse & John
    Ma wanted I should write you a few lines to let you know we are all well. not anything new or strange only we have had more hard winds this spring than usual and not much rain the wheat and gardins need rain bad we wont have much wheat if it dosent rain soon, say Mira you spoke about a man by the name of McIntosh being at your place his father & mother live down by Herndon and they came up yesterday to see if it was true about seeing him They have not heard from him for 4 years and did not know wher he was. they would lik to know what he is doing, so have Elmer find out if he has a claim and how far from your place how he is fixed, we told them we would write you & find out about him they are anxious to know just like any father & mother would be, they hadent heard from in so long was affraid he was dead-Nette has gone over to help clean the church guess she will go to Fairmont this week our place looks fine will have some appils & pears and appricots. not many cherries. I am glad you got the boxes all right. I thought Jessie would need the shoes as bad as any thing & little Johns shoes. how I would like to see him am glad he is so good baby it will be a great help to you and now accept lots of love & well wishes to all. how long does father Gant expect to be gon. how much will the Late Pension law help him I will get 18.00 a month untill the 10. of
Oct 12- when I will be 70 years old & will get 24.00 a month
    JH Chambers

On December 25, 1897, Ida wrote in Lulu Lambach's autograph book the following inscription, which was accompanied by a photo of Ida in a white bonnet: "Dear Lulu, May there ever be only enough Shadow about your life To make a beautiful sunset, is the wish of your friend, Ida B. Melugin. I wish you a Merry Xmas and Happy New Year." Photo courtesy of Inez Minney Walters.

Mira did return home for long visits, often staying for several months while the children attended school, but she always returned to Elmer and their sandhills home. In 1909, Ma wrote, "Mira come home March and went away May 30th Mira is very lonesome and dissatisfied." Living out on their prairie claim, Mira missed her parents and the close company of her sisters. The isolation of the long, cold winters was always difficult for her and there was also the additional concern of keeping the stock fed and sheltered. Without a healthy and growing cattle herd their very existence was threatened.

A February 1914 letter from Pa indicates that the family in Atwood was greatly concerned about Mira and Elmer: "Mira I am sending you a draft for 5.00 dollars & you use it wher it will do you the most good it looks as though we would get more snow, now dont worry about the loos of the cattle it my be for the best, what does Mr Gaunt think is the cause of the loos of the stock"
From Ma's 1910 journal:

    Mira came home June 13, 10 and stayed until Oct 11. 10 we have had such a nice time and now we mifs our baby so bad it is now 9 so I expect they are still waiting at Oxford O my the house is so quiet

Wed Oct 12, 1910 we finished the ironing this morning and chopped the green tomatoes this afternoon Paul [Paul Treadwell is the nephew John and Mary raised after his mother died from burns in 1892.] did not come to day dont know what is the matter it has been a windy day and awful dusty wish we could have a little rain

Oct 15 1910 I got up at 5 OK this morning we had our breakfast and done up the work as quick as we could and got ready to go to bean dinner I went to the dinner and had a real

Ida B. Meluzin

nice time but I was awful tired come home
about 4 OK and done some mending Ida was
down in the evening

Sunday Oct 16 1910 the folks all went to SS
and Church I stayed at home and got dinner
had the little white rooster for dinner cooked
it in the oven Ida got a card from Mira she
was in Anadarko would stay there till Elmer
got a horse in Chickesha I wrote to Jesse in
the afternoon dident feel very good layed
around and read and wrote to much they all
went to Church in evening

Monday Oct 17. 10 I got up and made the fire
and put on the wash water tried to help all I
could with washing the wind and dirt blew
awful bad but Nette got them all dry put out
a few and then took them down as soon as
they were dry I helped clean up we were
both tired Paul and Alice were here a while
in the evening

Tuesday 18. 10 Oct Nette washed for Mrs C
and it was a real bad day to so windy and
dusty it was just as bad on Mon but she got
them dry she was home in the afternoon and
Ida was down and Nerve was here a while
then she went down town she got her a new
hat and I think it is real pretty it begin to get
colder in the afternoon and was real cold at
night but it was cloudy and the wind blew
hard and it dident freeze we brought the
plants in when pa come home from Lodge I
done some patching today keeps me all the
time to mend Rodneys clothes

Wed Oct 19 1910 got up this morning at 5 OK
it was so cold thought I had better make a fire
early I got a good fire and then I went out
and fed the chickens and worked out doors a
while it was almost 8 before the folks got up
then we had breakfast and done up the work
then Nette cleaned up the dineing room a little and moved the cupboard so we can get the
stove up if it keeps cold I moped the floor
and then we got dinner and this afternoon I
have been mending some I dident feel a bit
good got a letter from Mira and one from
Jesse they are all pretty well just now

Friday Oct 21. 10 it was real cold this morning froze hard killed the four O clocks we
done the house work there is always something extra to do the work kept us busy till
noon in the afternoon Nette went to Mrs
Mungers she entertained about 40 the HS
boys from Colby played our boys foot ball
ours boys beat 12 to 0 Nette went to Lodge in
the evening they took in some new members
they were out real late

Monday Oct 24 1910 Nette done quite a big
washing I done up the work and then helped
some with the washing after dinner we
cleaned out the coal house a little and put out
the gasoline stove and then pa and Nette put
up the heater in the front room it was real
cold last Thursday but is warmer now wont
make a fire till we need it

Tuesday Oct 25 1910 we got up early I had
breakfast about ready when Nette got up she
ate her breakfast and then went over to Mrs
Corrells and done her washing I done up the
work and got dinner I was pretty tired but
Nette washed the dishes made some mince
pie for dinner I thought they were real good
Nette went to society in the afternoon they
met at the Parsonage. the[y] tied a comfortable it has turned cold this afternoon was
real cold at night it was so cold pa says let
the stove go till it warms up a little

Thursday morning Oct 27 it was real cold
and the wind blew terrible all day and the
dust was just awful Nette washed the windows in the dineing room and kitchen I went
out side and turned the hose on them we
made them look pretty good in the afternoon
Nette went to see Mrs Frank Robinson Ida
was here and I done some mending Ida was
down again in the evening Nette went to the
Church to practice for the consert it was real

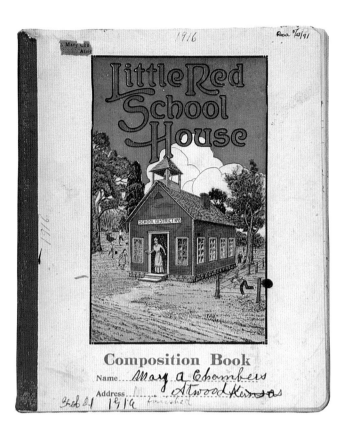

Mary Chambers's journal. On Friday, March 28, 1919, Mary wrote: "we got our dinner Ida and I were alone we eat our dinner and done up the work then we went out and watered the chickens and then I raked up the chips out where Henry cut kindlings. when we come in Ida was quilting on the society quilt I have been writing."

cold for this time of year we must get the stove up it is now 6.30 Friday morning I must stop and get the breakfast it is awful cold we cleaned the house all over purty near dident get done till the middle of the afternoon then Nette went over to the Church and I went and fed the chickens and cleaned out the barn and yard then we put up the stove in the dineing room then had supper and I went to the Church to the consert I thought it was real nice Bert sung

Sat Oct 29 1910 Sat was a nice morning we done up the morning work and then done some bakeing made some pumpkin pies for the Social at Mrs Reeves made a mince pie and an apple pie for home after dinner Nette had to go over to the Church and I was alone a little while and then Aunt Mollie come and we had a good visit Eva and Ida [Lambach] come and after a while Ida and Nerve come

Sunday Oct 30 1910 got up and had breakfast and done up the work Nette dressed a chicken last night for dinner to day I had dinner all ready when they come home we had our dinner and then I just set around for a while and then I wrote a long letter to Mira she is still in Chickasha they all went to Church in the evening I was home and wrote some

Monday 31 1910 I got up at 5.30 made a fire and put on the wash water dident have a very big washing At helped some I hung up the clothes and rubed the stockings I emptied the water and cleaned up the coal house and back steps Mrs Jacobs and Mrs Boyer called in the afternoon Nette went to the show in the evening

Wed Nov 2 we done our ironing I had all the underware mended and put away the girls [Ida and Nette] both went to society at Mrs Cochrans they tied a comforter for Mrs George I took my basket of stockings and went over to Mrs Corrells and spent the afternoon

Mira's longing for her family was a result of the physical separation. For all of their adult lives there was a constant stream of letters and gifts between the sisters and parents and long visits home with the Chambers. But for Ida there was a loneliness that was caused through the demands of the doctor's profession. Because of weather, distance, and the needs of his patients, John spent long hours and even days and nights away from home. There were many lonely hours for Ida, who at times must have found it difficult to be a country physician's wife. Time after time there are entries in Ma's journals that mention the many demands on the doctor and the hours that Ida was alone: "May 15 10 had a big rain this evening begun just time to go to Endevor rained real hard is raining now almost 10.....6 OK Dr had to go in the country to embalm Mr Palmer dont see how he can get home" "Tuesday June 15, 1915 Ida and I visited a little bit then she went home and stayed alone Dr was away in the country"

On a Thursday in February 1915, Ida had taken the quilt frames to the Ladies' Aid Society, where they were going to "put on a comfortable to tie." Ma received a message from the doctor: "Dr phoned a little while ago and said tell Ida I am going to Herndon he will be gone all night." Just a few days later Ma wrote: "Ida was here a little while Dr was home and she dont like to leave him when he is home for he is home so little" When the doctor was done with his work he continued to stop by his in-laws' home to get Ida. Without Nette and her parents and her quilting friends Ida's days would have been long and lonely.

Mira Chambers, Nette Chambers, Ida Chambers Melugin, and Nancy Chambers Eastwood, c. 1899. Photo courtesy of Inez Minney Walters.

Although Ida always longed for Mira's presence, three of her brothers had also left Atwood. Henry was an engineer with Southern Pacific and he and his wife, Minnie (Mary Martha), lived in a number of towns in Nebraska, Colorado, and Kansas. Jesse was a telegraph operator for the Burlington Railroad in McCook, Nebraska, where he lived with his wife, Ona. John and his wife, Cora, lived in Stratton, Nebraska, where he was an agent for the B & N Railroad. One advantage, however, was that as employees of the railroad, Ida's brothers and their families could easily travel to Atwood for visits. Interestingly, it was to John and Mary's home that the daughters-in-law went when their babies were born. Ida and Nette were very close to their sisters-in-law and loved to spoil and pamper their new nieces and nephews.

Charlie stayed in the country and farmed the claims until 1901. He and Nerve then spent a few years in Oklahoma, but by 1907 he had returned to Atwood, where he worked in the feed store with his father. Just a few years later he was elected mayor of Atwood.

The two decades of her marriage were busy and fulfilling for Ida. In addition to keeping her house and helping with John's erratic schedule she was active in her clubs and with the "M.E. Church," where she held various offices over the years in the Sunday School and the Ladies' Aid Society. "We done our ironing I had all the underware mended and put away the girls [Ida and Nette] both went to society at Mrs Cochrans they tied a

comforter for Mrs George" (11-2-10) Ida occasionally took in boarders, many of whom were students attending high school in town. The Lambachs were lifelong friends with the Chambers family, and their daughter Lulu lived with Ma and Pa or Ida all through her high school years. A surviving report card from 1900-1901 shows that Lulu lived with the Melugins during her ninth-grade year and that Ida signed off on each monthly report.

By 1902 Louise York was living with the Melugins, but there are few mentions of her after 1910. It is likely that those are the years when she went away to school and later to study medicine. On September 16, 1917, Ida noted that she had written a letter to Louise York, and in 1920 Ida listed in her journal the expenses related to a quilt she pieced for Louise and had quilted by the Ladies' Aid Society:

> March 5 1920 For Louise quilt
> Cotton batten   .50
> unbleached muslin 5 yds   1.75
> For quilting   3.00
> $5.25

> Mrs Nickols helped me bind it July 24th 1920
> July 27th mailed Louise quilt postage .15
> Gave Louise $2.25

Three months later Louise was in Atwood for a visit with Ida, who wrote in mid October: "Pleasant but little windy. In P.M. Louise and I took a walk out south of town went out to the rocks." And on October 20, Ida noted an expense of $1.10. "For Louise and I to go to the show. The eyes of the world." The quilt and that last visit are the final references to Louise. Although it is clear that Ida and John did care for her for many of her childhood years, after she left Atwood contacts became very sporadic. Clearly, however, the gift of the quilt reveals the affection that Ida felt for her.

In 1910 Ma noted in her journal the income earned by the Ladies' Aid Society of the M. E. Church through quilting and tying quilt tops:

July 30 Mrs Hacker for quilt.	$1.00
Aug 4 Mrs McCormick	.75
Sept 14 Mrs Pilnacek quilt	1.00
Sept 28 Mrs Yager comforter	.60
Nov 16 Comforter	.50
Nov 30 Mrs Harper quilt	.10
Dec 7 Mrs Mather rags	.25
Jan 11-11 Mrs Fisher sewing	.75
Jan 25 Mrs Preder Comforters	1.00
Feb 1 Mrs Chambers quilt	1.00
Feb 1 Mrs Munger quilt	1.00
Feb 15 Mrs Briney Comforter	.50

In 1912 Mira was in Atwood with her new son, John, born on New Year's day. She stayed with Ida for several

Dec 25th 1900.

Christmas at Home.
Pa and Ma. Charlie and Nerve
Frank and Eva. Uncle Ike,
John, George Lambach, Lulu,
Nettie, Mira, Rodney, Little Ida
Is and I.
I recieved for xmas. a nice
rug from Pa and Ma. fancy
plate from pa. cracker jar
from the girls and ma.
a fancy little-dish from Lulu,
a wish bone breast pin from Mira
a book. (Meadow Brook) from
Mrs Noble. a pretty handkerchief
Mrs Buster. perfume from John.
Minnie brought me a dog.
aunt nancy sent me an apron,

weeks and the sisters sewed for the baby. Ma wrote the following entry:

March 7. Thursday I got up at 5 OK this morning still cloudy and misting just disagreeable all day Nette and I done up the work and finished the ironing I have the mending most all done and the clothes all put away I went up to Idas about 11 OK and stayed till 7 this evening had a nice time with the girls and the baby they were sewing all day Mira has been makeing the baby new short dresses and today she cut out corset covers for herself Ida wants to help her get her sewing all done up good before she goes home.

When the baby was nearly two months old Mira began to make plans to return to her home in Nebraska, in spite of the concerns of her parents and sisters. Ma was already beginning to mourn her leaving when she wrote on March 2, 1912: "Now I begin to worrie Mira has got to go home away up in the Sand Hills I dont know what she will do away up there with little baby"

The early months of 1912 brought an exceptionally harsh winter with deep snows, and the families were often housebound. On March 15 Ma wrote: "I got up at 5:30 it was not very cold but snow till you could not see out they shoveled what they could." Three days later the weather warmed up and Nette put on a quilt and planned to have the society at their house. In the afternoon she wanted to go to Ida's, but "there was so much water she could not get there it was nice and warm but the snow had melted till it was almost impossible to go

On October 2, 1911, John and Mary Chambers celebrated their fiftieth wedding anniversary. All of their children came home for the occasion and more than 150 friends gathered at their home. The newspaper described it as "an event which will long be remembered as this is the first celebration of this character in Atwood." Mary's children gave her a "gold brooche" and John received a gold-headed cane. In addition, they were given a rocking chair, which is still a treasured family heirloom.

any where a foot." The following day there was a blizzard and only one lady came to quilt. The following week they had another quilting and a third one on April 3. Ida and Mira and the baby came for the day. They had "quite a crowd" and finished Nette's quilt.

Interestingly, although it was recorded some twenty years earlier in the Homestead Application that the family possessed a sewing machine, Ma wrote that Nette was making a "Light Mother Hubbard," and had gone up to Ida's to sew on the machine. (A Mother Hubbard was a casual, loose, long cover-up. It was comfortable, less fitted than a dress and required no bustles, hoops, or corsets. With a high neck and long sleeves, it could be worn loose or sashed at the waist.) Most likely, Ida's was

a newer model and may have been easier to use. Ida made a lot of clothing on her sewing machine, but she continued to piece her quilt tops by hand. Sometimes, however, she did note in her diary that she stitched up a lining for a quilt on the sewing machine.

One Thursday in January 1914, the Chambers women hosted a quilting for the Ladies Aid Society and Mary wrote of all the preparations:

> 1-21-14 has been a bad stormy day I got up at 5:30 OK fixed the fire in the heater and made the fire in kitchen and got coff and oatmeal ready for breakfast. then done what I could put more coal in heater and fixed the table so we could have our breakfast when it was 7 OK I called Nette and we had our breakfast then Nette called Goldean [a student boarder] and Nette baked cakes for pa and Goldean then Goldean fed chickens and tended to cow. Charlie got up Nette made cakes for him they come to the office with coal and pa went over to weigh it. Ida come down to help. they were in the front room putting on the quilt the top dident fit very good so Ida took it up home and fixed it and she dident come back till after dinner we finished up the work and got dinner as early as we could for it was society day but it was so cold and stormy we dident expect many but there was over 20 they seemed to have a good time and I think they had a good lunch they seemed to enjoy it any way they dident all get away till 5:30 then we got supper for Charlie and pa and we all eat some Goldean had her work all done before supper it was pretty cold and stormy after supper Nette and Goldean washed all the dishes and there was a pile of them all went to bed 11 OK

Through the winter and spring of 1915, Ma recorded a number of Ida's and Nette's quilts and sewing projects. "Nette was working on her log cabin quilt Ida was fixing a pair of unmentionabels for me." "Ida cut and made me a pair of outing pants Nette was working on her log cabin." "Ida was down a little while she was cutting pieces for Charlies slumber robe." "Ida was down a little while pieced two blocks." "Nette put a new faceing on her black pettecoat yesterday afternoon and this afternoon she worked on her log cabin quilt Ida was here and she made some blocks for Charlies slumber robe she has the blocks all made now we had two callers Mrs Cooper and then Mrs Charlie Brown come after the quilt that was made of tobacco sacks." "Ida was sewing made the lineing to Charlies slumber robe and sewed the binding on the quilt Nerve pieced when Nette come back she went to work on her Hardanger." "Ida come they went they took the quilt frames they went down to Mrs Hines they were going to put on a comfortable to tie."

The doctor continued working long, grueling hours and Ida tried to spend as much time as possible with him when he could be at home. "Ida went to Church this morning and she wants to go to night to hear the boys report of the convention but she dont like to leave the Dr alone." (2-14-15) "Ida come down and pa set up with us a little while then he went to bed and Ida and I visited a little but then she went home and stayed alone Dr was away in the country I set up and wrote some in my book." (6-15-15) "Ida was here with me but she went home she thought Dr would be home before morning but he dident so I was alone quite a while then I went to bed." (6-24-15) "Aunt Mollie come and brought a comforter and a quilt she wants the society to quilt when ever they can she stayed quite a little while and we had a real good visit she is so much more cheer ful than I would think she could be." (6-26-15) But the stress and demands of being a country doctor were taking a heavy toll on John's health. He had never been in great health, and he had originally gone west in the 1880s in the hope that the climate would be beneficial and his strength would improve. By 1910 when he was in his mid fifties, the long hours and travel to visit patients through hostile weather had had a serious effect on John's health. Although he continued to work, he was severely weakened and began to suffer from a habitual cough and shortness of breath.

Dec 24, 1911 we all eat dinner here there was just Dr and Ida she stayed a little while and then she went home Dr went down town again he is not very well has an awful bad cough the snow is so deep we can hardly get around.

In a February 1914 letter to Mira, Pa wrote: "the Dr is bad with his lungs he bleads a good deal. if he dont get better soon, he wont live long lots of days he dont go to his office, and stays at home nights"

One year later Ma wrote:

Feb 27 1915 Sat PM when Nette got up she washed the dishes and Ida come down a while the snow is about a foot deep the girls both have all the out door work to do the Dr or pa are not able to do a thing and I am not as well as usual and the snow is so deep that I dont try to do any thing. Ida was doing some of her fancy work Nette to work on her Hardanger and I made a pair of pillow cases out of flower sacks my pillows are small when it was chore time Ida went home and Nette fixed up and done all of our chores got in coal and kindlings watered the cow and done the milking I had every thing ready to get supper we just warmed up potatoes and

Ida and Nette sent this Christmas card to their young nephew Jesse Gaunt in Ellsworth, Nebraska, in 1908. Twenty years later Ida wrote about her Christmas celebration: "December 25, 1928. A fine day. we ate dinner with Thorne and Mary. Mrs. Kelley, Mary E. Ruth, Irene, Lonnie, Eve, Mr and Mrs Frank Hoover, John, myself and Thorne's family. we had a nice time and good dinner. Mrs Allen was there. we had turkey, chicken dressing, gravy, irish and sweet potatoes, gravy, corn, mince and pumpkin pie, light rolls, angel food and fruit cake, cabbage, slaw, water melon pickles, dill pickles, cranberries, plum jell."

cooked pa an egg pa was asleep and we didlent wake him till we was pretty near done eating when we were all done eating Nette cleared up the table and washed up the dishes alone I was so tired but I didlent go to bed I finished my pillow cases I sewed on the lace Ida didlent come down in the evening but the Dr come from down town about 9 and he stoped in and rested a while he was so short of breath just panted like every thing he went on up to the house and Ida said he just leaned up against the side of the house till he got his breath a little I think he is bad off pa went to bed when the Dr went home Nette went to the show but she come home about that time she worked a while we set up over an hour after she come home it was 11 OK when I put out the light it was clear enough so we could

Nette and Mira Chambers, Rodney Gillette, age four, and Ida Chambers Melugin, June 6, 1900. Photo courtesy of Audry Gaunt.

see the moon it looked so pretty on the moon
I mean the moon shineing on the snow.

While John's health quickly declined, Pa also grew more frail. He ate less and less and had no energy. Ma grew very despondent over his failing health and always cooked his favorite foods in an effort to get him to eat more. "Feb 18, 1915 pa come just now and has gone to bed again I do get so blue he is so poorly all the time I cant fix any thing he can eat just sets around and then goes to bed and just lays and sleeps"

While John's health declined, Ida filled her hours with quilting. Among the quilts she made during John's last years was one pieced of tobacco sacks and one for her brother Charlie, a pieced "slumber robe." And although the names of her other quilts were not recorded by Ma, there were almost daily mentions that Ida was piecing or quilting. Her work would have been a great solace to Ida while she waited through the silent hours while John

was away and later as she observed the daily signs of his ebbing strength and vitality.

On September 1, 1915, Pa caught a cold and never recovered from his last illness. Nette recorded his final days and the gathering of his family. Perhaps Nette wrote of Pa's death after the fact, because of the finality of her entries ("The last time he was down town"). Or perhaps she was aware that Pa sensed he would not recover, and that he would "be ready when the good Lord cals."

September 1, 1915 Pa took cold and was real hoarse.

9/2/15 Pa went to a party to Mae Scott's for John Hayes, his 75 birthday. The old soldiers give him a chair and pa made the presentation speech. Charlie went after him with auto.

9/3/15 Pa was no better went down town little while.

9/4/15 Pa went down town and did not stay long. come home & went to bed. The last time he was down town.

9/5/15 Pa got up and dressed and then stayed a bed all day.

9/8/15 Pa went out doors the last time.

9/12/15 I washed pa's neck and he changed his clothes the last time.

9/13/15 Pa asked Ida to have Aunt Nancy come. [Nancy Eastwood was John's youngest sister. She lived in Fairmont, Nebraska.]

9/16/15 I went to Grace Reeves to society. Aunt Nancy & Uncle Ike come. Pa was glad to see them.

9/18/15 Dr sent telegram to Henry & Jesse & John.

9/19/15 Jesse, Ona, John, Cora & Burdett come about 5:45. the girls went to bed and the boys eat breakfast then went to bed. Pa visited with them little. Charlie took John, Cora, B. & Ona to Stratton. Jesse set up with pa.

9/20/15 Pa continued to fail. Charlie & John come about 10:30. Jesse sit up that night, and Ma stayed by Pa and sit in rocker. Rodney come home.

9/21/15 Pa continued to grow weaker. Mr Johnson come & read chapter & had prayer.

Jesse & John sit up all night. Ma sit in rocking chair after 12 oclock.

9/22/15 Pa very low the boys went to bed. We called them. Pa talked to all of us and bid us goodbye. Thot he could not live until Henry come. Henry got here about 1:20 & Pa died about 1:30 just lived to see him. Cora come over after John, they went back to Stratton.

9/23/15 John, Cora, & Burdette come in P.M. about two oclock. brought some flowers from McCook, Rec'd nice pillow of flowers from Fairmont.

9/24/15 Pa was buried at 10 A.M. windy day. Paul & Alice come down. Bert, Celsus, Ruby & Edith Guy sung. They sung Nearer still Nearer, In the hour of Trial, Blest Be the Tie. We all eat supper here. There was 18 of us. Lots of lovely flowers

Five months later Nette wrote in her red journal: "Feb-11-1916 Dr Melugin passed away." Just two weeks after her forty-ninth birthday, Ida became a widow as her mother had just the previous fall. Ida immediately went to stay with Ma and Nette, and she never returned to live in her own home.

On the day of John Melugin's funeral, Ma began a new journal. Her entry for that day covered two pages and listed the activities, guests, and sleeping arrangements for the visitors. The only clue as to the grief and sorrow that Ida was feeling on the loss of her husband was in Ma's comment that Ida went to bed because she was "sick with her stomach trouble."

Mira Chambers, Atwood High School graduation, June 6, 1900. Photo courtesy of Audry Gaunt.

Sunday 2-13-16 Sunday morning Ida went up home as soon as she could get ready after breakfast then I got ready as soon as I could Nette had to help me so I was a little longer for there was so much to do Nette got me ready to go up to Ida's and then she and Cora got dinner and got ready to go they all come up to the house we were there quite a while before it was time to go to the Church the Family took our last look of the Dr. and then we went to the Church at 2:30 the house was full and away out side there was a big crowd Paul brought Mira home from the Church because she couldent leave Doris so long we went up to the cemetery and the Masons had a short service it was very nice Emma was not able to go out only come here to stay with Pauline and the little ones John and Doris and Jessie Wilson come and stayed part of the time when we got home we got dinner just as quick as we could. we only had a lunch before the funeral Paul and Alice set down first they were in a hurry to start home then we all had supper for it was almost night when we got through the girls Nette Cora and Mira washed the dishes Ida went right to bed she felt so bad and then she was sick with her stomach trouble Charlie and Emma went home right after supper she dident feel very well the rest of us set here and visited quite a while then Henry and Ike went up to Ida's house and slept Jesse and John slept over to Charlies and Cora and Burdette in the front room bedroom and the rest as we always did Ida slept with little John and the rest of us in the other bedroom

Embroidered Flower Basket quilt, 68" x 83", c. 1937. Ida's niece Doris Gaunt Shaeffer embroidered sixty flower basket blocks for her quilt. She then sent the top to Atwood, where Ida and Nette quilted it for her. In 1937 Ida noted in her diary: "I went downtown got lining and batten for Doris Quilt." (9/25/37) "we put one in for Doris. one she embroidered." (10/12/37) According to family records, Ida worked on at least three other basket quilts. In the late 1920s, Nette went to Eagle Rock, California, to care for her uncle, Henry Chambers. She stayed with the family until Henry's death. Henry's daughter-in-law, Vinnie Chambers, embroidered fifty blocks for her quilt and Nette wrote in her journal: "Put the embroidery quilt together." (9/20/29) Having fewer blocks, this quilt had a double border of pink and white. The quilt top was then sent to Ida in Kansas to be quilted. Ida also made another set of embroidered quilts for Rodney Gillette's daughters. One quilt was set with alternating blue blocks and then quilted, and the other is an unquilted pink top. Quilt courtesy of Doris Gaunt Shaeffer. Photography by Brian S. Birlauf, Birlauf and Steen Photo, Denver, Colorado.

Done Little Sewing

Ida received $1,000 in insurance money and she rented out her house, eventually selling it in 1922. "Saturday July 1st 1922   Sold the old home place signed the deed this P.M. sold to Roy E Stires"

the abstract cost	$12.25
the deed	1.50
the notary fees	.25
	$14.00

After John's death, money was increasingly scarce for the remaining years of Ida's life. Other than quilting and domestic work, there were few opportunities for a woman of Ida's age to earn an income. She frugally noted her expenses in her journals, revealing her interests and causes. In 1920 she recorded $1.00 for Women's Christian Temperance Union dues and another entry for "Anti Saloon $3.00." Ma, Nette, and Ida were all dedicated members of the Women's Christian Temperance Union. Ida paid fifty cents a week to the church fund for the pastor's salary, increasing the amount to $1.00 when she could manage it. She also recorded money paid to the mission fund and the building fund:

Oct 10th to help put furnace under church $2.00

Jan 16 1921 For the starving children $1.00

April 25, 1921 To the children's home finder $1.00

Food costs were often recorded:

Mar 10 1920 For eats $2.00
    meat .95
    blackberries 1.45
    cucumbers .60
    coffee .60
    Postum .35
Aug 9, 20 Flour 3.75
    tomatoes .50
    bacon 2.25
Wed Sept 23 1920
    milk 1.00
    meat .45
    sugar .60

And of course cloth, thread, and needlework magazines and other sewing supplies were frequent expenses:

April 18th 1918 Shirting for John [Mira's six-year-old boy] some shirts 4½ yds $1.35
Jan 9 1921 gingham 1.40
    rick rack .20
Mar 6 1921 pillow tubing 2 yds 1.30

2 spools thread .25
crochet thread .30
Mar 27 1921 unbleached muslin five yds 1.75
April 16 1921 needles .10
Dec 29, 1921 2 balls crochet thread .30
1 ball crochet thread .15
1 ball crochet thread .15
Jan 9 1922 percale for dress 5 yds .90

On February 3, 1921, Ida purchased "a new electric washing machine." Less frequently she bought shoes or a "pretty hat," but clothing was a much less common expense:

April 19th 1919 got new hat $6.50
Sat 2 Feb 1924 bought pair of low shoes
$3.25
Aug 30 1924 3 suits underware and 2 pair
stockings $3.28

Ida subscribed to several magazines, most of which were sources for crochet, needlework, and quilt patterns:
Feb 1918 American Woman .50
3-6-21 Square deal -9 mos $1.50
4-16-20 Needlecraft .50
Feb 21 successful farming .70
Square Deal for 1921 $1.50

Ida also noted various medical expenses. In 1919 she paid $30.00 for new glasses and $1.00 to have her teeth cleaned. But she had trouble with her teeth and had to have several pulled ($.50), and eventually in the fall of that year Ida paid $35.00 and "got new teeth."

The earliest of Ida's surviving diaries begins in June 1916, just months after John's death, when she begins writing in one of his old red Physician's Daily Memorandum journals. The journals were issued each year by the makers of Pepto-Mangan, which "aids mightily in restoring normal conditions by 1. Increasing appetite and improving digestion. 2. Rebuilding old and creating new red cells. 3. Increasing the hemoglobin. As a result, such causative therapy as is underway is encouraged and assisted in such conditions as Chlorosis, Bright's Disease, Tuberculosis, Chorea, Post-Operative Devitalization, Convalescence, etc." On the heading of each page one could find "a miscellaneous jumble of facts and suggestions of interest and assistance to the physician as the days fly by." Five of these volumes exist; two were used by Ida, one by her mother, and two by Nette. As an example of the Chambers' frugality, one of the books that Nette used was issued in 1902 and was saved for thirty-four years until she began making daily entries in 1936.

Other journals of Ida's have entries written on scrap paper, envelopes, and the backs of Christmas and birthday cards and stuck into the books. While many of the books were meant to be kept as diaries, others, besides John's physician's memorandum books, were school tablets and ledgers for church or clubs with unused pages. One of Ma's journals was an old geography notebook that Rodney had used in the third grade. The first dozen pages contain his homework assignments and several maps that he drew.

The timing of the entry in Ida's earliest surviving diary, just four months into her widowhood, suggests the possibility of the diary as an outlet for Ida. It was not as a means of expression for her private thoughts and grief, because with the exception of the occasional terse comment, Ida's journals were similar to Mary's in that they were comprised of the work and visits and events of each day. But a daily recording could have given a validity and comfort to her life after John's death. On the other hand, it seems unusual that Ida would have become a faithful diarist suddenly at the age of forty-nine, and in fact, there have been references to earlier diaries that seem to be lost. Ida's later journals have regular entries, increasingly relating to her quiltmaking, but until or unless additional journals are discovered, it will be impossible to know just when Ida's journal keeping began. And if it is true that she destroyed some of her earlier journals, then a great portion of her life will forever be lost. It is apparent, however, that writing was a daily activity for Ida, and there are existing diaries for almost all of the next forty years of her life, with the last entry just seventeen days before her death.

The unassuming entry that follows comprises the first lines from Ida's earliest surviving diary:

Monday June 19th 1916. picked enough cherries in Ma's south lots for two pies.

Wednesday June 21st Mrs Pilnacek picked some on lower lots. Friday Lucy Wallace and Mrs Dumond picked some up home finished the early ones. Mrs Pilnacek finished the early ones on lower lots

June 24th canned 6½ qts early cherries.

As the months of her first year of widowhood passed, Ida noted various domestic tasks in her journal:

9/11/16 took care of plums from up home. made two dozen glasses of jell and about six qts of butter.

11/2/16 Charlie and I put up base burner in dining-room. I started a fire Nov 11th

11/12/16 ground white with snow, and snowed some during the day.

Ida also recorded her first Christmas without the doctor:

12/25/16 a cold frosty day. had dinner at Ma's. There were ten of us. Ma, Charlie,

Mira and James Elmer Gaunt wedding, September 1904. Top Row: Mrs. Jesse (Ona) Chambers, Mrs. Henry (Minnie) Chambers, Nette Chambers, Mrs. John (Cora) Chambers, John Chambers, Baby Burdette Chambers, Mrs. Charlie (Minerva) Chambers, Mrs. John (Ida) Melugin. Middle Row: Jesse Chambers, Mrs. John H. (Mary) Chambers, John H. Chambers, Charlie Chambers, Dr. John Melugin. Front Row: Merle Chambers, James Elmer Gaunt, Mira Chambers Gaunt, Rodney Gillette, Thorne Chambers. Photo courtesy of Pat Chambers Thomas.

Emma, Paul, Alice, Erma, Mrs Thomas, Nette, Rodney and myself. Emma gave me pair black silk stockings, Jesse's folks a handkerchief. sister Minnie a handkerchief. Mrs Dumond a handkerchief. Minnie Bodin a white apron. Edith Willsie a bath towel. Hettie a box of writing paper. Maud Melugin a box of 3 hankerchief. Carl bottle of perfume. Mrs Pilnacek three balls of crochet cotton. Mrs King a little book Ruby a cake pan. Cara a combing jacket. little book from Mira.

There is no mention of quilting in Ida's 1916 journal, but from Ma's diary entries for the following year it is evident that Ida pieced or quilted nearly every day:

3-10-17 Ida done some mending and cut out dark for four blocks and croched some I mended some and made some holders

3-12-17 cold in am we all helped with the morning work and then Ida went to peicing on her quilt.

3-21-17 Ida eat a little and then she went to work on her quilt blocks she worked a little bit and then she took her work and went over to Emmas and was gone till chore time.

3-22-17 the girls were up about 6 and we had our breakfast and then begun the work Ida washed the dishes Nette tended to the chickens then she fixed the meat in to bake then she went and made the fire in front room and dusted out some of the dirt that blowed in wed they fixed the table with dishes on and got every thing ready that they could Ida moped both rooms I made both beds and we put some of the plants and every thing away in my bedroom that we could to get it out of the way for the PM I went over to Mrs Corrells a while then when I come Nette was getting dinner and when she had it ready we eat and then we done up the work as quick as we could and we all got ready for the PM. the society met here and I tell you there was a crowd here they served 42 plates I just set around all PM till I was awful tired but Ida washed all the dishes and she done the out door chores and Nette stayed in the front room with Grace and Mrs Overholt they stayed and quilted till 7:30 they put on the lights [the house had been wired for electricity in 1916] and quilted when they went home the girls fixed us a cup of coffee and we had a lunch then At come for Nette and they went to the show but she said she dident like it a bit Miss Anderson and Nette got home about 10 they heat up the coffee and had another cup and then we kept on talking till it was 11 OK

3-23-17 it was real cold and windy Ida done some peicing then she cut out some and she worked with her peices most of the day only crocheted some

3-26-17 Ida was makeing Doris [her niece] an apron it is awful cute.

3-28-17 Ida is makeing Doris two calico aprons this week

4-9-17 Ida washed the dishes and then took her rest and then she cleaned up and went to sewing but she bent the needle so she couldent sew much but she was buisy until most 5 Ida done a little mending and about 5:30 Ida went over to Mrs Mungers a little bit

4-11-17 the girls went over to Lucys to see angel food cake she had made Ida done a little sewing on machine Nette got the dinner and Ida washed the dishes then she rested a while before Ida got cleaned up Mrs Thomas come and stayed till almost five Ida basted up the hem in my new gingham dress

Journal keeping does seem to have been a family activity for the Chambers females, since there are no existing diaries that were kept by the men, and the gift of a journal was often a favorite Christmas present. Ida received a five-year diary from John and Cora on December 25, 1932, and one from Jesse Gaunt for the Christmas of 1938. Nette gave Ida another five-year diary on September 14, 1944. Ma also received a diary as a gift from Pa in January 1903. When Nette received a small, black book with lined pages for Christmas in 1926 she made the following entry:

> As this was the day on which the record book was given to us I think it desearves special notice. Besides this it was one of the best Christmases I ever had. We got up about six o'clock and had our stockings. Carl went down after Antie Minnie and we distributed the presents.

Perhaps the most poignant gift was the five-year diary that Ida and Nette gave to Anita McAvoy in 1932. Six years after Mary Chambers' sister, Celestia Thorne Treadwell, died, her husband, Charles Treadwell, remarried in 1900. Anita was the granddaughter of Charles and Elda, his second wife, related only by marriage to the Chambers family, but because of the close ties with the Treadwells through Paul, who had lived with them for so many years as a young boy, they were all a very close, extended family. In 1932 Anita was eighteen years old and living in Fairmont, Nebraska, with her grandmother, Elda Treadwell. She was very small and rather frail and suffered from poor health, and she had attended school only through the eighth grade. But she made lovely oil paintings, an occupation that filled many of her hours, and she also spent much of her time piecing and quilting. Anita's "aunts" Nette and Ida gave the diary to her at Christmas in 1931. They were staying with their father's youngest sister, Nancy Chambers Eastwood, who also lived in Fairmont, Nebraska. On the cover page Ida had inscribed: "Love to Anita. From Aunt Ida and Aunt Nette. 1932."

Anita made faithful daily entries in her red leather journal from January through May. Ida and Nette had been visiting their relatives in Fairmont for several months, but on May 18 they returned to Kansas. Here Anita's entries end and there is no more word of her until fall. On September 13, when she was gravely ill with pneumonia there is an entry in Ida's hand: "Anita took bad had the Dr for her little dear" Four weeks later Ida wrote: "Anita passed away Dear little girl so sweet"

Here are some entries from Anita McAvoy's diary, which she began keeping when she was eighteen years old:

> 2/10/32 Pleasent. Like spring. Aunt Ida and I went out to Oledene's. Went in A.M. Come back with them after supper. Aunt Ida helped Oledine put in a quilt.

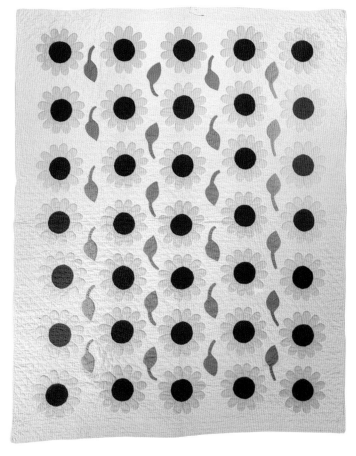

Sunflower quilt, 71½" x 87", c. 1940. Mira Chambers Gaunt designed and appliqued the delightful Sunflower quilt in the early 1940s. The brown centers are 4½" in diameter, and each of the twelve encircling yellow petals are appliqued on separately. The backing of the quilt is green, and the quilting is in white thread. Quilt courtesy of Doris Gaunt Shaeffer. Photography by Brian S. Birlauf, Birlauf and Steen Photo, Denver, Colorado.

3/1/32 Cloudy and rainy. Grandma isnt feeling very good. Her heart bothering her. I made a block and a half on my quilt today. Nette was down a while in P.M.

3/3/32 Cloudy all day. It misted nearly all day. Fogg in the evening. Went up town in P.M. I made two blocks and a half today on my quilt. Nette down while in P.M.

3/4/32 Misting early this A.M. Then turned to snow. It is snowing hard this A.M. Snowed all day. Cold. I made three and a half blocks today.

3/5/32 Clear and cold in A.M. Clouding up some in P.M. but warmer. I washed dishes, dusted and went downtown. Gma made pies and cookies. Oledine was here in P.M.

3/6/32 Cloudy and snowed some in A.M. Cleared off in P.M. Then clouded up in eve. Aunt Ida went to church and S.S. Then ate dinner to Aunt Nancy's. Grandma and I alone all day.

3/7/32 Clear in A.M. Partly cloudy in P.M. Cold all day. I went down town in P.M. worked some on my quilt. Mrs S. Porter was over while in A.M. and in P.M.

3/8/32 Cloudy and cold this morning. Wind blowing hard. Down to Zero last night. Cloudy in P.M. Spitting snow nearly all day. Grandma finished twin Star quilt.

5/15/32 Aunt Ida and I went to church and S.S. Maurice [Anita's half-brother] came from his school today. Welcome was here for dinner. Aunt Ida took her grips and stayed up to Eastwoods until they go home.

5/16/32 Maurice and Grandma washed up all the dirty quilts and blankets. An awful nice day today. Mrs S Porter did our washing today.

5/17/32 Grandma done the ironing in A.M. I helped a little with it. Aunt Ida and Aunt Nette was down in the evening. Partly cloudy today.

5/18/32 Pleasant Maurice, Grandma and I done up the work. Then Maurice tied up some bundles for Aunt Ida and we all rode down town with him. Aunt Ida and Nette went home today.

Anita's diary was tucked away, forgotten for five years until her grandmother passed away in 1937. Nette, Paul Treadwell, and his wife, Ruth, went to Fairmont for the funeral. Here Nette discovered Anita's abandoned journal and took it back to Kansas with her. The following year she began writing her own entries in it.

Like Ma, Ida saw her journals as a record of her daily activities and, of course, visits with family and friends. Weather observations were frequent, which would be expected because the weather dictated much of their daily work. There was no washing on rainy days, because the clothes couldn't be hung out to dry, and the summer dust storms were also a concern on wash days. In winter Ma or Ida often noted that when the clothes were hung outside they quickly froze and had to be spread about inside the house to finish drying. Keeping warm was always a consideration. Ida often noted purchasing a load of corncobs to burn in the stove. "Cool all day. done up work, then went over to Ruby's a while, sewed mended and pieced some. got load or rather part of a load of cobs. Joe Pinegar passed away at 8:40 p.m." (4/16/34 Ida) In later years Rodney bought "his girls" a load of coal each fall. That was a gift that Ida gratefully acknowledged in her book. Money was always a consideration, so stoves were not lit until it was absolutely necessary. Even kerosene lamps or electric lights were used sparingly, and quilting was done in the mornings and afternoons when the light was best. On a stormy afternoon Ida sometimes noted that it was too dark to sew.

Besides the expense of buying fuel for the stoves there was always the work of hauling it in each day, heavy work for a woman. In the fall after Pa and John had passed away, Ma wrote that the days were turning colder, and what would become of them when winter came, three women in a house with no man to help them. Ma made the following poignant entries in her diary: "every body is so good to us since Pa and Dr died we miss them so much." (2-24-16) "we had our dinner and just as we were about done Charlie Phoned and asked us if we would like to take a ride if we did to be ready at 2 OK. ...we started 20 minutes after 2 and got home 10 minutes to 4 we went down to the Depot and around where their Oil tank is. ...we went up to the cemetery Ida and I got out and went to Pa and Dr's grave O my it is so sad to think they have gone and we wont see them any more here but O my Father grant that we may meet in that home above." (3-5-16) "O dear how awful cold it is. ...I do dread this winter I dont know what will become of us so much to do and no man on the place." (10-23-16) In the spring of 1917 Ma wrote:

Rodney come on Sat March 31 and he went down town in PM come across Jimmie Curtain and brought him home to supper with him they seemed to have a good time we all like Jimmie so well. Sunday April 1 it was Spring like the girls done up the work and then Cora and Ina went to the Baptist Church an we had our dinner and then they rested a while and we wrote some all but Rodney he was reading Ida Nette and Cora went to the ME Church to hear a WCTU lady speak they liked her ever so much when they got home Johns folks were here then in a little while they all but Cora and I went up to the cemetery and when they got back Ida and Nette got supper Charlie and Emma Cora and Marshall come and eat supper with us we had a real good time but O how we do miss some of the dear faces then they all went to Church but Nette ma Rodney and Ida and when they had all gone Ida wrote some to Mira I dont know what I done but I was awfuly tired

At that time Rodney had moved away and was teaching school. Later he went into the army. While Ma didn't indicate whether her feelings for Nette's beau, Atwood Cochran, had changed, he did step in to help the ladies with the heavy work. For nearly all of the previous two decades, Nette and At had "kept company," attending church, movies, and social events together. He came by every day and did a bit of work, often staying for dinner, and in the evenings he and Nette went out together or stayed at home and played the piano and sang or just read the papers.

When World War I came there was never a mention of the earth-shaking international events. Rodney went into the service and they noted his letters from Paris Island, as well as going down to the train depot to see off a trainload of the local boys. Ida also mentioned a letter that she received from her nephew Thorne Chambers, written while on an army ship en route to Europe: "Received Thorne's card telling of his safe arrival July 16th 1918 then received his first letter written, Aug 2nd It was written while yet on board ship." "I am here

The little red doll's chair was a gift to Hazel Gaunt nearly seventy years ago from her aunt, Ida Melugin. The chair is sitting on Hazel's grandmother's Blazing Star quilt, c. 1880. In one corner of the quilt the name "Gaunt" is stitched in blue thread.

Mira Gaunt's homestead in the Nebraska sand hills, 1926. Photo courtesy of Hazel Gaunt.

alone it has snowed all P.M. and is still snowing we got a letter from Rodney to day he was in Paris Island SC" (3/7/19 Ida) And in their own contribution to the war effort, Ida and Nette went every week to help make quilts for the Red Cross. "Minnie come down here for dinner so she helped Nette wash dishes then in a little bit they got ready to go to Red Cross they tied a comforter." (2-19-19 Ma) "when it was time Minnie and Nette went to the Red Cross they tied a comfortor and finished all up." (2-26-19 Ma)

Nette was the only one of the three to record the end of the war: "Nov-7. Snowed this A.M. Jesse wired about noon Germany had signed the Armistice had big time Bonfire in eve. At was up this P.M."

After John's death, Ida found solace and companionship with her family. She visited her aunts in Fairmont, Nebraska, and John's brother, Frank Melugin, in Iowa. And of course, she went to Mira's. Ida adored her nieces and nephews, and with her sewing skills she could provide the very much needed clothing for Mira's growing family. Doris, or "Toodles" as she was affectionately known, was born just a month after Pa died. Ida went to Ellsworth to help her sister with the births of her children, sometimes acting as midwife, and with all the work and sewing that she could do.

Two years later, Mira wrote in Ida's journal:

Sewing we done after Ida came Sat, October 12-18 Ellsworth Nebr.
    1) Made 2 pairs of ticks for pillows changed one pair of pillows and put new

feathers in other one.
    2) Made 6 pairs of pillow slips 3 had lace on.
    3) 3 pairs of outing panties for Doris
    4) 2 waists for Doris
    5) 3 pairs of stockings for Doris
    6) finished red dress, made one blue dress 2 aprons for Doris
    7) 2 underwaists for me
    8) put collar on shirt for John also made him 2 flannel shirts.
Ida
    9) hemed table cloth
    10) bound quilt Aunt Mollie made me
    11) we made 2 shirts for Doris.

Ida spent several weeks with Mira, who was expecting another child in the fall of 1918. In true pioneer fashion Mira kept up with her heavy load of work right up to the day little Hazel was born, and since she was born at 10:45 AM on Christmas Eve, the only inconvenience seems to have been that Ida and Mira ran out of time and "dident get our turkey ready to eat."

11/21/18 Cold and stormy. snowed some. I helped celebrate Mira's birthday she worked on a sugar sack for her machine. I tore off two pair of pillow cases, sewed my butterfly yoke together and crocheted one sleeve and started to put on the edge.

11/22/18 Thanksgiving day. Ellsworth, Nebr. A sunshiny day, but cold & windy. I went with Mira & family over to Mr Moore's. we had a splendid dinner. she had the Ellsworth teacher there, Miss Tylor. we had mashed potatoes, sweet potatoes, turkey, gravy, dressing, peas, celery, cranberries, chow, chow, white, and raisin bread, pumpkin pie, and coffee.

Sunday Dec 8th like a spring morning but got cloudy and cool. looked like rain and did commence to rain about two P.M. Elmer went to town. Monday ground all white with snow but soon disappeared, sun shone out nice about noon and a little after. I made bread. Mira done little mending then in P.M. Mira cut out a black and white gingham dress for Doris. I made her doll a little comfortor out of outing flannel. Tuesday cold and windy. we washed. Elmer went to town. Wednesday still cold. we ironed in A.M then sewed on gingham dress and apron for Doris. Thursday clear and cold. Mr and Mrs Moore over. Mr Moore helped Elmer shingle west side of house I mended some then sewed on Doris apron. they went home about five Friday frosty and little windy. Mira and I cleaned up stairs in A.M. we sewed in P.M. Elmer butchered pig. Saturday pleasant. we done up Saturday work. made bread and churned done little mending in P.M. Elmer went to town. Sunday a very pleasant day. we were busy all A.M. had dinner about one. then we went for a ride, Mira the children and I, Mrs Hill and one of the boys come over this P.M. come while we were gone. Monday cloudy, frosty and a cold wind. boys went to school, but no teacher, so they come back home. Mira and I sewed for Doris dolls. Tuesday still cloudy, frosty and cold. we done up work then wrote some. we both wrote home. Mira wrote to Luella. I wrote card to John, Eva, Maude Melugin Mrs Yates and Mrs Sites. we about finished up work for Doris dolls.

Wednesday Dec 18th 1918 cloudy and frosty in A.M. snowed up until about noon, sun shone out a while. we washed and baked bread. Mira got up early to get the boys off to school. they were gone about an hour then come home. teacher not feeling well yet. Thursday pleasant, thawed some. we were buisy all A.M. Mira made pair of curtains and put up. we got our clothes about all dry. I crocheted some in P.M.

Friday 20th John's birthday. [Ida's brother John Garfield Chambers was forty years old.] Still stormy acting. rained some in A.M.

thawed all day. then in P.M. commenced to snow, and kept it up until after dark. we ironed. Mira fixed hogs head and put on to cook. in P.M. we both mended some. then in evening we crocheted.

Saturday 21st 1918 A cold, stormy day. snowed some. we done our regular work. baked bread and churned. Mira made scrapple. done little mending in P.M. crocheted some in evening. Sunday.. still cold, but cleared off was real cold in A.M. we just done up work and got the meals. I wrote some in P.M. we read stories in eve in Needlecraft Monday frosty and cloudy when we got up. but the sun shone out some during the day. we done up work then got dinner, right after dinner Elmer killed the turkey and picked the feathers off. then Mira finished dressing it.

Tuesday Dec 24th 1918 A nice winter day. I got up at five o'clock. built fire in kitchen got breakfast, then Elmer took boys over to Hills, but brought them back, also Mrs Hill. he took them then over to Mr Moore's. come back home. a baby girl was born at ten forty five. Elmer went to town about twelve. was busy rest of day. Elmer took Mrs Hill home toward night. baby dident rest very well was up and down all night.

Wednesday Christmas day. was busy all day. dident get our turkey ready to eat. Mrs Hill come over in P.M. stayed all night and took care of baby. I was pretty tired. thursday. was buisy all day. had our turkey for supper. Elmer took Mrs Hill home. she got dinner for them then come back with Elmer and stayed all night.

As much as the sisters visited, Ida never stopped missing Mira and her adored children. Perhaps because Ida herself could never leave her family, she found it difficult to accept the idea that Mira had made a home away from them. She wrote often about Mira's children. Through them she could express the great love and affection for the children that she had always wanted to have herself. Of course, the family never stopped worrying about the loneliness and hardships that Mira faced living "away up in the Sand Hills," but Ida never stopped urging Mira to bring the children back to Kansas for as long as she could stay. In letters written to Mira in 1919, Ida used every reason available to urge her to visit. In Ida's favor, however, is the fact that her brother Charlie had recently died. Now the three women were truly alone in Atwood with no man to help them or support them, obviously a daunting situation at that time, when jobs for women were virtually nonexistent, and a visit

Four Point Star quilt, 67" x 79", c. 1935. Quilt courtesy of Doris Gaunt Shaeffer. Photography by Brian S. Birlauf, Birlauf and Steen Photo, Denver, Colorado.

from Mira and her family would have been a welcome distraction and a relief from the loneliness caused by Charlie's death.

Atwood Kans

June 22nd 1919

Dear Mira

Well here it is five thirty and this is the first I have wrote today. we got up before six o'clock. dont know why should find something to do until time to get ready for S.S. but did just fussed around. Nette went with Grace Reeves to a funeral. they started from here little after nine. they havent got home yet. Henry was here for dinner, just Ma, Henry and I. Minnie and Thorne started for Fremont Friday P.M. they expect to be gone two weeks. Well Mira I got so sleepy, I went and laid down. just seems like here lately, since the weather has got so warm, if I sit down a few minutes, I can hardly keep awake. I laid down after got the dinner work done up, took a nap. then Paul and Erma come. want Ma and I to go with them over to Mrs Thomas. we did, was gone some over an hour. I wanted to write another letter besides

one to you. We recieved your letter O.K. with pictures in, was so glad to get them. how nice of baby. just think she will be six months old Tuesday. has been now over three months since I see her. am so glad you had them taken. wish you could have all the children picture taken.

Oh Mira I think of you so much, and of my stay with you. how wish was nearer so could do something for you. of course I see plenty to do here all the time, lots more than I feel like doing. now today, it just seems an effort for me to do any thing. what will it be when we get to picking and canning cherries. I do wish we dident have so much to do. no I musent say that for guess its a good thing cant think so much. I get the blues so easy these days, and know I shouldent. Nette went to McDonald to S.S. convention last Tuesday P.M. and got home Thurs noon. went to society in P.M. then down to Henry's Friday. we never done a thing toward cleaning the kitchen. so guess it will have to go for a while. was so in hopes we could get it cleaned. yesterday I worked up to the other house. got quite a little done. begins to look as though could see my way through for all I dident get the walls all wiped, nor the windows washed. but got things unpacked and straightened around some. I made another apron for Doris, will send it if can some time this week. am afraid I made the button holes to low, if so just leave the last one unbottoned, or cut the button off. then to, dont believe I got a good do on the neck. Mira what color gingham would you like for her. wish I could make her a pretty dress. you dont need to by anything to make her white shirts for some time. wish I could do all your sewing.

I have the yoke made for aunt Nancy, so now must finish it up ready for use and send it to her. I am just finishing the second little bonnet. I sent one to Hettie, just heard from it the other day. I havent made any thing yet for Minnie Bodin's babies would like to but every thing looks so big to me now. I dont see how you get through. how is my John? has he forgotten his Aunt Ida. wish he was here to help me pick cherries, and Jess too. I'll have to go up to the home place and pick some. the trees sure look pretty. Monday evening. little after nine o'clock. well Mira I never took time this morning as I should and finish your letter. we got up early, but we sure done a big washing. has been a very warm day. the clothes hung still, made them look nice. tomorrow Nette says we are going to clean the kitchen or do as much of it as we can. wish could of done it

Four Point Star quilt, 67" x 79", c. 1935. In the late 1930s Ida made two Four Point Star quilts for her nieces Hazel and Doris Gaunt. The two quilts are similar, although Hazel's is set with alternating blocks of solid yellow fabric and yellow binding, while Doris's quilt is set with pink. The stars in each quilt are hand pieced, and the 5–3/4" blocks are stitched together by machine. The straight grain bindings are both machine sewn, turned, and stitched down by hand. There is a wide sampling of 1930s fabrics in the seventy-one stars that comprise each quilt. Quilt courtesy of Hazel Gaunt. Photography by Brian S. Birlauf, Birlauf and Steen Photo, Denver, Colorado.

last week. Sanford was up today and picked cherries off of one tree. I will have to pit and can them tomorrow. we rested some this P.M. I done a little sewing, and thought was going to crochet some, but only got to do just a little. I hoed some in the garden after supper. I planted sweet corn twice. it is doing fine since the weather has got so warm, and have four hills of cucumbers. wish could have the good luck to raise a few cucumbers.

Ma recieved your card today. always glad to hear. hope you wasent disapointed because dident hear from us Saturday. I know I should write so you would get some work, but dont always do it. my feet hurt me so tonight can hardly sit still. so must quit and get ready for bed. just think Mira the days are at thier longest now.

Tuesday A.M. another warm day cleaning kitchen. baby six months today how would love to see her

lots of love to all   Ida.

Atwood Kans
Oct 8th 1919

Dear Mira,

Recieved your letter today and sure was glad to get it. we have been so anxious to hear how Doris was. but thought must be better or would of heard. but am so sorry to hear you think you cant come down this winter. for do want you to come so bad. think it would do you and the children all good. but of course dont feel like I must say to much. for you know what you can do better than I do. but it will be awful lonely for us this winter. know Ma is grieving all the time, but dont say very much. and you know Mira how lost we all feel with out Charlie. at times I just think it cant be so if you were down here we could help you with the children clothes, I want to make Doris some winter gowns. of course we find plenty to do all the time, but would be so much company to have you here with us. the boys could wear their overalls here just the same to school. of course its not the best thing to do, to change them from one school to another but think would be alright. and how nice for us to see and enjoy the baby. Ma would love to see her. she isent very well and would be nice for you to be with her a while. Aunt Nancy is still with us. but expects to go home the last of week. we sure have enjoyed having her with us. not so lonesome. we'll miss her so much. Nette entertains the society tomorrow will be glad when its over with. we have put up so much fruit and fixed pickles of different kinds, enough so could let you have some. I got beets yesterday of Mrs Beck's, and Nette canned them this morning, flour of course is high, and potatoes are going to be awful high. not many potatoes raised.

Dr. John Melugin, 1905. Photo courtesy of Audry Gaunt.

think you could live as cheap down here as up there. only you have your own milk and butter, which of course is awful nice. we pay fifty cents for butter, and ten cents a quart for milk and hard to get at that. Henry Turner died at Stratton last Sunday. was buried Mon, P.M. very sad. Madison's only boy. he had an operation for appendicites. Thursday A.M. have just had breakfast. think had a frost last night. have been trying to get the plants fixed in shape for winter. Mrs Will Holcomb come and got a lot yesterday evening. now Mira I dont know just what more to say about your coming down here. but we all do wish you could come. I think you ought to come if possible, for you know we may not have Ma with us long. and of course one ought not to say those things, but still we know how uncertain life is. little did we think two months ago Charlie would be taken. and as time goes on it seems harder to realize. now we were just planing and talking, the money that it would take for one of us to go up there would go quite a ways toward getting things for the children, and havent you all got clothes that you could wear down here. you know it dont

matter what one has on to travel in, just so its whole and clean. the boys clothes would be alright, and your coat is. but now Mira, maybe I hadent ought to write this way. but its just the way I feel, we all feel. Nette has been planing on going up there if you cant come down, but just think how lonely we will be here with out her. I would just as soon go again if dident hate to go so far from Ma. now maybe I have said to much, but you know its hard to write just as you would like to. nice that you are putting down a lot of butter. I found some thing to make Doris a nice wool dress. must hurry and make her some warmer gowns. we are sending her a birthday present today. hope they will be alright. now dont know just what more I can say, but do wish it would be possible for you to come. you wouldent need to stop off any place on way down and maybe Henry could meet you in Stratton. Doris present is from us all. you [sic] and I wish the little ones could stay in my house. think could get along fine.

lots of love
Ida.

In March of 1921, Ma passed away, just a month short of her seventy-seventh birthday. On March 1, Ida made her last entry for the month; Ma died eighteen days later: "Sibbie Giles come to see us today. Lena Smith come to see us Sun, eve. ma walked over to Emma. she went about eleven o'clock. got back before twelve Emma come with her, then she went on to town. Ma got pieces to mend Jesse's overalls." Her death was a great loss to her entire family; she was the center of the family. In addition to her own children, Paul Treadwell and Rodney Gillette, the boys she had so lovingly taken into her own family and raised, also mourned her loss. As was the situation six years earlier when Pa died, Mira was expecting another baby, Rodney Hall, born just a month after Ma's passing. Ida went to Nebraska to be with Mira, but it was a sad time for her, especially on "Decoration Day," a time when she had never been away from home, and with the remembrance of the ones she had loved who were now gone:

Tuesday April 26th 1921 Pleasant in A.M. Minnie and Joe Gahley took me to Trenton we left home about nine got to Trenton in plenty of time for the train. stopped off at Akron. found them all well. was surprised to see me. left there early in A.M. made good connections and got into Ellsworth about twelve thirty. Elmer met me at the train. we come right out to their place Mrs Moore was with Mira. Thursday pleasant but cool, Baby boy born at ten A.M. Mrs Hill and Dr with us.

all concerned got along fine. Mrs Hill stayed Saturday P.M. baby was real good.

Ida stayed for an extended visit with Mira, and one month later on "Decoration Day" she wrote: "we mended and sewed some in P.M. after supper went with Doris and Hazel after chips. was the first Decoration day I was away from home in years if ever was before. A very sad day for me." The death of her mother was a terrible blow to Ida. It took a great deal of time for her to reconcile herself to her loss. Her diaries mention her grief, and she copied down poems and verses dealing with the loss of a loved one.

Sadly, Ida's second oldest brother, Henry, died on April 16, 1922, just twelve months after Ma's death. A further blow was the death of Mira's new baby four months later. Rodney Hall Gaunt lived only sixteen months before he died in August 1922. Ida wrote in her diary: "got word from Mira that baby was quite sick. Nette got ready and started up there that night. dident get to Mira's until Sunday P.M." (Friday, 8/11/22) Little Rodney died two days after Nette arrived.

Ida was fifty-four years old when her mother died. She had been a widow for five years and had also experienced the loss of her oldest brother, Charlie, who perhaps had been closest of the boys because he had spent most of his adult years in Atwood, living in a house just across the street from his parents' home. Like many mature women, Ida now found herself at a time in her life when the needs of her loved ones were in the past. The creative energies that had previously been saved for the precious and few free moments of the day could now be unleashed, and she could increasingly devote herself to her lifelong love of needlework and quilting. From this time on, until the end of her life, Ida was rarely without a sewing project or a quilt on the frame and one or two others in some stage of progress. Ida quilted every day of the week, except Sunday, when she refrained from picking up a needle, perhaps because of her religious beliefs or perhaps because, like many stitchers who were taught by an older generation, she grew up with the old admonition that "every stitch you make on the Lord's day you will have to remove in the afterlife—with your nose!"

For the last several decades of her life, quilting became the major creative focus of Ida's existence. Quilting for others provided her only cash income, quilting was her significant social outlet, and of course, quilting served her need to incorporate beauty and creativity into her daily life. There was always a quilt on the frames set up in the parlor in front of the window. From this vantage point Ida could see all the way downtown, she could quilt and watch the comings and goings of the town, and she enjoyed the companionship of her neighbors, who often stopped by to visit and quilt for a while. One close neighbor, Mrs. Doty, was an especially dear friend and the two ladies spent many hours quilting together.

Although her first name was Mary Rose (she was usually called Matie) and she was a full ten years younger than Ida, she is never referred to in Ida's journals by her first name, only as "Mrs. Doty." Of course, that formality reflects a time when only children and family members called each other by their first names.

If Ida had gone to town, Mrs. Doty would let herself into the house and would often be sitting at the frame quilting when Ida returned. For two decades Mrs. Doty stitched on nearly every quilt that Ida put in her frames, and in many instances she also helped with the piecing and marking the quilting design. Upon completion of a quilt, Ida would remove it from the frame and walk to a neighbor's house to show the just-finished quilt. The many years of Ida's life that are documented in her journals are also narratives of the importance of the role that quilting played for her. Ida made quilts for her church, her clubs, her family, and all of their children. She made quilts for her friends and neighbors, to commemorate events, to raise money, to meet the challenge of a new or difficult design, to "make do," to use up fabric scraps, and, always, just for the love of quilting. Her diaries are remarkable chronicles of an ordinary woman living a fairly quiet life, a woman whose one creative love and passion speaks to us across the boundaries of time, a woman who becomes remarkable herself as she has documented her life one page at a time, one stitch at a time.

Ida's Corn Pudding

2 cups corn
1½ cup milk
2 eggs
1 tablespoon flour
1 tablespoon sugar
1 tablespoon butter
½ teaspoon salt

Make white sauce of butter, flour & milk add sugar to egg yolks and beat slightly. then add to white sauce. Add corn and seasoning. Fold in stiffly beaten egg whites. Pour into buttered baking dish and bake in moderate oven.

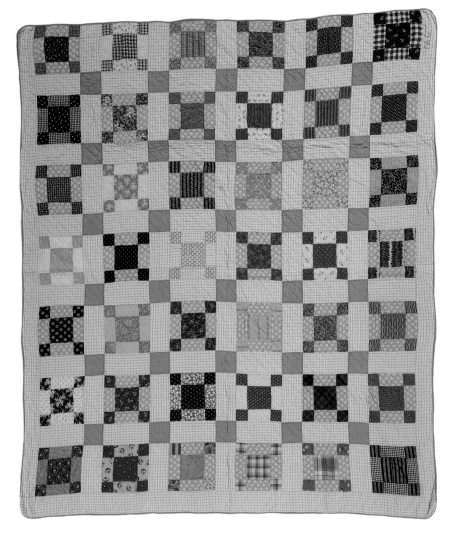

Puss in the Corner, 71½" x 79½", c. 1920. Mira and Ida may have traded patterns for at least two of the similar quilts they each made, the Kansas Dugout Friendship quilts and the Puss in the Corner quilts. Ida's 1890s Puss in the Corner is set on the point, and each pieced block alternates with a block of solid red fabric. Mira's quilt, made several years later, is set in rows and each pieced block is set off with a sashing strip and block. The quilt is hand-pieced and the backing fabric, which is older than some of the fabrics used in the top, is a lovely, soft greenish brown with a leaf-and-berry print. Mira embroidered her initials, "MG," on the front of the quilt in a corner. Quilt courtesy of Hazel Gaunt.

Photography by Brian S. Birlauf, Birlauf and Steen Photo, Denver, Colorado.

Quilted Some

The terse entry Ida made on Memorial Day, a year after Ma's death reveals the sorrow and loss she was still experiencing: "May 30th 1922 Decoration was a cloudy, cool rainy day." A few years later her description of the day is much more cheerful; Decoration Day had again become a time to remember loved ones who were gone and to join with dear family and friends. "Monday May 30th 1927 Decoration. was the most like it usto be, that it had been for years. had nice pro-gramme and a big crowd went to the cemetry. Eva, Ida, Mrs Thomas & Alice ate dinner with us."

Ida made note of a quilt she pieced for Rodney and then had quilted by the Ladies' Aid Society, as she had done with a quilt for Louise. In later years Ida never again paid to have a top quilted because money became increasingly scarce, and in fact, quilting for others was nearly her only source of income.

> 1922 Aug 31 Last Thursday P.M. Put
> Rodney's quilt in frames at Agnes Berrier.

Took quilt out of the frames Nov 10th here at home. quilted on it every society day, but two. I paid $4.50 to have it quilted.

Dec 1st 1922 Mrs Nickles, Minnie Nette and I tied my wool comfort, the nine patch.

Ida also enjoyed crocheting and in addition to table mats, vanity sets, and doilies, she often made crocheted yokes: "commenced a butterfly yoke, that was in American woman, Nette sent up. finished it the 14th of Feb. ready for the string. finished it all complete Feb 20th commenced another one Feb 24th commenced a yoke Mch 24th like the one Jessie Blood loaned Mrs Correll."

> June 1919
> Sold two yokes one for $1.50
> the other for $2.00
> Sold a crocheted hood for baby $1.75
> Finished my butterfly yoke Friday Nov 29th

commenced to make little crocheted bonnet
Nov 30th 1919

Two years later Ida listed "Crocheted yokes I have made:"

1 Emma Chambers
2 Minnie Chambers
3 Minnie Bodin
4 Alice Treadwell
5 Edith Willsie
6 Minnie Chambers
7 Cara Gillette
8 Aunt Nancy
9 one for myself
10 Jeanette Price
11 Maud Melugin
12 Eva Lamback
13 another one to give away or sell
14 one for ma
15 one for Nette
16 one for myself
17 one for Mira
18 one for Mrs Dumond
19 a butterfly yoke for myself
20 another butterfly

Ida and Nette lived on in the house on the corner of Sixth and State streets, two very different women who found a loving and compatible balance in their lives. Nette continued to see Atwood and her circle of friends in the Eastern Star and her other clubs. She also became an avid fan of picture shows in spite of the fact that her first impression of a movie with "all talking" in 1929 was not favorable:

June 12 Tried to make cake. helped at Temple for Rotarians. Mrs. Mettler, Wallace, Brown Frank Brown, Anna Reeves & myself. Cloudy, Ida took things out of her bedroom. went to picture Show with Mrs Brown & Harriett, "Desert Nights" See Mrs Fisher.

June 13 Helped Ida finish bedroom. went to church to quilt Had big rain. Took walk up the hill after supper

June 14 Beautiful morning. Finished Carl's quilt. went to see Mrs Robinson

June 15 Nice morning. Lulu, Frank & Robert here for dinner. went to town with Lulu, Noah's cousin Miss Gaunt, was here in P.M. Dust storm in evening.

June 16 Lovely morning. went to church. Dinner with Thorne & Mary. Fried chicken. Took ride to Lake. Did not have church in evening.

Thanksgiving postcard from Ida Melugin to her nephew Jesse Gaunt, November 17, 1912. Ida's message reads: "Dear little Jesse, How are you these days? We are having winter here, snow quite deep. What are you going to have for dinner Thanksgiving? Wish you could be with us. With lots of love From Aunt Ida." Postcard courtesy of Audry Gaunt.

June 17 Got new washing machine. Had the washing done by 10 oclock. Put quilt in. one Charlie bought of Mrs Larrabee in 1915. went to Rebekah's.

June 18 Done the ironing. wrote letter to Vinnie. Cleaned little in my bedroom. Mailed Quilt to Carl.

June 19 Helped clean woodwork in dinning room. Bought Congoleum Rug of Grace. went to Show with Kate L. All talking did not like it.

Nette seemed to attend most of the movies that played in Atwood. She often noted enjoying Jeanette McDonald and Nelson Eddy and was especially enthusiastic about Gene Autry, attending virtually every movie he made. In the early years of cinema an actor could make almost a movie a month, so in 1940 Nette went to see Gene Autry in nine movies.

Both sisters enjoyed Will Rogers—"Mrs Doty and I went to see Will Rogers best and last picture" (2/18/36)—

Nette Chambers, April 1898. Photo courtesy of Audry Gaunt.

and although she went to the movies less frequently than Nette, Ida recorded many of the classics that she enjoyed such as *Little Women* and *Gone with the Wind*. But as Nette continued her active life-style, Ida always stayed closer to home. She visited with her neighbors every day or they called on her, but when Nette went away from Atwood, generally to stay with the Nebraska branch of the family, Ida often recorded that without Nette in the house she felt lonely and sometimes the days were long. "Pleasant, got up little early. Mrs Kelley took Nette to McCook in A.M. left here about eleven. was a long day to me. for all was busy. Clara was over while in evening. I sewed some on Nette's Star quilt little cool" (10/25/33) "Nette away all P.M. and gone again this eve in P.M. I quilted." (3/31/48)

Money was a growing problem for the sisters and to earn a bit of cash they rented the two north rooms of their house and occasionally did washing for other families. A widowed neighbor, Irene Henderson Kelley, who taught school, had three daughters who ate their noon meal with Ida and Nette. Mrs. Kelley hired Ida and Nette to iron and do light housecleaning, and the two families of females enjoyed a long friendship. The sisters provided cooking and cleaning and childcare for the widow, who was raising her daughters alone, and Mrs. Kelley helped with a small income desperately needed by Ida and Nette. They also shared meals, picnics, outings, and holidays. Ida recorded many quilts and tied comforters made for the Kelleys.

Ida and Nette had many boarders over the years, often the newly married sons and daughters of their friends,

or young people from the country who lived in town with the sisters while they attended high school. Those young people had very fond memories of the time spent with the Chambers sisters and years afterward would often come for visits, bringing their own new babies and families. Ida kept a guest book where they recorded their visits. In 1951, Billy Thorne Henderson wrote: "All my love to two dear old aunts." The following year Arthur David noted: "My wonderful home when I went to High School. Never to be forgotten."

In 1933 Ida began a diary that took the general form seen in her journals for the next two decades. Entries are regular but fairly short, and as with Ma's diaries, they describe concisely the work, weather, and events of the day. Ida comments more frequently on her feelings than Ma did, although Ma always recorded her worry over her large family and her failing health and energy as she grew older. Ida, however, seemed to deal throughout her life with feelings of loneliness. She always notes when she is alone and there are often times when she writes that she is lonely. In April 1933 Ida wrote "my wedding day," thirty-nine years after her marriage to John. Ida also sometimes mentions that she had been thinking of her parents. Perhaps her loneliness was not always caused by solitude as much as a longing for her beloved family members who had passed away and for the ones who no longer lived close by.

In March 1934, Nette went to stay with her elderly Aunt Nancy in Fairmont, Nebraska. On the evening of the day she left, Ida wrote in a letter to their sister Mira how she hated to see Nette go, that even though she was generally gone most evenings, at least Ida had the consolation of knowing that she would eventually be coming in and that she would not be alone all through the night.

Wednesday eve (3/28/34)

Dear Mira,
    Well, here I am alone again. Nette started back this P.M. she hated to go too, and, I hated to see her go. I dont want to complain, but dont look like we should live apart so much. but suppose will be this way as long as we are all spared.
    of course she has been home most six weeks. think she had a good time while here. and believe she is feeling better, I hope so John, Cora, Harry and Ann drove in Sunday A.M. before we got away from the breakfast table. then they went back that P.M. at five thirty. Nette had wrote to John saying she was starting back Monday. They thought then she could go with them, but Mrs Dillon had a turkey dinner for her, Monday evening, so of course she couldent go then. it sure pretty quiet here tonight. of course Nette has been gone evenings about as much as she has been home. but I was expecting her in some time,

Judge John H. Chambers with his sons and grandsons. Back Row, L to R: Thorne Chambers, Jesse Chambers, Rodney Gillette. Front row, L to R: Charlie Chambers, John H. Chambers, Burdette Chambers, and William Henry Chambers (Thorne's father), December 29, 1909. Photo courtesy of Audry Gaunt.

even though would be late. Mr & Mrs Berry are both away this evening. the children are asleep. dont think she will be gone long, they are getting a programme ready for Easter. got your letter Monday, glad to hear, and glad to get Jesse's. this a spring day. sure great, but yesterday cloudy, windy and cold. we heard today another spell of winter coming. rain then snow. the fire in heater went out about noon. had the house all open, until little while ago. it just struck half past eight. we cant have so very much more cold weather.

April will soon be here. do you remember when Easter was on the first day of April before? I dont. think its so long ago dont remember.

Friday P.M. well, must add a few more lines then go to P.O. after a while, I have been quilting some this A.M. [Ida was working on

a baby quilt for her friend Ruby's daughter, Elaine] want to quilt some this afternoon. have it half done or maybe a little more wish could finish it, this week, but dont suppose I can. well, we have had another touch of winter. was so nice Wednesday, and until in the night, then turned cold, and cold was right. it was cloudy yesterday, last night after dark it rained some then sleeted and snowed, sure was bad for a while was cloudy and cold for a while this A.M. but has cleared off, and is warming up some. maybe March will go out nice after all. you wont hear from Nette this week, but she will get around to write next likely. know the folks will be awful glad to see her.

Ruby was over a few minutes this A.M. to show me a dress she was making Elaine's baby. sure pretty. said was going to finish it so

*Postage Stamp quilt, 68" x 83½,"
c. 1935-40. Ida hand-pieced the
Postage Stamp quilt with more
than 4,200 – 1⅛" squares for her
niece Hazel Gaunt. She quilted it
diagonally with two parallel quilting rows going through each
square. The quilt is backed with
muslin. Ida used a red bias binding because red was always
Hazel's favorite color.*

*Quilt courtesy of Hazel Gaunt.
Photography by Brian S. Birlauf,
Birlauf and Steen Photo, Denver,
Colorado.*

could mail it out this P.M. she must have it for
Sunday I suppose, although may not go to
church. I'll be surprised if she does. Lon and
Ruby dont care for church, and dont think
thier girls do. that the way with so many here
in town, but, can they go to card parties, two
and three times a week. well I must keep still,
even though I feel like I would explode some
times. I am going to try and send Doris some
velvet pieces before long. must get busy. Love
to all. Ida

When Ida writes that she hopes that Nette is feeling
better it is possible that her suffering was not so much
from physical causes as it was from an emotional loss. It
was about this time in 1934, that her longtime companion, Atwood Cochran, left Kansas for a visit with his
brother out West. While he was there, At met a "widow
with gorgeous eyes" and married her after a brief
courtship. He never returned to Kansas. For more than
three decades, Atwood had been Nette's companion and
steady escort and while it is tempting to speculate that
his marriage to another woman may have broken her
heart, at the least his absence must have left a huge void
in her life. The poem she copied in her journal may provide a clue to her unspoken feelings.

A Confession

Do you suppose, if the world some day
   should come
and stand beside my grave and say,

"Here lies one who can ne'er be forgot."
I would care aught for it, if you came not.
But if alone you came, and said with tears,
"Here lies one that I loved"—
Ah! then the years since we had met would
    quickly
    fade away,
And heaven for me be reckoned from that
    day.
              Author Unknown

Thanksgiving postcard to Jesse and John Gaunt, 1913. On November 28, 1935, Ida wrote of her Thanksgiving Day: "Thanksgiving. An ideal a.m. Nette and I went to the church at 7:30 for communion, Mrs. Doty ate dinner and supper with us. she made sleeves for one of Nette's dresses. I done little sewing. Mrs Doty and I went to see Clara in p.m. I walked down home with Mrs. Doty."

Pleasant only little windy and dusty. Elmer and Mira started for the Sand Hills a little after nine. we dident do much, but straighten around. I quilted some in P.M. no company. lonesome. (4/19/48)

In March of 1933 Ida listened to Franklin D. Roosevelt on the radio as he took his oath of office and then gave his address. In later years she also noted when she went to vote in presidential elections. And on April 12, 1945, Ida wrote: "President Roosevelt passed away this P.M." Except for these rare exceptions, she makes no references to national events. Besides quilting, one interest of Ida's that appeared often in her journals was her love of flowers and gardening. She grew a few vegetables each season and there was the cherry orchard behind the house, but her real passion was for flowers. She made notes of planting flower seeds or starts and bulbs that had been given to her by friends. "Helped with work, then went to Mrs Campbell's after yellow chrysanthemum." (10/10/36) "Stopped at Mrs Crist to get a root of Chrysanthemum, white." (4/28/37) She also commented on which of her plants were blooming or that she walked to a neighbor's home to see a flowering plant. "I went to see Goldie Howard's flowers in A.M. they are sure lovely. she gave me a nice bouquet." (6/5/40) Each spring, as a prelude to her gardening season, she noted the occasion of seeing the first robin of the year. Ida planted border lilies, cosmos, petunias, chrysanthemum, Star of Bethlehem, tulips, zinnias, iris, and lilacs. In the late spring, she spaced the planting of flower seeds so there would be blooming plants all through the summer. "I set out some four o'clock's and cosmos." (6/3/36) "Nette's pretty red cactus is in bloom." (7/25/45) "Nette's barrel cactus has 2 blossoms on it." (8/6/45) In late September 1942 Ida noted the end of her summer: "Cloudy in A.M. and real cold, froze last night. killed the flowers."

Of course, in addition to the flowers there was also the fruit to preserve, and beginning in June with the early cherries, Ida preserved jars of cherries, peaches, apricots, beets, tomatoes, jams and jellies of wild plums and crab apples, watermelon, peach, and cucumber pickles. One September Ida noted that she made some "end of garden relish." Ida sold the cherries; people from town and even from the country came to pick the fruit.

The overwhelming theme of Ida's diaries, however, is quilting. On the rare days when she wasn't quilting or piecing, Ida mentions crocheting or sewing dresses, aprons, nightgowns, smocks, pillow cases, holders, and tea towels. Generally though, there was a quilt in the frame, and sometimes there was more than one frame with a quilt on it in the house. Many times Ida writes of putting aside a quilt she is quilting for a day or two and putting a comforter on a second frame to tie. She would also stop working on a quilt of her own to quilt a top for a neighbor. Very likely, her monetary needs dictated that she finish the neighbor's quilt before her own. Interestingly, in spite of the importance of quilting as a source of income for the sisters, there is only one instance in all of the diaries where the amount paid for a quilt is recorded. In 1939 Ida and Nette quilted an unnamed quilt for Mrs. Hayden and received $3.10 for their labors. Ida often went to a neighbor's to help sew a quilt into the frame, and she occasionally brought home from society a quilt rolled up in a frame to store or work on herself. Ida and Nette sometimes worked on each other's quilts and tops; Ida would quilt a top that Nette had pieced and Nette generally quilted on the quilts that Ida had set up in the house. Nette did piece and quilt a great deal and she would mention quilting in her journals. However, a comparison of the sisters' diaries reveals that quilting held a much greater place in Ida's life than in Nette's. Nette made lovely quilts, but she had numerous other interests and was simply gone from the house much more than her sister. When Ida left the house it often was to go quilting or to buy "batten" or

The broom brigade: Women of Atwood ready to march on the saloons in Atwood. Rawlins County High School in background. Photo courtesy of Rawlins County Historical Society.

WOMEN'S CHRISTIAN TEMPERANCE UNION

Taste not, Handle not, touch not the wine!

For every girl like me the temperance pledge should sign.

Minnie Colgon
(From Ida's
Autograph Book,
December 16, 1881)

The Women's Christian Temperance Union was founded in 1874, but it was through the leadership of its second president, Frances Willard, who came to the office in 1879 and led the union for nearly two decades, that it became the largest of all nineteenth-century women's movements. Most famous for the war its members waged against alcohol, the W.C.T.U. also worked for suffrage, vocational training for women, child care and child labor laws, and prison reform. Willard encouraged members to use their traditional needlework skills to promote and fund the causes championed by the W.C.T.U..

Quilts were a natural vehicle to support the cause so vital to thousands of nineteenth-century women, and several patterns became popular symbols of the movement. Blue and white became the union's colors: white for purity and blue for water, the purest beverage. There was a pieced W.C.T.U. block that was used often, and of course the Drunkard's Path quilt was a popular symbol with the organization. Another pattern was the Goblet quilt. Turned one way the blue pieced image looks like a whiskey bottle, turned upside down, the bottle becomes a goblet, intended to hold only pure water. Ten-cent signature quilts were a common means of fund-raising and friendship quilts were inscribed with names of local chapter members.

Mary Chambers was vehemently against alcohol, a passion she instilled early in her daughters. She reportedly even refused to allow a newspaper or magazine in her home if it had advertisements for liquor. There are repeated mentions of W.C.T.U. meetings in her journals over the years. "I done some mending and in the evening we all went to Church to hear the Temperance Lecture it was just fine." (9/11/02) "done up our chores and went over to the lecture Lulu come home with us to go to the Church. It was a grand talk to young men there was a good many signed the pledge." (Thanksgiving Day, 11/27/02) "We went to the WCTU meeting I enjoyed it ever so much and we had a nice little visit after the meeting was out some of the ladies stayed and quilted a while." (12/2/02) "Nette washed the dishes and then got

ready and went to WCTU it was over to Mrs Wirmers." (3/7/17) "Ida Nette and Cora went to the M E Church to hear a WCTU Lady speak they liked her ever so much." (3/31/17)

Ida supported the ideals of the temperance movement all of her life. She went to meetings and made quilts and even noted cash donations to the organization from her meager income. In 1920 Ida recorded $1.00 for W.C.T.U. dues and another expense of $3.00 for "Anti Saloon." "I quilted some, went to the W.C.T.U. in afternoon." (3/8/35) "I quilted some in a.m. and p.m. went over to Ruby's in a.m. went to the Christian church in evening to a W.C.T.U. programme." (3/26/40)

Although liquor was generally illegal in most Kansas counties it was possible to get a drink through a doctor's prescription or by registering with a druggist. Some men made several trips a day to the druggist, signing false names for each drink and listing the particular ailment that would be aided by a shot of John Barleycorn. There were clandestine

saloons or "blind tigers" reached through alleys and back doors. The Red Heifer, or Atwood Social Club as it was also known, was run by the Twillegar brothers. On February 22, 1901, it was reported in the *Republican Citizen* that the ladies of the town met at the Christian Church, summoned by the church bells ringing at high noon, and marched to the Red Heifer for the purpose of ridding their town of that evil. They had resolved to sweep their town clean.

Bud Twillegar met the ladies at his door and gave a promise to close up his business. "The citizens, mostly business men, raised a purse for the Twillegar Brothers to help them remove everything from the city in order to avoid a Mrs. Nation scene by the W.C.T.U. on Wednesday noon."

Information on quilting and the WCTU courtesy of Hearts and Hands *by Pat Ferrero, Elaine Hedges, and Julie Silber. Information on Atwood and the WCTU courtesy of Ruth Kelley Hayden, author of* The Time That Was.

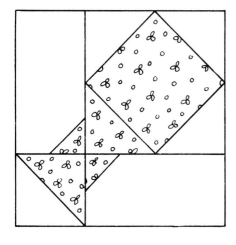

Goblet

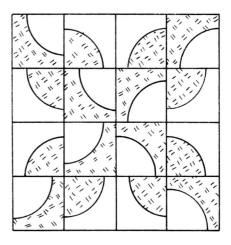

Drunkard's Path

fabric for her quilts. Ida lived by choice a more confined life than Nette. Quilting filled more emotional and creative needs for Ida and therefore occupied a much greater importance in her journals.

In mid January of 1933, Ida and Nette went to Fairmont, Nebraska, where they spent the next three months with Pa's youngest sister, Nancy Eastwood. Even there Ida continued to make quilts:

1/23/33 A peach of a day. we washed. had quite a big one. worked on holders in P.M. Nette went to see Aunt Elda. we went after mail in evening. I sewed some on my double wedding ring.

1/24/33 Another nice day. we ironed. that about all besides the A.M. work Aunt Nancy feeling better. went with Nette after mail in evening. I done little sewing in P.M. making holders.

1/25/33 A peach of a day. helped Nette clean the front room. she dressed a chicken. then made a cake after dinner, while I washed the dishes. I wrote to Clara, then went for a walk. visited with Mrs Philson, then went to see Aunt Elda, then to see Dr Bert about my glasses. had my frames changed. went to P.O.

1/26/33 Cloudy and colder. made soap after washed breakfast dishes. then went for a walk. went to see Mollie and Mrs Palmer, visited with Ethel Prescott on street, after dinner sewed on apron for Nette, then went to see Dr Bert to have my frames adjusted. went to P.O.

Nette and I went down to Mrs Prescott's in evening, then to P.O.

1/27/33 Pleasant. I helped with the A.M. work. cut pattern for Aunt Nancy's smock. then wrote to Jesse Gaunt and Mira. cut out some pieces, sewed on double wedding ring in evening.

1/28/33 Cloudy, some colder. helped with the A.M. work. cut out some pieces. Nette and I went to town after supper. Nette done little shopping. got the mail.

1/29/33 Some cloudy, not so cold. helped with work. wrote to Lucy, went to M.E. church in A.M. wrote to cousin Idie in P.M. Nette and I went to Federated church in evening.

1/30/33 A peach of a day. we washed. I went to P.O. stopped to see Dr Bert about my glasses, took them down to him about five o'clock. getting new frames. cut out a smock for Aunt Nancy in P.M. went with Nette to P.O. in evening.

1/31/33 Pleasant in A.M. cloudy and stormy acting in P.M. I went to see Mrs Chapin and Mollie in A.M. helped Nette iron. dident do much rest of day, helped some with work. snowed little during the night. Oledine come to see me in P.M. weighed 162

2/1/33 Cool, but pleasant again. went to Dr office got my glasses. had nice visit with Mrs

Ashby. went to see Aunt Elda in A.M. sewed some on Aunt Nancy's smock in P.M. Nette and I went down to Mrs Prescott's in evening.

2/2/33 Pleasant, helped with A.M. work, then sewed on Aunt Nancy's smock, finished it after dinner, then wrote 2 letter. worked on holders [pot holders] and my pieces. went with Nette to P.O. in evening.

2/3/33 Cloudy in A.M. snowed some. I went to Mollie to get Pete some sand, called to see Bell Pult. marked off an ironing board cover in P.M. finished a holder. went with Nette to P.O. in eve.

2/4/33 Cloudy a regular March day. snowed at different times. I helped with work. then cut out some pieces. in P.M. worked on ironing sheet, then worked with my pieces. Nette & I went to see Aunt Elda, then to get mail.

2/5/33 Pleasant, helped with work. wrote few lines to Ann and Harry Jones. Nette and I went down to the noon train to see John and Cora, they going to see Burdette. in P.M. I wrote to Mrs Reeves. after lunch Nette and I went down to Mrs Prescotts then to train to see John & Cora again.

2/6/33 Monday, not as warm. we washed, was windy and got colder. so dried the clothes in the house. I worked on ironing sheet in P.M. pieced some in evening. got lots colder in P.M. & evening.

2/7/33 Still cold, snowing some and blowing. we ironed in A.M. I finished ironing sheet in P.M. worked with my pieces. still awful cold 20 below last night.

2/8/33 Some cloudy. helped with work, then sewed lining in frames in P.M. Nette and I tied it, then after supper I fixed it around the edge.

2/9/33 Pleasant, not quite so cold. I helped with the work, then put the protector on the comfortor. [A protector was also known as a whisker guard. It was an extra strip of fabric sewn across the top edge of a quilt to keep it clean and protect the area where it got the most wear and handling.] sewed on 2 holders. pieced some.

2/10/33 Pleasant, not so cold. helped with A.M. work. went up to Mollie's few minutes in A.M. took mail to her. wrote to Mira in P.M. then worked with my pieces.

Christmas card sent to Jesse Gaunt, 1913. Ida's Christmas entry in 1917: "real cold but no snow on the ground. we ate dinner at Ma's. there were eight of us. Charlie, Emma, Henry, Minnie, Ma, At, Nette and myself. what I got this xmas. Handkerchief from Lulu Minney. two little pins from John's folks. pair of black silk stockings from Minnie Bodin. nice ribbon hand bag from Lucy W. nice morning cap from Provie. Pocket book & handkerchief from Hettie. handkerchief from Maude. Violet Dulce combination from Carl. Box of writing paper from Ida L. card from Cora, Idie and Edith."

2/11/33 Pleasant but little cool. helped with A.M. dident do much else the rest of day. worked some with pieces. took a walk in P.M.

2/12/33 Pleasant. helped with work. then got ready and went to Federated church. rested some in P.M. wrote to Mrs Doty. Nette and I went to P.O. then to see Aunt Elda a while.

2/13/33 Cloudy, colder, snowed in A.M. we washed. got through at ten o'clock. worked some with my pieces.

2/14/33 Cloudy in A.M. snowed some during the night. Nette and I ironed in A.M. I worked some on tea towel. Nette & I went down to Mrs Prescott's in evening then after the mail. wrote Lulu Minney in P.M.

2/15/33 Pleasant, but little cool. I helped do up the A.M. work, then went to see Mrs Chapin. wrote to Hazel in P.M. finished a holder and worked on tea towel. Mollie was here for supper. Nette and I went after the mail.

2/16/33 Pleasant, not so cold. I helped with A.M. work. Nette made soap. I took a walk in A.M. they brought half hog in from the farm. Uncle Ike and Nette took care of it after dinner. quite cloudy about five. Nette and I took some the fresh meat to Mrs Prescott and Aunt Elda then went to P.O.

2/17/33 Pleasant. I helped with A.M. work, then went to see Dr Bert. helped with dinner and the dishes when got back. worked on tea towels in P.M. went with Nette to P.O. and for a walk after supper.

2/18/33 Pleasant, but little windy. helped with work then went to see Dr Bert. not feeling my best. went to see Aunt Elda a few minutes. wrote letter to Mrs Roberts in P.M. Nette and I went after mail in evening.

2/19/33 Pleasant, cool north wind. I went to S.S. and church at Federated church. wrote to Mrs Allen in P.M. was quite windy, Nette and I went to M.E. in evening.

2/20/33 Pleasant but little cool wind, we washed I wrote to Cady in P.M. worked on tea towel we went down to Aunt Elda's in evening. then after mail.

2/21/33 Pleasant in A.M. windy in P.M. we ironed, Mollie was in few minutes. I started to join Aunt Nancy flower garden quilt in P.M. Nette & I took walk after supper then went after mail.

2/22/33 Pleasant, little windy. helped do up the work then took a walk. went to see Mrs Prescott and Aunt Elda. Nette made soap. worked on Aunt Nancy's quilt in P.M. went for little walk then the mail after supper.

2/23/33 Pleasant, helped do up the work then sewed on Aunt Nancy's quilt. after dinner I rested a while then went for a walk.

Ida Melugin and Inez Minney Walters, c. 1915. Photo courtesy of Inez Walters.

worked on quilt, finished another tea towel. up to 70 [degrees] in P.M. we went for a walk then got the mail after supper.

2/24/33 Pleasant, worked on Aunt Nancy's quilt, then took a walk, went to see Mrs Palmer a while. worked on doily, Mr Stutzman died very sudden about six P.M.

2/25/33 Pleasant. helped with A.M. work. then went for walk. went to see Aunt Elda & Mrs Prescott. both quite poorly. started my pie quilt in P.M. we went for walk, then Nette done little trading and got the mail. [Research has failed to locate a Pie Quilt pattern in published quilt block directories. However, interviews with Ida's family and former neighbors indicate that the Pie Quilt block did indeed look like a pie pieced of eight equal sections, much as you would cut a piece of pie. At the top of the block or sometimes across the center of the pie was embroidered the name of the pie, such as Cherrie, Apple or Peach. Ida made at least three additional Pie Quilts.]

2/26/33 Fine. helped do up A.M. work. wrote to Marshall. Uncle Ike and I went to train to meet John and Cora. we had good dinner, and nice visit, John and I took little walk. had lunch. Nette and I went to train with them, was little tired when got back.

2/27/33 Pleasant, little windy a while, we washed. got through early. worked on tea towel, and pieces. we took walk and went after the mail, after supper.

2/28/33 Pleasant, we ironed. I cut out some pieces for my pie quilt. did do much in P.M. finished working Nette tea towels we went down to Mrs Prescotts in evening and after the mail.

3/1/33 Pleasant in A.M. then little blustry a while in P.M. I hemmed the last 2 tea towels, and put border on Aunt Nancy's quilt in A.M. Nette went to York with Ethel this P.M.

3/2/33 Pleasant helped with A.M. work, done little mending. wrote to Clara. in P.M. called on Mrs Miller, then went to Mollie's and she helped me to start joining the wedding ring. we went for a walk and after the mail. Uncle Ike not feeling well.

3/3/33 A peach of a day. helped with the work. then went for a walk. went to see Aunt Elda and Mrs Prescott. I worked some on wedding ring quilt. Nette went to see Mrs Chapin. we went after mail in evening.

Ida and Nette stayed on with Ike and Nancy Eastwood until April 19, when they returned to Atwood. One month later Ida wrote that she "got the sad news of bro Jesse's death about eight thirty." The family gathered in McCook, Nebraska, for the funeral on May 19. Jesse was only fifty-eight years old. (His brothers Charlie and Henry had also died young, at ages fifty-six and fifty-seven.) Now the remaining family numbered only four: Ida, Nette, Mira, and their brother John.

On May first Ida had written: "went to town got material [lining or backing fabric] for the wedding ring quilt." Four days later Mrs. Doty came over and helped her put the Wedding Ring quilt in the frame. Twenty days later the quilting was completed and Ida stitched on the binding. The Wedding Ring quilt that she began in Nebraska in January was finished on the fifth of June. Ida made at least three additional Wedding Ring quilts and quilted two more that had been pieced by her neighbor, Mrs. Ruby Nichols.

Nette Chambers. Photo courtesy of Audry Gaunt.

After the Wedding Ring quilt was done in early June, Ida pieced a Star of Bethlehem quilt for her nephew, Burdette Chambers. She always referred to these quilts as Star quilts or Lone Star, and as with the Wedding Ring quilts, she made at least six additional Star quilts. Ida pieced Burdette's Star quilt in twelve days, and on July 6 she began another: "we all worked on the Star quilt, Nette cut out Mrs. Doty and I sewed." The ladies "got the Star together" in four days. On the fifth day they added a white background, and on the sixth day "Mrs Doty and I went to Mrs Gaines & Mrs Dominy to see about pattern to quilt the border and plain blocks. Mrs Doty and I finished putting on the border." July 13 "Warm. Mrs Doty come in A.M. helped put the quilt in the frames. we quilted some in P.M." They worked on the quilt every day for the following week or so. Then on July 25, Ida wrote: "Pleasant in A.M. warm in afternoon. I swept the cave steps. [Behind the house was a storm cellar that mostly served as a storage area for fruits and vegetables. They were kept cool in the summer and would not freeze during winter. The below-ground room

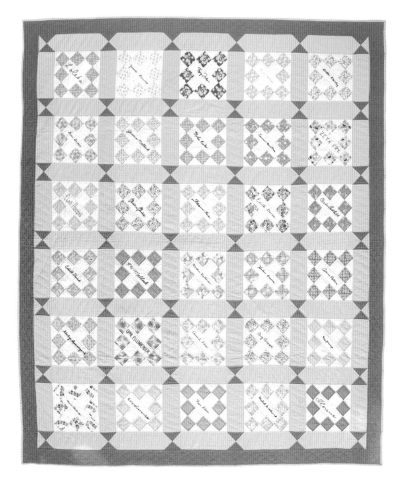

also gave protection from the violent prairie storms and tornadoes.] then went to quilting. Mrs Doty come in A.M. we all quilted in A.M. Mrs Doty and I quilted in P.M. took it out of the frames at 3:30" After Ida had "trimmed" the Star quilt "Several were in to see it." ("Trimmed" may have referred to stitching on the quilt binding, or it may been that Ida trimmed off any uneven edges of the quilt or excess batting.)

August was no less productive; the ladies quilted Aunt Nancy's Flower Garden quilt, pieced a Flower Garden and a Wedding Ring for Nette and began quilting another Flower Garden for Mrs. Nichols. That quilt was put in on August 28 and was finished on September 8 at fifteen to two. In the fall Ida pieced a yellow-and-white Nine Patch and quilted an unnamed quilt for Mrs Paulson, a neighbor.

> 10/2/33 Cool. I washed with Mrs Berry. Lulu and Frank were in a few minutes. Mrs Doty come and helped me put in Mrs Paulson quilt. then we quilted some before and after supper. Mrs Doty went home about eight o'clock.

> 10/3/33 Cloudy, cool and rainy in P.M. wasent bad in A.M. just little cloudy. I quilted a while then went to see Mrs Plantz, then Dr Dowler. come home got dinner, Mrs Doty

come in A.M. we didn't get very much quilted in P.M. was so dark.

10/4/33 Pleasant. done up the work then quilted some in A.M. Mrs Doty come in morning. we went to out S.S. class meeting in P.M. at Mrs Dominy's had nice time. a good number out. 14

10/5/33 A wonderful day. made pie to take to the pot luck dinner at Mrs Brown's the Aid met there. we quilted on Aid quilt. had election of officers. Mrs Frye president, Mrs Plantz first vice Pres Clara Bump second vice Pres, Mrs Elmer Mullen Sec and Treasurer.

10/6/7 Pleasant but little cool. I ironed in A.M. Mrs Doty come in A.M. went home about eight thirty. we quilted pretty steady in P.M. we both quilted some in A.M. Clara come over in evening. we walked home with Mrs Doty.

10/7/33 Pleasant, but cool north wind. cleaned up house some. done few odd things. quilted some in A.M. then till four in P.M. Lulu and Eva were here few minutes, Clara come over in evening we took little walk. I done some trading. they had the water shut off working on one of the mains.

10/8/33 Pleasant but quite cool. warmed up some in P.M. I went to S.S. and church, went home with Mrs Doty for dinner. come home about three, rested a while then wrote to Nette. went to church in evening.

10/9/33 Cool in A.M. but fine in afternoon. I dident do much in A.M. but little work, then quilted some. Mrs Doty come in A.M. we quilted in P.M. I went piece with Mrs Doty after supper. when she went home.

10/10/33 A peach of a day. Fine A.M. done up part of my work, then went to hear the gospel singers. Mrs Doty was here when I got back. I quilted in A.M. until time to get dinner, then after I rested went down to Mrs Preders to see about a hat. then from there went up Clara Walts. she sent for me. said she was sick. I come home about five. went over to Mrs Kelley's while in evening to stay with girls

10/11/33 Some cloudy, cool wind. done up work, went over to Ruby's few minutes, then to Mrs Haydens to get some Jennica seeds. quilted in A.M. and P.M. Mrs Doty went home about seven thirty.

10/12/33 Pleasant. done part of my work, then went to hear the gospel singers. washed out a few pieces when come home. then quilted some in A.M. and P.M. then went with Mrs Dominy to see Mrs Reeves. then from there I stopped to see Lucy. when got home Mrs Doty was here quilting. we quilted some after supper. then I went a piece with her. [Matie Doty lived several blocks to the east of Ida's house and she often mentioned walking part of the way home with her after they had spent the day quilting together.]

10/13/33 Pleasant, I done up work. Mrs Doty come about eight. we quilted in A.M. and P.M. Mrs Doty went home about four o'clock. Mrs Swaney, Mrs Doty and I went to the Seth Parker programe

10/14/33 Pleasant, I done up part of my A.M. work then went to town. went to see Mr Birrer, paid him some on my lumber bill. Mrs Doty come little after eight. I took Nette letter to P.O. went to George McDougal's funeral in P.M. Clara was over in evening went down town with her.

10/15/33 Pleasant in A.M. but got windy in P.M. disagreeable. Mrs Doty come in P.M. we went to band concert. I went to S.S. had no church Dr Plantz was sick. Mrs Doty and I went to the Nazarene church. I come home after dinner rested a while then wrote some. about four o'clock Mrs Doty come and we went to band concert.

10/16/33 Pleasant, quilted some in A.M. and P.M. Mrs Doty come in morning. I washed with Mrs Berry. Lulu and Eva here few minutes. Ruby in a while.

10/17/33 Partly cloudy, little cooler. Mrs Doty come in A.M. we both quilted in A.M. and P.M. then while after supper. finished the quilt and took it out of the frames about seven thirty. I went over to Mrs Dominy's few minutes in A.M.

10/18/33 Cool, windy and dusty. I done odd jobs. sewed some in P.M. pieced on little nine patch. stayed with Ruth and Lonnie [Kelley] while Mary Elizabeth went to practice. I made fried cakes in A.M.

10/19/33 Cool, ironed, Mrs Dominy come over to tell that Mrs Doty's brother in law had passed away. we had little party for Mrs Gerald and Mrs Swaney, for thier birthday's at Mrs Dominy's, had nice time. Mrs Doty come by to go up to Mrs Swaney's. I went with her

10/20/33 Windy and cool. I cleaned the bedroom and washed bathroom window on in side, also the west window. got Mira's letter ready and took to P.O. Mrs Doty was in few minutes. I went to see Lucy, then stopped at Mrs Dominy's a few minutes. Clara was over in evening we took a walk.

10/21/33 Cool all day. I cleaned up the room some, then went to town on few errands. went over to Mrs Dominy's about eleven to hear a programme. Eva and Lulu were in P.M. Mrs Paulson come and got her quilt. she seemed well pleased. Clara come over in evening. we went to town, done little trading, then walked up to Mrs Swaney, and stopped at Cady's

Ida's diaries from the 1930s show an intense dedication to quiltmaking; they are also rare and extraordinary volumes depicting years in a pioneer woman's life. Generally, the mention of quilting in a diary is very unusual, and the references are often brief when they do appear. Ida's diaires, however, mention quilt after quilt, year after year. She talks of buying fabric and batting, borrowing patterns, piecing, sewing in linings, putting on borders—all the steps required in construction of a quilt are in her journals. Many women make quilts in an attempt to create works that will live beyond their lifetime. Ida documents her work and her life in a body of writings that speaks to us beyond the boundaries of the years. Besides being a chronicle of her quilts, a sense of her dignity and personal integrity in her daily life comes through. There is also the obvious love and caring she expresses for her family and friends. Though she lived a fairly secluded life, it was also a life full of friendship and love, work and creativity.

Nette kept journals sporadically through her life. Sometimes she made faithful daily entries for months and years and other times there are gaps of several days and even years between entries. It is likely that there were lost journals as there were with Mary Chambers and Ida. Nette's earliest surviving diary is dated 1902, but there are huge gaps between the journals. The next one is dated 1915 with occasional entries in 1916 and 1918, then there is a space of a decade. There is a 1929-1930 record book with two years of regular entries. This book includes a number of Nette's favorite recipes for cakes and salads, and also "Ida's Soap Receipt." In February 1930, Nette indicated that she was working on a quilt; regretably, she never mentions the name of the quilt, just "worked on my block." Three days later she wrote: "finished my tenth block," and on March 5: "Finished my 12th block." Perhaps the twelfth block completed her quilt, but it is not mentioned again in the main body of the journal and there are no further clues as to which quilt she was piecing, except for the listing below, which states that on March 20, she had "Finished

blocks for my quilt." On the last pages of this record book there is an interesting listing of the sewing projects Nette had stitched over several years. This list indicates that although she quilted frequently, embroidery, hardanger, and other types of fancywork occupied a much greater portion of her time than piecing and quilting:

Jan-1929
made Apron for Irma.
2 pair butterfly pillow cases for Lucy Wallace.
1 pair of Pillow cases with water lily on.
Started lunch cloth for little Ida.
　Feb
Helped to make 3 rugs. sent one Lois Chambers & one to Irma Gillette & two for Aunt Nancy.
　March.
Made two pair pillow slips for Lucy Wallace with yellow butterfly. Pair pillow slips with water lily on and yellow border. Pillow slips. pink butterfly. Ida's lunchen cloth & four napkins. Aunt Elda & I made me two slips.
　April
Table runner.
　June
Pillow slips for Emma. Two quilts
　July. '29
Comforter Protector for Aunt Nancy. Pair of pillow slips Comforter Protector for Ethel Mahroney
Pillow slips for Ida Walters
　Aug-
Rug for Alice Chambers.
　Sept-20-29. Put the embriery quilt together.
　Sept 28- Finished pair of pillow slip with water lilies on
　Oct-5. Pair Pillow slips.
　Oct-12. Pair of pillow slips
　Nov-12 Pair of pillow slips for L. Marie
　Nov-28 Pond Lilly Pillow cases for Aid at home
　Dec-5. Pond Lily pillow cases for Ethel.

Nette used one of Dr. Melugin's Physician's Daily Memorandums, dated 1902, to keep her journal. The first entry is dated January 1, 1936. Her comments in this volume are varied and sometimes extremely brief: "Ironed" or "Ironed. cloudy in morning. quilted." or "Hot day. quilted. went to show." Other times she writes more extensively: "Nice morning. we ironed. I went with Ruby to farm bureau meeting at Legion Hall. see lot of quilt blocks went to picture show with Fannie. Professional Soldier."

In July 1936, Nette wrote about a quilt that she and Ida worked on for their neighbor Ruby Nichols:

7-8-36 Ida & I quilted. windy. finished quilt.

Nette and Ida, 1921. Photo courtesy of Audry Gaunt.

Put in Ruby's quilt.

7-9-36 Ironed for Mrs Kelley.

7-10-36 Cleaned my bedroom quilted. had company in morning. Mrs Reardon, Bertie MC. Ruby.

7-11-36 Cleaned little & quilted Bad windy day. big crowd in town in evening. cool wind.

7-12-36 Cool this morning went to church. Hollis Hayward preached. went to Christian Church in evening.

7-13-36 Washed. went with Mrs Kelley to picnic B.W.

7-14-36 Ironed.

7-17-36 Sure have had hot days. went to see Lucy.

7-18-36 Made cake, cleaned my bedroom.

7-19-36 Another hot day.

7-20-36 Washed.

7-21-36 Ironed. Mrs Dillon walked up here.

7-22-36 Mrs Doty come, we quilted.

7-23-36 Ironed for Mrs Kelley did not feel good in P.M.

7-24-36 Hottest day of year 116 Mr Cooper was buried. See Lyda's bro. Mrs Doty here we quilted went to Arthur's for dinner.

7-25-36 Another hot day.

7-26-36 Very warm day. Mr Strayer preached this morning. Had pot luck dinner and good time. Mrs Paulson died.

7-27-36 Washed. Hot day. Donal Horton hurt last nite in Auto accident. went to see Trail of Lonesome Pine. Went to Mrs Paulson's funeral.

7-28-36 Ironed & finish Mrs Howards quilt. Had ice cream over to Mrs Kelley's. Little cooler.

Whenever there is an overlapping of Ida and Nette's journals, it is always fascinating to compare the daily entries that each sister made. There is often a clarification of events, such as on July 8, where Nette wrote: "finished quilt." Ida's entry for the same day was: "we finished quilting Jesse Gaunt's quilt about noon. put in a baby quilt for Ruby. but dident quilt any." Obviously, the sister's interests become clearer through a comparison of their diaries. Ida writes much more extensively about her quilting projects, while Nette's entries record her visits to friends, trips to town, picture shows, clubs, and outings. She went out a great deal more than Ida; a wider social life and larger circle of friends and activities was clearly more important to her.

The last journal that Nette kept was the little book that had belonged to Anita McAvoy before her early death in 1932. Five years later Nette began making entries in the small red diary that she maintained through 1941. There is quilting in her diary: "May 6, 1938 rained, nearly all day. Kenneth finished painting Kitchen. snowed this evening we quilted nearly all day. August 16, 1939 Nice day. did not do very much but quilt. June 4, 1940 Hung all quilts on line. put trunk in middle room. Mae, Scott & Grace Hill here to see quilts. put them in trunk. Clara stayed with Ida I went to show." Nette went to shows, Rebekah Lodge, Pinochle Club, and Eastern Star. Like

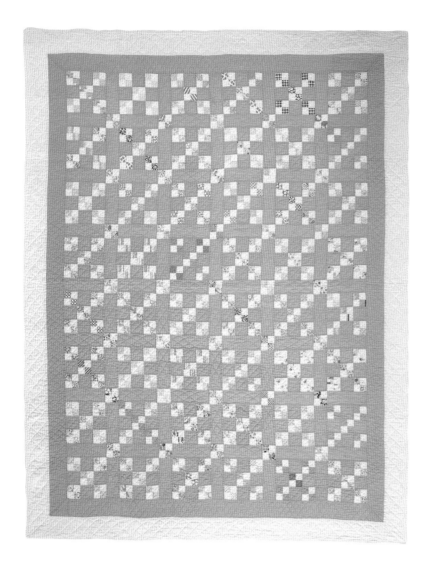

Nine Patch quilt, c. 1935. The Nine Patch pattern has always been a favorite with quilt-makers and was often chosen as a first quilt for beginning quilters. Ida's Nine Patch quilt, however, has interesting variations that enhance the overall graphics of the piece. Five of the squares that make up the nine-patch blocks are further divided into a four-patch grid, so each of the forty-eight blocks is composed of twenty-four squares. Ida also added a four-patch setting square that intersects the sashing pieces and allows the diagonal movement to flow out of the block and out to the edges of the quilt. The placement of the four- and nine-patch squares creates a dynamic grid in a deceptively simple quilt, which is, surprisingly, constructed with nearly 1,400 pieces. Ida's journals contain several mentions of four-patch patterns that may refer to this quilt: "I started to join the little four patch." (6/17/35) "I finished a tea towel, then cut off three more. I pieced some in evening. four patch." (11/16/35) "I went to town on several errands. then went to see Mrs Doty. dident do much in p.m. pieced some or rather joining my little four patches." (9/16/38)

Quilt courtesy of Pat Chambers Thomas. Photography by Jack Mathieson Photography.

Ida, Nette did not record events of national importance. During World War II there are only two references to the war. On July 1, 1941, Nette noted that she had finished a Red Cross shawl and on December 24 of the same year she went to a "military funeral for the Finley boy."

It is apparent from Ida's journals that quilting did more than earn an income and nurture a creative outlet. It provided for Ida a very important social focus that may have been much narrower than would have suited Nette, but was for Ida a comfortable circle of friends and companionable work that she loved. Ida quilted at the parsonage, Ladies' Aid, W.C.T.U. meetings, for church bazaars, and with all of her friends. "A wonderful day. made pie to take to the pot luck dinner at Mrs Brown's the Aid met there. we quilted on Aid quilt." (10/5/33) She often "invited a few in to quilt," or went to a quilting at a neighbor's. She enjoyed an especially close friendship with Matie Doty, who shared her passion for quilts. Next to Nette, Matie occupied a special place in Ida's life. The two women spent hours together day after day, year upon year. They pieced quilts together and spent long hours seated across from each other at the quilting frame, and miles of stitching held their lives together. They shared holiday meals and summer picnics,

and because Matie lived on the opposite end of town, Ida generally walked halfway home with her in the evening after a long day seated at the quilting frame. The following entries from Ida's journals reveal the close friendship the two women enjoyed and the many hours of quilting they shared.

Cloudy, sun come out just few minutes. Mrs Doty come about nine thirty, helped quilt. I went to town in A.M. Mrs Doty stayed till most dark. (5/6/33)

Cool, done up work. went over to Ruby's a while. brought her quilt over. Mrs Doty come up in P.M. we put quilt in the frames. Ruby was over in P.M. and evening. we quilted some after got it in the frames. Mrs Doty went home about nine o'clock. (10/23/33)

Pleasant, but little cool. I washed out a few pieces. Mrs Doty come in A.M. she quilted before and after dinner. I quilted in P.M. til about five or after. went after mail. Mrs Doty went home about 5:30. (2/15/34)

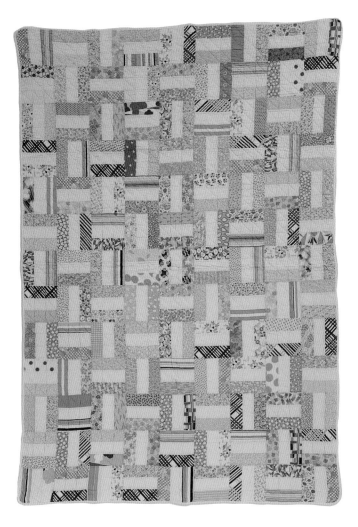

Spirit of St. Louis quilt, 53³/₄" x 77¹/₄", c. 1940. Ida listed three Spirit of St. Louis quilts in her life list, including one "for myself, small size Lindy." The small lap quilt she hand pieced for Hazel Gaunt is a "scrap quilt" constructed of a wide variety of fabrics rather than one or two fabrics, often color coordinated and specially purchased for a planned quilt. The basic block of the Spirit of St. Louis quilt is composed of four equal 6-inch squares. Each of these squares is made of three 2" x 6" strips. These four blocks are set at right angles to each other and the overall effect is of a spinning propeller blade. This quilt has a muslin backing and is quilted in a triangular grid. There are several references to other Spirit of St. Louis quilts in Ida's journals. "we done up work, then I sewed quilt lining on sides, in p.m. we put the quilt in frames. the Spirit of St. Louis, for John Gaunt." (10/27/36) "we helped with a.m. work. was busy all morning. in p.m. worked some on quilt. Spirit of St. Louis. snowed." (1/19/37) "finished the quilt. my Spirit of St. Louis, the one joined with green and white." (6/17/37)

Cloudy and cool north wind. rained and hailed some in p.m. Mrs Doty come in a.m. helped quilt. we finished it little after six. Mrs Doty here until after supper. (4/24/35)

Pleasant like spring. done up work, Mrs Doty come little after eight. we both quilted in A.M. and P.M. quilted the most I guess we have any day yet. (3/2/36)

Pleasant, not so warm. we washed. Mrs Doty come, she brought a few pieces. Mrs Doty and I filling in the top of Jesse's star quilt. (6/22/36)

I went to Mrs Doty's in P.M. to help her put in a quilt. stayed for supper. (11/15/37)

Year after year Ida and Mrs. Doty quilted together through the long days. In February 1938, Matie Doty was hospitalized, and although she was able to go home she never recovered from her illness. Ida visited her all through the spring and summer. At that time, however, it was believed that cancer was contagious and Ida could

Mrs Doty's Devils Food Cake

2 cups Brown Sugar
¹/₃ cup butter
2 cups flour
2 eggs beaten seperately
3 tbs cocoa, dissolved in ¹/₂ cup boiling water, let cool. 1 level tps soda dissolved in ¹/₂ cup sour milk.
Carmel filling:
Butter size of egg
Pint b. sugar
¹/₂ cup milk or water
¹/₂ cup cocoa.

only stand near her friend's bedroom window and talk with her from outside the house. Faye Doty Makings nursed her mother through those long months and sadly recalled how Matie would have loved the companionship of her friend to ease the pain and loneliness of those last days, but doctors refused to allow visitors into the

Charles A. Lindbergh, Jr., Little Falls, Minnesota. From the Collection of the Minnesota Historical Society.

Charles A. Lindbergh

Charles Lindbergh's amazing solo flight across the Atlantic in 1927 instantly made him one of America's best-loved heroes. His brave feat was cheered by people everywhere and his quiet manner and dashing good looks appealed to women of all ages. On February 2, 1929, even Nette made a brief, underlined entry in her journal: "Lindberg 27 years old." It is no wonder that quilters also succumbed to his charm and began to fashion quilts to celebrate the flight of the Lone Eagle. Shortly after the event, quilt block designs based on the Spirit of St. Louis, Lindbergh's airplane, became wildly popular. For the next decade Lone Eagle, Spirit of St. Louis and Lindy quilts were stitched by quiltmakers across the country. Of course, the tragic kidnapping of Lindbergh's baby a few years later only added to the love and empathy felt by the American public for their hero. In her diary, eighteen year old Anita McAvoy recorded the following: "March 1, 1932 Charles A. Lindbergh's baby was kidnaped."

Perhaps Ida set a small record with her completion of three Lindy and four Spirit of St. Louis quilts, but there was a personal connection that many Atwood residents felt with Charles Lindbergh because of his earlier residence in Bird City just a few miles to the west. A local wheat farmer, Banty Rogers, met twenty-year-old Lindbergh at a fair, and being an aviation enthusiast, he invited Charles to come to Bird City and join a group Banty was putting together to do aerial shows in western Kansas and neighboring states. Lindbergh took on the summer job as a stuntman. Billed as "Daredevil Lindbergh," he was a wing-walker, parachutist and at times, a mechanic. Local residents were thrilled with feats of the daring barnstormers and braver souls paid the not inconsequential fee of $5.00 for a brief ride in an airplane often piloted by Lindy himself. Bird City inhabitants watched as he practiced "balancing on the wings of a moving plane, floating downward a determined distance with a parachute; jerking a slender rope. Then downward! Downward! Landing if possible free of incumbrance."

Lindbergh slept in a huge barn on Banty Rogers' farm that also served as an airplane hanger. Mornings he bathed in a watering trough and then walked a mile to town for breakfast at the Nichols' drugstore. Patrice Nichols, just a few years younger than Charles, served his favorite morning drink of a malt with a raw egg. Patrice and Charles dated casually over the summer, he walked her home and was often invited to stay for dinner. He was a tall, lanky young man, very pleasant, remembered as being a "nice fellow," and interestingly, he and Patrice both shared the distinction of having auburn hair. Lindbergh spent many evenings visiting on the Nichols' front porch and eating Ruby's chocolate cake. In the months after Lindbergh's record setting flight he flew across the country, stopping at major towns and giving brief speeches to huge crowds of fans and well-wishers. Officials scheduling Lindy's flight would not allow him to land in Bird City, but to the delight of the residents he "circled the town 12 times and flew low for people to get a good view of him and his plane, Spirit of St. Louis, which transported him across the Atlantic Ocean to fame in May, 1927."

It is no wonder that when the Nickols family moved to Atwood a few years later and lived in the new house neighboring the Chambers home, that Ida felt an increased connection to the famous aviator that possibly was expressed through the many quilts she stitched commemorating Lindbergh's flight. Certainly, that link was on her mind when Ida pieced Patrice's wedding quilt in 1931. For the girl who dated Charles Lindbergh, Ida stitched a quilt with red and white airplanes, a Spirit of St. Louis quilt.

Quotes and some information from an article by Doris Minney, January 19, 1979, *The Daily Free Press,* Colby, Kansas. Titled: "Charles Lindbergh's Bird City Interlude."

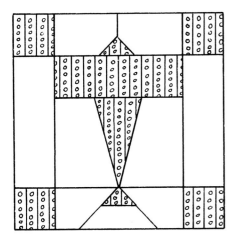

Airplane

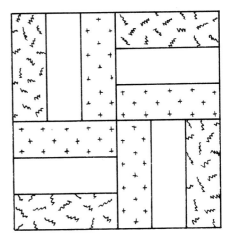

Spirit of St. Louis

On December 20, 1924, Ida wrote a card to Master Audry C. Gaunt: "Dear little Audry, I am anxious to be with you. do wish wasent so cold. with lots of love and xmas wishes from Aunt Ida."

house. In mid July Ida wrote: "the last time Mrs Doty was here, about noon." When she passed away on the first of October Ida lost not only a dear friend but a true companion whose heart shared the same path, whose hands loved the same labor.

Ida made quilts to celebrate friendships and family ties; her quilts observed all the passages of life. As the children of her friends and family grew they all received quilts from "Aunt Ida" as she was fondly called. In 1936 Ida made a baby quilt and pillow for Erma Treadwell LaDuke. Erma's father was Mary Chambers' nephew, Paul, who had come to live with the Chambers family after his mother died in a fire. Paul always called Ida and Nette his "aunts" and maintained lifelong ties with the sisters. As Paul's daughter awaited the birth of her first child, Ida "worked some on baby quilt for Erma Treadwell. got pillow tick ready to wash." "fixed little pillow for Erma Treadwell's baby." "done up work, then worked on little quilt." Sadly, the anticipated event brought sorrow. Erma gave birth to a son, named Paul after her father, but in December of that year Ida wrote, "when got home got the sad news of Erma Treadwell's death."

Fortunately, there were many joyous occasions to celebrate, and the gift of a quilt from Ida was truly a gift from her heart. Living on a very limited income restricted Ida's resources, but in each quilt Ida had stitched hours of herself and days of caring. A quilt from Ida was unquestionably a gift of her love and affection.

Although Ida faithfully recorded in her journals most aspects of the construction of a quilt and exact times that she sat at the quilting frames, she often failed to list the name of the quilt she was working on. On June 26, 1940, Ida even wrote about purchasing, stitching, and shrinking a lining for a quilt, but it remains anonymous: "Pleasant in A.M. warm in P.M. I went to town in A.M. got material for Mr Franklin's quilt sewed up the lining then shrunk and ironed it. worked some on Audry's quilt." It seemed to be especially true with the quilts of her neighbors that she quilted for money, but it was often the case with her own quilts as well. Her "life list" identifies some of the quilts, but we can only wonder about many of them as we read of the hours Ida sat, day after day, at her frames stitching the nameless quilts.

There was a surge in popularity of quiltmaking in the 1920s and 1930s, and many of the quilts Ida made reflect the styles and patterns that were the rage at that time. Although the quilts no longer exist, Ida made a Log Cabin quilt for Ruby Nichols' daughter, at least two Sunbonnet Sue quilts for nieces, and for Mira's daughters, two Trip Around the World quilts. The colors she chose for the two Trip Around the World quilts are bolder, especially the reds and blues, than was common for the times, but other colors in her Trip Around the World and Postage Stamp quilts—the soft greens, pinks, and purples—show the lovely pastel colors so popular in depression-era quilts. These new colors were a result of technological improvements in the textile dyes. After World War I pastels dominated the color range of quilts for at least two decades. Ida's Water Lily quilt is a fine example of the popular pinks and greens. The subdued colors of this lovely quilt are graceful and feminine.

Ida never recorded a Grandmother's Flower Garden in her life list of quilts, but she did quilt at least three of them for Nette, Ruby Nichols, and Aunt Nancy Eastwood. And as for the other amazingly popular quilt of the depression years, the Double Wedding Ring, Ida made three or four and quilted at least three others for friends. The Wedding Ring quilt had its origins in a nineteenth-century pattern, Pickle Dish, according to quilt historian Merikay Waldvogel, who also noted that the twentieth-century version became one of the most popular of all quilt patterns.[4] Unfortunately, none of the Wedding Ring quilts that Ida pieced or quilted exist today.

> I cut out some pieces and pieced on my wedding ring. Mrs Doty over in evening. I walked home with her. (6/25/34)
>
> I pieced some on my wedding ring. (6/29/34)
>
> I went to town to get muslin and pink and green print to join wedding ring. (7/12/34)

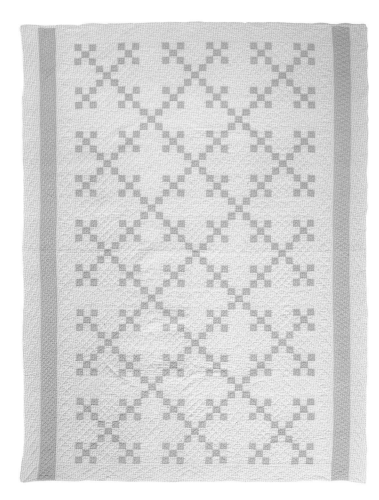

Nine Patch quilt, c. 1941. In the fall of 1933, Ida noted that she had completed the yellow and white nine-patch top she had been piecing. "finished Nette's lone star about two o'clock, after that pieced few of my yellow and white nine patches" (9/30/33) "sewed some on nine patch in p.m. finished joining it." (11/20/33) There are no further references to the Nine Patch quilt, although Ida did mention piecing several Four Patch quilts during the next four years. It is not clear whether this Nine Patch top was soon quilted or put away for nearly a decade. Given Ida's tendency to make several of her favorite patterns, it could be assumed that she made more than one version of the Nine Patch quilt, and indeed, there is a blue Nine Patch quilt, although it is pieced with smaller blocks.

Ida's yellow-and-white Nine Patch quilt is joined in an unusual and possibly original setting. The fifteen nine-patch blocks are set with plain white sashing strips, which are intersected with a nine-patch setting block. The unusual variation of this block and sashing gives a striking, graphic look to a very popular and traditional pattern.

In the summer of 1941, when Ida was quilting a quilt for Pat Chambers' birthday, the name of the quilt she was working on was never mentioned. However, in one corner on the back of the quilt she did embroider the date: "Aug '41." Several of her diary entries refer to the quilt: "A grand a.m. quilted some in a.m. then finished it and took out of frames at six o'clock. Patty Chambers quilt." (8/8/41) "I ironed my dress and slip, then sewed some on binding Patty's quilt." (8/11/41) "Finished binding Patty's quilt." (8/13/41) Two days later Nette wrote in her journal: "mailed Patty's quilt to her."

Quilt courtesy of Pat Chambers Thomas.
Photography by Jack Mathieson.

Four years later Ida worked on another Wedding Ring quilt:

> Pleasant but cold in A.M. we done a big washing. went to town in P.M. to get lining and batten for wedding ring quilt. (10/24/38)

> A grand day. we put wedding ring quilt in the frames this A.M. had the heater set up in P.M. (10/25/38)

Of the several Star quilts that Ida made, one has been located. Again, the Lone Star or Star of Bethlehem was a popular nineteenth-century pattern given a very new look with the soft colors of the twentieth century. Star patterns enjoyed great popularity in the Midwest and have traditionally been among the most popular of all pieced patterns. The yellow-and-white Star quilt owned by Mira's daughters is pieced with four shades of light yellow to deep gold. This quilt is similar to another Star quilt Ida pieced with a rich orange and brown. This quilt was the backdrop for the photo of the three sisters, Ida, Nette, and Mira, on the occasion of a visit Mira made to Atwood in 1953, one of the last times the sisters were together. The location of this quilt is unknown. Ida also made Star quilts for Rodney Gillette, John Burdette Chambers, and Cora Chambers.

> sewed binding down on Mrs Moors quilt
> sewed border on Rodney's quilt. (2/13/35)

> put Rodney's quilt in frames. the Lone Star. (2/15/35)

> Cloudy a while in A.M. then cleared off nice. we were busy all A.M. invited in a few to quilt in P.M. Mrs Dominy, Clara, Bell Sawer, Mrs Berry, Mrs Doty, and Ruby. Nette had lunch. had nice time. (2/19/35)

Ida made several four-patch and nine-patch quilts. There are two of these quilts in existence that Ida used as a light cover when she took an afternoon rest. They have been well worn and washed until there is virtually no color left in the fabrics, and just the piecing lines show the pattern where the pieces were hand stitched together. Another pattern that Ida wrote of often was the Pie quilt. Curiously, there is no mention of this quilt in quilt pattern directories; the only clue as to its image comes from interviews with current and former Atwood residents. Patrice Nichols Lilley, Ruby Nichols' daughter, exclaimed, "Well, it's just like a pie divided into eight

Ida C. Melugin. "October 7th 1928 Taken just as I was leaving for Fairmont." Photo courtesy of Hazel Gaunt.

equal pie-shaped sections, and they embroidered the name, like cherry or apple, across it." Sometimes the pies were padded and trimmed around the edge with lace or embroidery. Pie patterns were especially popular for doll covers for little girls. The pattern certainly captured Ida's imagination; she made at least four Pie quilts over a thirteen-year period.

worked on my pie quilt in P.M. (4/17/34)

Warm. helped with work, then went to town, got muslin and batten for my pie quilt, sewed up lining and sewed on the frames. (8/22/35)

Warm and windy. done up work then put my pie quilt in the frames. (8/23/35)

Cloudy and cool all day. we done quite a big washing. got through early. started to quilt on my pie quilt in P.M. (8/28/35)

Three years after Aunt Nancy Eastwood's death, Ida finished her Pie quilt top: "Pleasant, washed a few pieces, went over to Ruby's a while, in P.M. hemmed 3 tea towels and started to sew Aunt Nancys pie quilt in the frames. finished a lunch cloth. went to picture show, Mrs Bastian invited me." (3/4/40) Exactly one month later, Ida completed the quilting at nine o'clock in the morning of April fourth.

Another unusual quilt mentioned in Ida's list is a Radio quilt. Patrice Nichols Lilley described this pattern as an applique block, based on the old Cathedral Radios with a gothic window which were popular in the mid 1930s. Each block had a radio appliqued on it using various colored fabrics and alternated with a solid block.

Certainly among the most fascinating of Ida's quilts are the Lindy and Spirit of St. Louis quilts that she wrote of in her life list of quilts and journals. Charles Lindbergh's flight across the Atlantic captivated the American public and he instantly became a national hero, but because of his earlier residence in nearby Bird City, his feat had a personal impact on the people of Rawlins County. Many had paid five dollars for a short ride in Lindy's plane when he flew at local fairs, or had watched as he did aerial stunts or parachuted from his plane in air shows. And when the Nichols family had lived in Bird City in the 1920s, Charles Lindbergh had been a guest in their home and had been invited to join them for meals (he especially loved Ruby's chocolate cake) and had dated her daughter, Patrice. As she made her Lindy and Spirit of St. Louis quilts, Ida must have felt a personal connection to the man who became one of our great American heroes.

Based on research done by quilt historian Cuesta Benberry, there were several versions of these quilts designed to commemorate Lindbergh's flight. One of the earliest patterns to be published was The Lone Eagle by Emma S. Tyrell, which appeared in January 1929 in *Successful Farming*, a magazine Ida had subscribed to for many years. This was a realistic airplane design, alternating with a solid block quilted with an eagle. In 1933 the *Chicago Tribune* published a Nancy Cabot quilt design based on a pattern "originated by a clever needleworker in 1927, the year of the flight." This pattern is similar to a pinwheel and resembles the whirling propeller of an airplane. The Spirit of St. Louis quilt was published in a February 1929 issue of *Farm Journal Magazine* in an article titled "Quilts: Old and New" by Deborah Hale. This pattern comprised four equal squares made of three rectangles placed at right angles. The circling motion of the right angles represents an airplane propeller. The quilt names become rather confusing because later quilts with realistic pieced airplane blocks were also called Spirit of St. Louis.

Ida made three Spirit of St. Louis quilts, one for her nephew John Gaunt and two for her nieces Hazel and

Doris Gaunt. She listed three Lindy quilts, one for Hollis Hayward, one for her nephew Audry Gaunt and "for my-self, small size Lindy." Appropriately, for the girl who dated Charles Lindbergh, Patrice Nichols, Ida made a Spirit of St. Louis quilt for a wedding gift on the occasion of her marriage in 1931. This wedding quilt was probably based on the earlier Lone Eagle design, which had appeared in 1929 in *Successful Farming Magazine,* rather than the four-part block from *Farm Journal Magazine,* although that quilt was always called the Spirit of St. Louis by its owner. The blocks were composed of realistic red pieced airplanes on a white background. These pieced blocks were set in vertical and horizontal rows as Ida did not alternate them with the quilted eagle block, which had appeared in the earlier pattern. Unfortunately, this quilt was lost in a house fire in 1953, along with several other quilts that Ida had quilted for her friend Ruby Nichols.

Other versions of the Spirit of St. Louis or Lindy quilt alternate the pieced block with a solid block quilted with an eagle. The Kansas Quilt Project located a Spirit of St. Louis quilt made by another Kansas quilter in 1937. Lora Housholder Wedd's quilt was pieced with red, white, and blue fabric, but the pattern resembled a Nazi swasti-ka so during World War II the quilt was stored away and never used. [5] In *Women and Their Quilts,* historian Nancyann Twelker wrote of a swastika doll quilt made in 1915. Her research indicated that the swastika symbol was "used all over the world in ancient cultures and even in the Christian Church as a symbol of the Greek cross."[6] "For American Indians, the swastika represent-ed the four winds, rivers, mountains and rains." In the American Southwest the swastika symbol appears on rock walls and boulders painstakingly carved in prehis-toric petroglyphs. Ida's surviving Spirit of St. Louis quilt was pieced of scraps, and each block was set together without alternating plain blocks, thus the propeller—and the swastika image—is lost in the overall graphics of the quilt. In 1937 Ida wrote: "finished the quilt. my Spirit of St Louis, the one joined with green and white." It would be interesting to know whether her quilt pieced of two colors rather than scrap fabrics evoked a reaction as the graphics of the block became apparent.

Cover of a popular quilting book which contained patterns for Lindy's plane. Information courtesy of Cuesta Benberry. Quilting by Alice Beyer, Chicago: South Park Commissioners, 1934.

Trip Around the World quilt, 71" x 84³/₄", c. 1935-40. In the late 1930s, Ida hand-pieced the Trip Around the World quilt for her niece, Doris Gaunt Shaeffer, who was often referred to as "Toodles" in Ida's early journals (written when Doris was a baby). Each tiny piece measures 1³/₄" and is outline quilted inside each square ³/₈" in from the seam line. The backing is solid yellow and the bias binding is machine applied, turned to the back and stitched down by hand.

Quilt courtesy of Doris Gaunt Shaeffer. Photography by Brian S. Birlauf, Birlauf and Steen Photo, Denver, Colorado.

My Best Girls

Two days before Christmas in 1940, Ida had a severe heart attack and was bedridden for weeks. She never went to the hospital—Dr. Gertson came to the house every day, and Nette cared for her. On December 9 Ida wrote: "Got up in A.M. dident feel good went back to bed. got up in evening put on my gown. Dr come to see me. wasent up and dressed again until Feb 13th [1941]." Nette feared for Ida's life and called Mira and their brother John to come to Atwood right away. Nette wrote: "Ida had very severe attack of the heart. Mira, John and Audry come about 9:30." Ida slowly recovered, and Mira stayed on with the sisters for several weeks as Ida regained her strength. Ida didn't write in her book again until January 12, 1941. She noted that her brother John, with his wife, Cora, and their daughter and grandbaby came by for a short visit: "was only here a little while, guess I was still pretty sick."

Toward the end of February, Ida began writing again. Her entries are brief and it is apparent that her illness took a great deal of her vigor. Still, on February 27, Ida noted: "I worked some with pieces I had cut out years ago. calico pieces."

From Nette's book:

> 4-8-41 washed few pieces. quilted a little. First time since Ida was sick.

> 4-11-41 windy. quilted most the day.

> 4-15-41 done part of ironing. Ida finished E.A. [Elisabeth Ann Kelley] quilt. cloudy.

Ida's journal entries also indicate that as her quilting increased her health and energy returned:

3/18/41 Pleasant, I helped little with the work. pieced a few blocks for Ruby. Mrs Preder here in afternoon.

3/27/41 Some cloudy and cool. I finished my outing slumber robe top Ruby and Pauline were here this P.M. Mrs Mullen was here few minutes this evening.

4/12/41 Some cloudy. little windy and dusty. I helped dust and clean some. Frank and Lulu were here. Mrs Daisy Dominy here in evening, she brought me a nice red geranium with three blossoms on.

4/15/41 Cloudy. had good rain in P.M. Nette ironed, and I finished the quilt about ten thirty. E. Ann's quilt. I trimed it in P.M. and started to sew the border on. Clara and Ruby here in evening.

Postcard sent to Jesse Gaunt, dated October 31, 1914. Two decades later Ida made an interesting notation about Halloween in her diary: "I got dinner for Mrs K then quilted some in p.m. and evening. Clara and I went up to bond fire last night." (10/31/34)

The tone of Ida's diaries changes after her heart attack in 1940. Ida was seventy-three, and although she had many more productive years, she never seemed to regain her strength and energy to the full extent that she had previously enjoyed. One indication of how seriously her health had declined was her dramatic weight loss. Ida often noted her weight in her journals. In 1917 she was a buxom 175 pounds. Through the following years her weight wavered between 160 and 168 pounds. Shortly after her heart attack her weight was down to 120 pounds. Ida had no appetite during her illness and no stamina. Fortunately, her strength came back slowly, and as she put on a bit more weight some of her old energy returned.

Quilting was still an almost daily activity and she continued to quilt for others, but she pieced fewer quilts for herself than in the previous decade. The other change is the importance Ida attaches to her family and friends. Ida had always valued her relationships, but after her illness and through the following years they became even more dear to her. Because they had no immediate family in Atwood, Ida and Nette were very dependent on their friends and neighbors, and they seemed to have been cared for and looked after in a way that people in a small town often do. They always had rides to their clubs and meetings and church. Ida especially loved a ride around the lake just north of town and up to the cemetery. Their friends rarely came empty-handed. Ida mentions gifts of flowers, peaches, a gooseberry pie, fresh meat, and even a bucket of lard.

Jessie Hale brought me a nice violet. (5/4/41)

Agnes Birrer brought me a nice bouquet of yellow tulips. (5/6/41)

Mrs Dillon was here about noon. she brought us a pheasant. (10/29/41)

The sisters were desperately poor and eventually received county aid. But with the help of many friends, they got along well enough and were able to stay in their beloved home. Throughout both of their journals the much appreciated gifts are always recorded. In 1937, just as winter was beginning to set in, Nette wrote: "Rodney had 4200 lbs coal sent to us. Third time he has give load of coal." Ida also noted: "they brought us the coal Rodney sent us." (9/30/42) An undated letter to her nephew Jesse Gaunt reveals some of the despair they felt over their finances:

Wednesday eve.

Dear Jesse,
    Recieved your letter this P.M. sure was glad to get it. your mother was disappointed yesterday because was no letter from you. we were all pretty much excited over the news your letter contained. sure hope you get along O.K. we'll sure miss you tomorrow, these holidays make one think of what has been. Thanksgiving evening. better try and write

a few more lines. has been cloudy and rained some today. I look for snow by morning. well we had a very nice time considering. guess some of the rest how many were here. I let your Mother go to the lecture course last night. the girls went to the show with your father. I stayed home. have been going quite a little lately. the more I go the more want to go. Yes, Mary hears quite often from Mrs Kelley. she is getting along fine. dont think Nette plans on going now. but no telling she may change her mind. she was pretty blue after she went to see about her taxes yesterday. it is to bad, I say. they are so high. well maybe better quit for now.

will write again soon lots of love from Aunt Ida.

In addition to the much appreciated coal that their nephew Rodney Gillette sent each winter, another gift was a gas range from Mrs. Kelley. Ida wrote: "A wonderful gift." The sisters had also gotten an "Electric refrigator" in 1941, but they very frugally only used it during the hot summer months. By October or early November of each year as the weather turned colder, they turned off the refrigerator and stored perishable food in the cave or sod dugout behind the house.

Just a year before Ida's heart attack Nette had written: "Went to Mrs Davis funeral. another old friend gone." (8-14-39) Ida was now in her seventies and her diaries clearly reflect the growing importance she put on her friends and family. Visiting and renewing old friendships was her greatest pleasure. Guests she was especially pleased to see are noted in her journals with their names underlined and little x's or stars drawn around the entry.

2/23/45 A spring like day. Orpha Reeves, Mrs Kelley, Mary and Mike were here this afternoon. Nette was away
.

2/28/45 Pleasant, like spring in P.M. I quilted some, Ruby in A.M. Clara was here little while in afternoon.

6/25/45 Grand day up untill late P.M. clouded up and rained some. I washed out a few pieces. went over to Mrs Dominy's. quilted in P.M. Ruby was over. who should come to see us but Frank Reed and wife. [3 stars]

3/11/46 An ideal day. we washed out a few pieces. I quilted some in P.M. Faye Makings [Matie Doty's daughter] here in P.M. Arthur David called to see us just as we were eating supper [4 stars]

Arthur David had been one of the young people whose parents lived on a farm in the country and who boarded with Ida and Nette in town while he attended Atwood High School. Ramon Horinek's mother had been a lifelong friend of the Chambers sisters. When Ramon was home on leave from the air force in the spring of 1954, he wrote in Ida's guest book: "To the most wonderful neighbors I have ever met God bless you." And at Christmas of the same year he wrote: "I'll always stop and see my best two girl friends."

Ida quilted nearly every day, but it took her longer to finish a quilt. Earlier she had been able to quilt a top in an average of four weeks, but as she neared her eighth decade it took at least twice as long to stitch most quilts. Every now and then her journal entries became less regular and once she noted: "feeling to bad to keep up my writing." That entry was made in 1941; fortunately she recovered enough to write fairly regularly for another dozen years.

Through the war years Ida occasionally writes of working on a Red Cross quilt. "started to put Mrs Grace Hill's quilt in frames. I sewed some on Red Cross block." (8/14/41) "went up to Mrs Frye's to help with Red Cross." (8/12/42) "done little work for the Red Cross." (11/11/42) There was always quilting to do for the Ladies' Aid: "went to Mrs Kelley's to get thier names for the church quilt." (9/7/44) Ida finished the church quilt two months later "about four thirty."

Curiously, while Ida rarely mentions the pattern name of the quilt she is working on, she always notes the time when the quilting is completed.

quilted some in a.m. then finished the quilt about three o'clock. sure glad. (7/19/39)

finished Grace Hill's quilt about 9:30 (9/23/41)

quilted some in P.M. then finished it after supper about seven forty five. Clara helped (11/4/41)

Ruby was over. we quilted in a.m. and p.m. finished it, about 3:30. (5/2/44)

very warm. I quilted most of a.m., then a while in P.M. Ruby's quilt. finished it a little after two o'clock. (8/3/44)

Ida tied many comforters or slumber robes; a silk spread that Aunt Nancy pieced before she died, an "outing slumber robe," "worked on slumber robe, the one with pink lining," and a "crazy top comfortor" were some she mentioned. Otherwise she just noted "tied a slumber robe" or comforter.

Cloudy, cold and snowy. we washed out a few piece this A.M. then I started to put little outing flannel comfortor in the frames. Nette helped me finish putting it in after dinner,

Ida and Nette's home in Atwood, Kansas, c. 1935. Photo courtesy of Pat Chambers Thomas.

and tied it, then I fixed it around the edge. its for Fern Briney's little girl. (2/23/42)

Pleasant. real warm in P.M. we finished the ironing, then I quilted some went over to Ruby's a minute. this P.M. went to Mrs Crist. our S.S. class met there. we tied a comfortor for the Red Cross. (10/7/42)

Other quilts seem to come alive for the time they are on Ida's frames:

6/9/42 Cloudy in A.M. and cool. I helped some with the work, then went to the P.O. from there to Zella Snyder and then to see Goldie Howards flowers, then to Dillon's store to get batten and lining for Mrs Preder's sister's quilt.

6/10/42 Pleasant, helped some with work. then went over to Mrs Preder's to see about her sister Kate's quilt. Nette was gone a while in P.M. Paul, Ruth and Charlie [Treadwell] were here in P.M. [Their names are underlined and bracketed by stars.]

6/11/42 Pleasant. real warm in P.M. started to clean the corner cupboard in A.M. then started to put in Mrs Preder's sister Kate's quilt. Cady here few minutes in evening.

Nette went to the show.

6/12/42 Cloudy and cool. big storm last night, we finished putting Mrs Preder's sister Kate's quilt in the frames this a.m. quilted some in P.M. I went over to Mrs Dominy's while in P.M. Ruby was over.

6/13/42 Pleasant, done little cleaning, took a bath. Morgan was here. Mrs Reardon was in, Frank & Lulu were here. Cady was in, we quilted a while in afternoon.

6/14/42 Cloudy and cool. went to S.S. and church. after dinner rested a while. Cady come little after four, stayed for supper. had good visit.

6/15/42 Cloudy early, but cleared off later, we washed, wasent very big. Mrs Mullen here a while in P.M. rested while, then quilted a while. Clara here few minutes. Nette went to Colby with Elmer and Eva.

6/16/42 Cloudy all day. rained some during the night. I ironed some, then went to town went to see Dr Wolfe. quilted some in P.M. then went over to Mrs Dominy's a while Mrs Morton was here while I was gone

Water Lily quilt, 73¼" x 99", c. 1937. The Water Lily was a popular quilt motif in the 1920s and 1930s and was available as a paper pattern or in kit form. Quilt historian Cuesta Benberry has traced the variation of Ida's Water Lily quilt to the Rainbow Quilt Block Company, owned by William Pinch, who originally printed the kits in the colors in which they were to be embroidered, hence the name of his company. Benberry also noted that the designs and kits were widely available in dry goods stores, ten-cent stores, and department stores, and would have been easily accessible to people in remote areas and small towns, such as Ida's hometown of Atwood in northwest Kansas. There were several popular versions of the water lily design. Some had butterflies and cattails, while others had more stylized buds and leaves. The Kansas Quilt Project, which documented 13,000 antique quilts in that state, located seven Water Lily quilts during the research. Five were made in Kansas and two others were made in Oklahoma and Colorado and later brought to Kansas.

Ida made her Water Lily quilt in 1937, and in July she wrote: "started to join the lily quilt Nette gave me." Each of the twelve lily blocks measures 16½" x 16½", and glimpses of the stamped stitching lines are visible in the embroidered area. The water lilies are embellished with french knots, a running backstitch and a blanket stitch around the appliqued flower petals and leaves. Ida's quilt is pieced of all new fabric, which may have come as a quilt kit or was purchased especially for the quilt. The backing fabric is a finely woven, soft white muslin. The quilt has never been used or washed.

Through the summer of 1937, Ida worked on the Water Lily quilt: "sewed up lining for my quilt." (8/18/37) "in p.m. started to put my Lily quilt in the frames." (8/19/37) "got the quilt in and quilted some." (8/20/37) Ida and Nette quilted on the Water Lily quilt for nearly eight weeks, but their sewing was often interrupted with work of the summer's end. They began cleaning in preparation for the coming winter and preserving the harvest from the summer gardens. Ida mentions canning plums, peaches, crab apples, pickles, "chille sauce" and peach pickles. On October 12, Ida noted, "we finished my lily quilt a little after ten." When that quilt was taken out of the frames a new quilt, "one for Doris," was immediately put in. In a corner on the back of the quilt, Ida embroidered the date, "Oct 37," but the quilt was not completely done until nearly three months later. On January 29, 1938, Ida wrote: "I finished the edge of my lily quilt in p.m."

Quilt courtesy of Hazel Gaunt. Photography by Brian S. Birlauf, Birlauf and Steen Photo, Denver, Colorado.

1 quilts I have pieced and helped quilt —
2 nine patch for myself.   don't know the name
3 another one for " " that pieced before we left Iowa
4 a charm quilt — gave it to Mira.
5 one, just pieces of my things
6 one, "   "   "   " the family things
7 one, pieced of Grandma Thorne's dress and mine
8 one I gave Lulu Minney
9 one for Charlie   38 one for Mary Chambers
10 "   " Henry   39 "   " E. Ann "   "
11 "   " Jesse   40 "   " Patty "   "
12 "   " John   41 "   " Ruby   Sky Rocket
13 "   " Angie   43 pieced Nellie (Radio quilt) quilts
14 "   " Nellie   Amy pieced a nine patch,
15 "   " Mira   I quilted it here sold it —
16 "   " myself.   42 I gave Ruby a quilt —
17 "   " Thorne neck tie
18 "   " Rodney   "
19 "   " Burdell — Lone Star,   for cross stitch pattern
20 "   " Myrtle just fixed the top   quilting
21 "   " Jesse Gaunt the lone Star
22 "   " John "   " Spirit of St Louis
23 "   " Doris "
24 "   " Hazel "
25 "   " Audry " Lindy
26 "   " Carl Chambers neck tie
27 "   " Hollis Hayward Lindy
28 "   " Jeannette Price wedding ring
29 "   " Roy & Louise Melugin Pie quilt —
30 "   " John and Cora Shooting Star
31 "   " Maud Melugin Fan quilt
32 "   " Nellie outing flannel
34 "   " one for myself, small size Lindy.
35 "   " Mrs Breder.
36 "   " Rodney and Irma Lone Star
37 "   " Cora Lone Star

Ida's "life list of quilts." Courtesy of Hazel Gaunt.

6/17/42 Cloudy in forenoon. sun out warm in P.M. we cleaned some in corner cupboard. I went over to Ella's a few minutes quilted some in P.M. Cady and Mrs Winters were here in P.M. Nette went to the show. Clara was here rained in even.

6/18/42 Sun shone in a.m. cloudy in afternoon I cleaned some in kitchen cupboard. quilted a while then went to see Mrs Luther. Jessie Hale come to see us right after dinner.

6/19/42 Pleasant but little windy. I quilted some then went to town, on few errands, quilted some in P.M. Clara and Mrs Preder were here after supper, also Mrs Kelley. I went up to see Cady.

6/20/42 Partly cloudy. had another big rain last night, lots of lightening. I cleaned some then quilted a while, quilted some in P.M. Clara here a few minutes, Mary Elizabeth come to see us.

6/21/42 Mostly cloudy, rained some again last night. went to S.S. and church. Cady ate dinner with us. rested a while. Mr Franklin passed away this A.M.

6/22/42 Cloudy, rained some during the night started to rain some time in A.M. and kept it up till late P.M. Lulu come just as we were eating dinner, she ate some with us. we quilted some in P.M. Ruby was over.

6/23/42 Cool all day, quite cool by night. done a little house work, then quilted some. Ruby was over. quilted most of P.M. Clara here a few minutes. then come after supper. we went to see Jesse Hale. Nette was away.

6/24/42 Still cloudy and cool. quilted some in a.m. and p.m. Nette went to Star, Clara come over here.

6/25/42 Cloudy all a.m. sun come out in p.m. quilted some in a.m. went over to see the Franklins in a.m. went to Mrs Dominy's in p.m. to our Circle. Mrs Messmaker was here.

6/26/42 Some cloudy in a.m. but sun out in p.m. and real warm. I quilted some in a.m. then most of p.m. Mrs Mullen and Cady were here in p.m.

6/27/42 Pleasant, but warm. done little cleaning in dining room, then quilted some.

Ida and her niece Pat Chambers Thomas, 1939. Photo courtesy of Pat Chambers Thomas.

went over to Mrs Dominy's a few minutes. quilted in p.m. Clara here after supper.

6/28/42 Pleasant. went to S.S. and church after dinner rested a while, then wrote to JoAnn Melugin, we went for a nice ride with Lon and Ruby, Ella went with us. Nette went to Vespers at the lake.

6/29/42 Pleasant, we done a big washing quilted some in P.M. Thelma Adcock come over to see me. Irma Koontz was in.

6/30/42 Pleasant, we done our ironing. I went over to Ruby's. quilted some in a.m. and

Friendship quilt, 1946. In 1946, Ida assembled a Friendship quilt that represents the zenith of the thrifty nature of the true quilter. On February 15, she wrote: "pleasant, warmer. helped with the work, then put a quilt in the frames. the top one I pieced years ago." Indeed, nearly half a century earlier, Ida pieced blocks for a Friendship quilt that had names of family and neighbors stamped or inked in the center squares. Many of the blocks Ida used for her 1946 quilt date from that earlier work and very likely were left over from that project. In the newer quilt names were embroidered with red thread in the center squares. The very newest fabrics in the quilt are used for the sashing strips and setting blocks and can be dated to the year Ida embroidered in a corner on the back of the quilt: "April 1946." Ida also noted in her diary: "Pleasant, finished Mira's letter, then quilted some. we finished my quilt, about eleven o'clock. dident do much in p.m. worked some on yard after supper, raked leaves." (4/5/46) "I sewed down some of the binding on my quilt. finished it in p.m." (4/15/46)
Photography by Jack Mathieson.

most of p.m. Nette went to Mrs Frye's to a party for Mrs Lesh's mother. Jessie Franklin Davis come to tell me good bye.

7/1/42 Pleasant, some cloudy. got cool in p.m. I went to beauty parlor in a.m. quilted some in a.m. and p.m. went to Mrs Dominy's in p.m. to S.S. class meeting. Nette went to the show. Clara was over.

7/2/42 A grand day, from start to finish, Clara and I went to the store got something for lunch then walked down to Mrs Swaney's, stopped to see Mrs Cloe, spent the day with Mrs S. got home about 6

7/3/42 Pleasant, but warm. I quilted most of a.m. and p.m. Ruby here in a.m. Nette went to beauty shop, Nette and I rode up to the cemetery after supper with Mr and Mrs Mellick.

7/4/42 A grand day. little warm. Nette and I cleaned up the front part of the house, and the rest of the house for Saturday. Cora come driving in little after twelve, we quilted some in p.m. took little ride after supper.

7/5/42 Pleasant but warm. went to S.S. and church. come home had dinner, Cora left for home about three thirty. Mary and her mother stopped and took me to the lake, to the Vesper service.

7/6/42 Pleasant, done little washing on the board. quilted some in a.m. and most of p.m. George Henderson wanted a room here for a few days.

7/7/42 Pleasant, real warm in p.m. I quilted some in a.m. we both quilted in p.m. Ruby was over. we had a nice shower in p.m.

frames. Ruby had some more work to do on the top. Ruby and Nette to the Circle this P.M. I wrote some to Mira." On the following day, the twentieth, Ida wrote: "we got the cotton and top on quilt." The next day she finished putting in the quilt and began the quilting.

When Ida finished a quilt there was generally another one to put immediately on the frames. Sometimes she began a new quilt the next day, and other times she stitched the binding on before putting another quilt on the frames, but for years and years not more than six or seven days went by before another quilt was begun. The only exception was at Christmas. There was always a church bazaar just before the holiday that Ida and all the aid members sewed for. Ida made aprons, tea towels, pillow cases, holders, and crocheted doilies. She generally tried to finish her quilting by Christmas so the house could be cleaned for the company they had at that holiday. If there was a quilt on the frame it was rolled up and stored out of the way for a few days but was soon taken out again to be worked on.

> Cloudy and cold. I washed out a few pieces. helped with a.m. work. went over to Ruby's a few minutes. got out the quilt quilted some in a.m. and most of p.m. Nette gone to Star tonight. (12/27/39)

> 5/23/45 A grand day. we aired our quilts. I quilted some in forenoon and afternoon. Ruby was over and quilted. Cady was in. I went over to Ruby's.

> 5/24/45 A grand day. we done part of our ironing. I quilted some in a.m. and p.m. Ruby was over and quilted.

> 5/31/45 Some cloudy. we finished the ironing, Ruby was over. I finished the quilt. Nette went to Lena's for dinner, Toots was here Velma Cochran was here in p.m. Cady was in. Nette went to the show.

> 6/6/45 Still cloudy and cool. worked with tea towels, wrote to Paul and Ruth. started to put the lining to Mira's quilt in the frames. Cady was in. Goldie Howard brought a lovely bouquet.

> 6/7/45 Cloudy all day. I done little cleaning in by bedroom, then we put Mira's quilt in the frames, ready to pin, and got it partly pinned.

> 6/8/45 Cloudy most of the day, sun shone a few minutes, we finished pinning in Mira's quilt this a.m. I quilted some in p.m. I went to see Mrs Morton in p.m.

Marshall's birthday.

7/8/42 Pleasant but warm, we both quilted in a.m. and p.m. Ruby over in a.m. Clara here a few minutes after supper. rained some during the night.

7/9/42 Pleasant. a grand a.m. but plenty warm in p.m. we finished the quilt about nine a.m. dusted the room some, crocheted. went up to Cady's in evening. Nette went to the show. Velma Cochran & grand daughter. good supper and nice time
7/10/42 Cloudy all day. cleaned up the dining room, then went over to Burd's store. in p.m. finished binding Kate's quilt. went over to Mrs Dominy's in evening few minutes. warm.

7/11/41 Some cloudy. I cleaned some in my bedroom. took the quilt over to Mrs Preder.

At least one quilt gave Ida some problems. On October 12, 1944, Ida "put one of Grace Hill's quilts in the frame." Just a week later she took it back out of the frame. "Pleasant, we took the quilt out of the frames the one we had of Grace Hills but just got the lining in

Ida did not finish Mira's quilt until the morning of

July 20, the same day that a neighbor, Emma Briney, brought another pieced top to quilt. Life went on more slowly for Ida, but she quilted and visited, cleaned and canned, and planted her flowers each spring. On her eighty-first birthday in 1948, Ida wrote that she had a "wonderful birthday. got a lot of cards." Ida's last journal was a guest book begun on September 11, 1950, on the occasion of Nette's eightieth birthday. Forty-three guests called to give their birthday greetings to Nette. "A well spent 80 years-bless you."-Rev. R.L. Wells; "Keep on Keeping on With Us."-Alonzo B. Nichols; "To a wonderful person who has always been nice to me. Happy Birthday."-Bernadine Reardon; "So glad to visit faithful friends."-Rev. and Mrs. Plantz.

For the next few years friends called on the sisters and jotted messages of love and remembrance to Ida and Nette. "How much I love to be with my dear friends."-Goldie Carmichael; "A day for good friends."-Ruby Nickols; "Love to two Dear Friends."-Faye Doty Makings; "Be good, Dont work to hard."-Lulu Minney; "God Bless you dear Girls."-Katherine Luther; "Glad to see you 'gals' again. Be careful Nette & dont fall again."-Mr. & Mrs. Frank Reed; "Just dropped in to see how you girls were."-Goldie Carmichael; "First one to wish you happy new year may the good Lord be good to you both."-Mrs. A.E. Pilnacek.

In the volumes of Ida's journals that have survived the years an enduring presence of her spirit emerges from her plain words. Ida had no children and was widowed early, but she loved many and her caring and affection emerges as a dominant theme in her writings. She dealt bravely and sensibly with the loneliness that often comes with aging. She commented on her loneliness but reminded herself to be happy for her blessings and to keep busy. She was able to appreciate the affection of the people around her; if her old friends were gone she would still enjoy the company of their sons and daughters. Where Nette sought out people and activity for fulfillment, Ida found contentment in a much smaller circle. In the small prairie town of Atwood, Ida's writing reveals a rare appreciation of her life and blessings. While it may be an old-fashioned and disappearing trait to be content with the circumstances that life delivers, Ida seemed to have been more than content; she worked to find a wholeness in her world.

Perhaps that is a clue to the very existence of her diaries. Many writers make provisions for the surviving body of their work; some hope they will be published, and others request that they be destroyed. Some diarists have burned their writings as they neared the end of their years and yet others have placed them in archives to be preserved or directed that they will be passed on to children or friends. Ida made no such grand provisions for her work and possessions. Perhaps, as some people in the past viewed quilts, she possibly considered her journals as too unimportant, too ordinary, to ensure their survival. And yet she possessed a creative drive that urged her through most of her life to write and to quilt.

It may have been that the sense of self that she possessed was complete enough, complemented with her lifelong spirituality, that she did not feel a need to ensure an earthly immortality.

For Ida, the present was fulfilling. She had work and she was making a contribution. Her sense of responsibility to her church and community is plainly evident year after year. Lacking most financial resources, Ida made contributions in the form of her service and time and, of course, her needlework. In the past, quilts have often been dismissed as common domestic goods, perhaps because they were generally the work of women's hands and their purpose often was viewed as only utilitarian. And yet quilts are the artifacts, and many times the only records, of women's lives. Each quilt speaks volumes of the love and caring, the skill and artistry, and sometimes the sheer perseverance that went into its creation. With Ida's journals there is the added richness of the written lines that accompany the quilts: "We commenced to quilt." "I put in most of the day quilting." "Sewed border on Rodney's quilt." "We quilted all day." "Started to join my lily quilt." "An ideal day. we hung out our quilts."

In themselves, Ida's journals are rare and unprecedented documents of quilting history, but even more they are chronicles of the life of an ordinary woman, a woman who stayed at home and served her family and her church, a quiet woman symbolic of so many whose stories are never recorded. And the term "ordinary" is not at all derogatory, most people are ordinary, most people live lives of hard work and responsibility and caring for their families and communities. Theirs are the stories that are never recorded.[7]

Perhaps Ida was ordinary, but she was ordinary in the finest sense of that word. And although her journals may never win awards, and have even been dismissed by some historians as just unimportant entries about domestic work and sewing, Ida's decades of writing show an awareness of a strong sense of herself and her place in the world. Certainly, her quilts parallel that reality, the hours and hours of mundane stitching, line after line of daily entries. Ida was not doing this work with an immediate awareness of her legacy; she had no direct family that this body of work would pass on to. Nor did Nette, her sister and dearest companion. And yet she felt compelled to leave a record of her life in fabric and paper, a lifetime of work that endures beyond the physical boundaries of her world on the high plains of the western prairie and across the years to speak to new generations. Her work with a needle and a pen is a fine and enduring legacy.

By 1954 Ida had discontinued keeping a regular diary, but she made fairly regular entries in her Guest Book, interspersed with signatures and comments made by her guests. A number of friends called on her eighty-eighth birthday on January 28, 1955. Anna Beck wrote "Happy birthday dear friend," and Mabel Sticle wrote "Many more birthdays to you." Friends stopped by every day to visit with Ida and Nette: "Marie Cochran come to see

Nette. Lulu Minney come to see us." "A cloudy stormy day, snowing. Billy T. Henderson brought thier new baby girl to see us." "Till Taylor's two oldest girls come to see us." "Frank and Lulu were here. Ruth Kelley Hayden and little one come to see us."

The last entry is dated March 11, 1955: "Rev. Adams the Narizane minister come to see us." That night Ida had another heart attack and was taken to the hospital. Ida never recovered. She passed away seventeen days later on March 28, 1955. Left alone with no close family nearby, Nette failed rapidly in her health. She was moved to a nursing home, where she died on June 26, just eleven weeks after Ida's death.

The two sisters who had been so different yet had shared eight decades of love and companionship, were both gone. Their brother John and sister Mira came to the house to dispose of their possessions. Quilts, their treasured pieces of china, and the rocker from Ma and Pa's fiftieth wedding anniversary were shared among the nieces and nephews. Clothing and similar items were given away, rooms were cleaned out, and the house was closed up to await the impending auction when the house and its remaining contents would be sold. The box of diaries filled with five and a half decades of faithful entries, Ma's early journals with her daily rounds of work, five of Nette's books full of her clubs and shows and parties, and Ida's diaries containing decades of piecing and quilting, years of her work and friendships, were all left behind, overlooked in the dark, silent house.

Ida and Nette, 1948. Photo courtesy of Pat Chambers Thomas.

Lone Star quilt, 81½" x 85½", c. 1936. Ida made several Lone Star or Star of Bethlehem quilts. On February 15, 1935, Ida wrote: "in p.m. put Rodney's quilt in frames. the Lone Star." She also mentions quilting on Lone Star quilts with the Ladies' Aid Society and for her neighbor Ruby Nichols. Other Lone Star quilts were made for John Chambers and for her nephew Burdette Chambers. The yellow-and-white Lone Star quilt was pieced and quilted in 1936 by Ida and Nette for their nephew Jesse Gaunt. Each diamond shape in the star is outline quilted and the pattern is repeated in the diamond grid quilting in the solid white background. Ida, Nette, and Mrs. Doty quilted mornings and afternoons for twelve days to finish the quilt: "Mrs. Doty and I filling in the top of Jesse's star quilt. real tired after supper." (6/22/36) "Real warm. done little extra work around the house, then helped on the quilt. we got it ready to put in the frames in p.m." (6/24/36) "Warm. Mrs. Doty come, we all quilted some in a.m. and p.m." (6/26/36) "Still warm. Mrs. Doty come, we quilted in a.m. and p.m." (7/3/36) "Pleasant in a.m. we finished quilting Jesse Gaunt's quilt about noon. put in a baby quilt for Ruby." (7/8/36) The prairie point edging around the quilt repeats the pointed shapes of the diamonds in the star. The edging is made of fabric squares folded into triangles and inserted into the edges of the quilt. Quilt historian Barbara Brackman's research indicates that the prairie points were a less expensive alternative to lace edgings, and although there are a few examples from the nineteenth century, the triangle edge was most popular in cotton quilts made after 1925. Quilt courtesy of Hazel Gaunt. Photography by Brian S. Birlauf, Birlauf and Steen Photo, Denver, Colorado.

Diary

6/1/33 Cloudy and windy. John and Cora started home at 8:45 we washed over to Ruby's. washed some for her. we ate dinner over there. Nette went over to Ruby's in evening. I went over to Mrs Dominy's. I started to put binding on the quilt.
6/2/33 Pleasant. we ironed. I went up to Mrs Nickols a while in a.m. I finished baisting binding then stitched it on machine. I took little walk with Clara in evening. I stopped and visited with Mrs Mullen.
6/3/33 Pleasant but warm. we cleaned up the house some. I went to see Dr Dowler, and Mr Neifeld in a.m. sewed some on the quilt in p.m. Sadie Jones and little girl were here a few minutes. Eva was here for dinner, Clara and I took little walk.
6/4/33 Pleasant but warm. went to S.S. and church. then to Grandma Kisling's funeral in p.m. Nette and I took little ride with Ruby and Lon, then went to church. Ate lunch after we come home. Mrs Dominy not well.
6/5/33 Warm and little windy. I went over to hear the gospel singers. then helped Nette with washing, over to Ruby's in p.m. I finished binding the wedding ring quilt. Clara over in evening. we went for little walk.
6/6/33 Pleasant, but warm. we ironed, then I went to see how Mrs Dominy was, and on to see Lucy few minutes. Nette went to see Edith about some hemstitching. Ruby was over while in p.m. Mrs Berry was in, another dust storm. had little rain. we were home in evening.
6/7/33 Cloudy part of day. sprinkled several times. Nette and I cleaned our bedroom. she got new linoleum rug. turned little cool toward night. we were home in evening.
6/8/33 Pleasant not so warm. Nette helped with Lions dinner. I went to hear gospel singers. dident do much in a.m started to work on Burdette's quilt in p.m. Mrs Kelley, her girls, Nette & I had a picnic lunch in Mrs Kelley's back yard Thorne's folks come just as we were ready to eat. They went to the temple. Harry & Ann come to see us in evening.
6/9/33 Pleasant in a.m. but very warm in middle of day. I went to hear the gospel singers. Nette done some baking, we all ate together at Mrs Kelley's for dinner. I pieced some in p.m. Thorne's folks went out to Genie's for supper. Nette and I ate lunch over with Mrs K. and girls. Mrs Swaney & Mrs Doty stopped in few minutes in evening.
6/10/33 Pleasant. Thorne's folks started home little after five, not much to do this a.m. went to hear the singers. pieced some on Burdette's quilt. Frank, Lulu & Eva here in p.m. took little walk with Clara in even.
6/11/33 Children's Day. Pleasant but warm. went to S.S. and the exercises. rested and read in p.m. had a rain in late p.m. and evening.
6/12/33 Cloudy and cool. rained after I got up this a.m. worked on quilt. wrote to Mrs Roberts. was home in even.
6/13/33 Pleasant. we washed over to Ruby's. went over while in p.m. worked on quilt. listened to Radio. went riding in evening with Ruby and Lon.
6/14/33 Pleasant. went to hear the gospel singers. pieced some on quilt. Ruby, Nette, & I helped with Father and Son Banquet. got home about nine.
6/15/33 Pleasant. went to hear gospel

Lone Star quilt, June 1949. Photo courtesy of Audry Gaunt.

singers. worked on the Star quilt. went to see Mrs Doty in p.m. our S.S. social com. met here in evening. Nette went to the lake for picnic.
6/16/33 Friday. Pleasant. Swanie, Myrle and Ona come over. got here about nine thirty. Swanie painted a sign for Aura Tillett. we had good visit. they started home about eight thirty. Eva and Ida drove up about three thirty. stopped a few minutes, then went on out to Lulu's.
6/17/33 Windy and warm. I went to hear the gospel singers. we dident do much work. felt like resting up a little. Eva, Lulu and Ida were here in. p.m. Clara here few minutes, Mrs Doty here a while.
6/18/33 Windy & warm. went to S.S. and church. then to church again in evening. Mr Sites preached both times. we ate dinner with Ruby. I wrote to Aunt Elda. I stayed all night with Ruby. Lon away.
6/19/33 Some windy, still warm. we washed over to Ruby's. ate dinner with her worked on Star quilt. it blew bad in p.m. commenced to rain about six. was a good rain. Nette stayed all night with Ruby. we were over in evening.

6/20/33 A fine morning after the rain. we ironed, Ida Saurbach come in after us. we visited, had a good time. I finished putting star together.
6/21/33 Pleasant, some cloudy, looked like rain in p.m. Nette and I went with Frank's folks down to John's for supper. rained some before we went.
6/22/33 Pleasant. rained some during the night. Ida brought us home, as she was on her way back to Arkansas. we got home about ten, Ida went right on. Nette went with Will Giles, to their reunion, I went over to Ruby's while in p.m. Nette got back at eight. Clara and Cady were here little while.
6/23/33 Pleasant, partly cloudy. I went to hear the gospel singers. I made a slip out of an old dress. Clara come over in evening we took a walk. rained.
6/24/33 Pleasant but warm. went to hear the singers. then helped with the work. Eva and Lulu were here in p.m. went for little ride with Mrs Kelley in evening.
6/25/33 Sunday. warm, went to S.S. had no church. after dinner rested some. Mrs Berry was in a while. Nette went with Lon and Ruby for a ride. we went the play at church,

put on by the young folks.

6/26/33 Warm. we washed over to Ruby's. I wrote to Mrs Philson in p.m. worked some on pie quilt. went over to Mrs Dominy's in evening. Nette went to the show.

6/27/33 Warm. Pleasant in a.m. we ironed. I went to hear the gospel singers. Cora come in on the one o'clock train. I went with Mary Elizabeth to meet her. then we took her back for east train. Charles Wilson was here to see Nette when I got back. Rodney's cousin.

6/28/33 Nice in a.m. but very warm during the day. I went to hear the singers, then went to see about my taxes. sewed some on pie quilt. we had a neighborhood picnic in evening, between Lon's and Mr Hayden's. had good eats and nice time. it rained.

6/29/33 Real warm. I dident do much. went to hear gospel singers. then went to see Mrs Allen few minutes. Ruby over in p.m. I looked through some drawers. went to see Ella Greason and Mrs Giles little while in evening.

6/30/33 Pleasant in a.m. very warm in p.m. went to hear the gospel singers. Nette made me a cake to take to the ice cream social, I laid around most of p.m. after supper went over to the church. flies and mosquitoes were bad. we done fairly well, I got home most eleven o'clock.

7/1/33 Pleasant in a.m. then warm again in p.m. I went to hear the singers. come back helped finish up the work. Nette and I ate our dinner over to Mr & Mrs Hayden's home. they went this early a.m. to World fair. we are going to stay over there while they are gone. I laid around most of p.m. Eva, Lulu & Inez were here. Mrs Doty & Clara here in evening.

7/2/33 Sunday. Pleasant in a.m. warm in p.m. I went to S.S. and church. come over home after dinner, rested & slept long time. we went to church in evening.

7/3/33 Pleasant, but warm. we washed. ate lunch with Ruby. Mrs Doty was here in p.m. helped us on the star quilt. Clara here a while in evening. Nette went to Rebecca in evening.

7/4/33 Pleasant. warm. Nette made a cake, we dident any extra work. I sewed some on my pie quilt. we had picnic with Mr and Mrs Berry in evening, right at home in back yard. Ruby & Lon are with us.

7/5/33 Some cloudy. saw pretty rainbow in a.m. we ironed, Nette made me a cake for S.S. class meeting. Mrs Doty here in p.m. we had our class meeting at Mrs Frye's in evening.

7/6/33 Warm, helped with the little work. Mrs Doty come in a.m. was here till after band concert. we all worked on the Star quilt, Nette cut out Mrs Doty and I sewed.

7/7/33 Another warm day. I went over to Mrs Dominy's to hear the gospel singer. Mrs Doty come in a.m. helped us on the quilt. Ruby over while in p.m. Mrs Doty and I went to see Mrs Franklin after supper she is sick. I dident know it until today. we had good rain lots of thunder and lightening between ten and twelve o'clock p.m.

7/8/33 warm. we done up part of our work, then went to Grandma Dunn's funeral at M.E. church, ten o'clock. I got weighed on way. weighed 163 lbs. worked some on star quilt in p.m. Ada Gaunt come to see us. Lulu was here.

7/9/33 warm. went to S.S. and church rested some in p.m. Nette and I went with Ruby and Lon to see high water at Blakeman. we went to church in evening.

7/10/33 Another warm day. we washed with Ruby. Mrs Doty come in p.m. we got the Star together. we went down in basement while in p.m. was so warm. Ruby come over. Mrs Doty and I went with Lon and Ruby to see high water. looked like rain as we come back.

7/11/33 Pleasant, but going to be warm again. we ironed, Mrs Doty come to help with quilt. we are filling in with white. Clara, Mrs Doty, Nette and I walked over to the lake to see the high water. Mrs Doty and I rode back with Mrs Mullen and Mildred.

7/12/33 Pleasant in a.m. then plenty warm. Mrs Doty and I went to Mrs Gaines & Mrs Dominy to see about pattern to quilt the border and plain blocks. Mrs Doty and I finished putting on the border.

7/13/33 Warm. Mrs Doty come in a.m. helped put the quilt in the frames. we quilted some in p.m. Clara, Mrs Doty, Mrs Berry, Nette and I went to high school building to hear the Philharmonic choir.

7/14/33 Real warm early. then the wind blew up nice from north. Mrs Doty come in a.m. we quilted in forenoon and afternoon both. rolled the quilt up and brought it over home. we rested a while, then got ready and went to the lake for picnic. had nice lunch and good time. Mrs Swaney, Mrs Doty, Clara Bump, Nette and I.

7/15/33 Pleasant, we cleaned and dusted Mrs Hayden's house. got all through before noon. after dinner we rested, took our bath. dident do much in p.m. Mr Hayden's folks got home little after eight. we finished bringing our things over home. Nette and Mrs Berry went to town. Clara was here. we walked down town a few minutes

7/16/33 Cool. I went to S.S. and church. after dinner rested, wrote and read some. we went to church in evening. Clara come over and went with us.

7/17/33 Some windy. we washed over to Ruby's Mrs Doty come in p.m. and we quilted. was home in evening.

7/18/33 Warm. we ironed. I went to hear the gospel singers. Mrs Doty come in a.m. we quilted in forenoon and p.m. to. Mrs Doty went up to Mrs Swaney, Nette for ride with Mrs Kelley. I went to see Lillian David.

7/19/33 Warm. Mrs Doty come in a.m. we quilted in forenoon and p.m. went to Mrs Dominy's in evening to a committee meeting. see about social.

7/20/33 Warm. Mrs Doty come in a.m. we quilted some in forenoon and p.m. I was real tired when we quit.

7/21/33 Warm. Mrs Doty come in a.m. we quilted in a.m. and p.m. Clara Walts here in p.m. Mrs Munger called. we went to lake on picnic. Mrs Swaney, Mrs Doty, Clara Bump, Nette and I. had good time, and plenty to eat.

7/22/33 Warm. I cleaned up our bed room and bath room. Nette ironed some for Mrs Berry. Lulu and Eva were here a while. Clara here few minutes in evening.

7/23/33 Cloudy and cool. went to S.S. and church. rested some in p.m. wrote to John & Cora. we went to church in evening.

7/24/33 Cloudy in a.m. cool, but warmed up by afternoon. Mrs Doty come about middle of a.m. we quilted. we quilted both a.m. and p.m. after supper, we went to see Mrs Dominy and Clara Clara was sick. then we went to see Mrs Reeves and Orpha. Mrs Reeves was out to Nette's. got home about dark.

7/25/33 Pleasant in a.m. warm in afternoon. I swept the cave steps. then went to quilting. Mrs Doty come in a.m. we all quilted in a.m. Mrs Doty and I quilted in p.m. took it out of the frames at 3:30

7/26/33 Pleasant, we washed in kitchen with Mrs Berry. I started to make a gown in p.m. Clara over in evening we took little walk.

7/27/33 Pleasant in a.m. warm in afternoon. Nette helped with Lions dinner, I ironed. trimmed the Star quilt in p.m. several were in to see it in afternoon. I went down to church in evening. My class had another ice cream social. took in over $12.00 Nette went out to Della Mettlers.

7/28/33 Pleasant in a.m. very warm in p.m. we opened big box in wash house and aired the bedding in a.m. I fixed a gown for Nette and myself. Clara and I took a walk in evening.

7/29/33 Pleasant in a.m. warm in afternoon I cleaned up the small room a little in a.m. done other cleaning. Eva & Lulu were here in p.m. I done some mending in p.m. Clara and I took another walk in evening.

7/30/33 Sunday. very warm again. I went to S.S. and church. rested in p.m. went to church again in evening.

7/31/33 Pleasant, but warm. we washed with Mrs Berry. in p.m. went to Mrs Haynes funeral. Mrs Dominy over after supper. I went home with her a few minutes.

8/1/33 Some cloudy. we ironed. I sewed some on binding star quilt. we put Aunt Nancy's grand mother's flower garden quilt in the frames in p.m. we had a good rain, between seven and eight thirty.

8/2/33 Pleasant. went to hear the gospel singers. Mrs Doty come in p.m. to quilt.

8/3/33 Cloudy and cool. Clara come over to tell me, I was invited to Mrs Reeves to spend the day. wasent feeling very good in a.m. but got to feeling better. we had a good dinner and a fine time. Mrs Doty, Clara and I. five of us. Mrs Reeves and Orpha. several were in in p.m. and evening to see the quilt.

8/4/33 Some cloudy. I went to hear the gospel singers. Mrs Doty come in a.m. to quilt. I made some dill pickles. went to Mrs Reeves and got some apples. several in in evening.

8/5/33 Pleasant. warmed up some. helped with a.m. work. then quilted some. Mrs Doty come in a.m. to quilt. had another good rain last night.

8/6/33 Pleasant. warm in p.m. went to S.S. then Nette and I went with Mrs Kelley & girls to Colby for picnic dinner, Thorne, Mary and girls were there. Mr & Mrs Hayward and Hollis ate with us. thirteen in all. Thorne's folks come home with us. got home about nine. we were at Mr Haywards home in p.m. Mrs Kelley and Mrs Hayward made ice cream. we had a nice time.

8/7/33 Had good rain last night, was raining early this a.m. was nice day. little warm in p.m. we dident do much in a.m. we all ate together over at Mrs K. Thorne's folks started home about four o'clock. Mary Elizabeth and Lonnie went with them. Nette and I quilted some in p.m. I went over to Mrs Dominy's little while after supper.

8/8/33 Had another good rain during the night. we washed on west porch. quilted some in a.m. and p.m. warm in afternoon.

8/9/33 Warm. we ironed in a.m. I went to hear gospel singers, then quilted. we quilted in p.m.

8/10/33 Warm. went to hear gospel singers. then quilted in forenoon and p.m. took it out of frames at four thirty. went to the Seth Parker programme at M. E. church in evening. was good.

8/11/33 Pleasant. done little work in cave then went to hear the gospel singers. went to town to see about getting some rent money.

sewed binding on quilt in a.m. then commenced to hem it down in p.m.

8/12/33 Pleasant. went to hear the gospel singers, then over to see Lucy. sewed some on binding in a.m. then finished it in p.m. Lulu was here in p.m. I done little mending. Clara here few minutes in evening.

8/13/33 Pleasant went to S.S. then to Christian church for preaching. Mrs Kelley & Ruth ate dinner with us. I rested, read, and wrote some in p.m. in evening Clara and I took long walk.

8/14/33 Pleasant. we done a little cleaning and straightening around. Nette cleaned the kitchen cabinet, I done little work in cave. finished up some holders in p.m. was home in even.

8/15/33 Pleasant, but little windy, we washed on west porch. joined Nette's grandmother's flower garden quilt in p.m. went over to Mrs Dominy's while in evening. Inez and Jim come to see us in evening. told us they were married

8/16/33 Pleasant and warm. we ironed I went to hear the gospel singers. put border around quilt. Mrs Kelley & Ruth went to meet Thorne's folks & Mary E. and Lonnie. Mary and girls come home with Mrs Kelley.

8/17/33 Pleasant. I went to hear the gospel singers, then looked through some of my beauru drawers. made a slip out of an old dress in p.m. Clara Walts here in p.m. Clara B. and I took a walk in evening. then to church for ice cream.

8/18/33 Pleasant, went to hear gospel singers. done little mending. and little odd jobs. our same bunch went on picnic in evening. Mrs Doty's oldest grand daughter went with us. we had a good time, and plenty to eat.

8/19/33 Cloudy and cool. rained a little, I went to hear the gospel singers. helped with work when come back. done little sewing in p.m. Lulu dident come until after supper.

8/20/33 Pleasant, warmed up again. went to S.S. and church. Dr Plantz preached a good sermon. we ate dinner with Mrs Kelley. we come home rested and wrote some. ate lunch with Mary, visited a while, I went up to Cady's few minutes.

8/21/33 Pleasant. some windy. we washed with Mrs Berry. I pieced some in p.m. started to piece on Nette's Star. went to Mrs Reeves after supper to help string beans.

8/22/33 Some cloudy and cool. went over to the church to help peel potatoes, went to hear band in afternoon. come home about six, went back again in little while, come home at ten thirty. Nette helped at the church.

8/23/33 Pleasant. dident do much in a.m. sewed some on Nette's star quilt in p.m. we went to the church in evening., to pot luck supper. last quarterly meeting. rained hard while we were at church. come home in the rain.

8/24/33 Pleasant, not much to do in a.m. went to Mrs Dominy's in p.m. to a comittee meeting. we had picnic supper for Mary here at our place. for her birthday. Mrs Kelley and girls Mary and girls. then we rode with Mrs Kelley over to the lake. I weighed 160 lbs.

8/25/33 Pleasant, dident do much in a.m. sewed some on Nette's star quilt. in p.m. our S.S. class had little party at the parsonage for Mrs William's, we had a nice time. I was alone in evening. Nette went to see Mrs Mullen.

8/26/33 Cloudy and gentle rain all day. I went to hear the gospel singers. then help with Sat. work. sewed on star. was home in p.m. and evening.

8/27/33 Sunday. Cloudy most of day. went to S.S. and church. Nette and I ate dinner with Mrs Kelley in p.m. went with Thorne and Mary over to Ziglers, they got lot of garden stuff. Thorne's folks started home ten to five.

8/28/33 Cloudy and rainy all day. we washed but dident hang out any clothes. put Ruby's flower garden quilt in the frames in p.m. quilted a little. Nette took a walk I stayed at home.in evening.

8/29/33 Still some cloudy. went to hear the gospel singers. then hung the clothes out. quilted some in a.m. and p.m. Mrs Doty come to quilt in afternoon. rained last night Mrs Doty, Clara and I took a walk after supper. went up to Mrs Swaney's

8/30/33 Cloudy most of the day. went to hear the gospel singers. Mrs Doty went with me. we ironed, we quilted in a.m. and p.m. both. Clara, Cady and Mrs Allen were here in evening.

8/31/33 Pleasant, went to hear the gospel singers, then come back and quilted. Mrs Doty come in a.m. she quilted, both a.m. and p.m. she went home right after supper. Clara and I went to band concert a while. I see Mr Price, Henretta and Jeannett Price. I stayed all night with Mrs Giles. Will and Irma both away.

9/1/33 nice day. Mrs Doty and I were invited to Mrs Dominy's for dinner. in p.m. most of our S.S. class come in to surprise Mrs Doty, but dident surprise her. we had nice time. Flora Turner and Mrs Price come to see us in a.m. real warm

9/2/33 Pleasant, stayed with Mrs Giles last night, helped with a.m. work. then quilted. Mrs Doty come about ten she quilted some in a.m. and p.m. we had a big rain between six and seven o clock.

9/3/33 Pleasant. went to S.S. and church. after dinner rested, then wrote to Mrs Roberts. went to church in evening. Clara come over and went with us.

9/4/33 Pleasant, we washed with Mrs Berry. we brought the quilt out. quilted some in a.m. and p.m. Mrs Doty come before dinner, and left before supper. I went over to Mrs Dominy's little while after supper. Clara and I took a walk.

9/5/33 Pleasant. we ironed, then I went to town on little business. come home quilted some before dinner. Mrs Doty come and quilted some in a.m. I went to see Lucy in p.m. quilted after I come back. Clara come over after supper, we took a walk. went down to Mrs Reeves and Mrs Doty.

9/6/33 Pleasant, quilted some in a.m. went to Mrs Gerald in p.m. to our S.S. class meeting, had nice time. quilted some when got home. Clara come over after supper. we took a walk. called on Mrs Morton and Mrs Gaines. warm in p.m.

9/7/33 Pleasant, but little windy and dusty. Mrs Doty come to quilt. I quilted in a.m. and some in p.m. Ona come over. drove over alone. got here about one thirty, started home four forty five. I went to church in evening, my S.S. class had an ice cream social. was awful tired when got home. Nette made me a cake. she went to social

9/8/33 warm, some windy and dusty. we quilted a while, then went over to Will Giles, to attend Irma's baby's funeral. we finished the quilt at fifteen to two. we wrote to Mira, rested some. Lulu was here few minutes. Clara come over in evening. we took little walk.

9/9/33 warm. I went to hear gospel singers then helped clean up the house. done little sewing. pieced some on Nette's star. Audry

Gaunt ten years old today.

9/10/33 Pleasant, went to S.S. and church. rested, read and wrote some after dinner. Clara come over and went to church with us in evening.

9/11/33 Some cloudy. Nette washed on west porch. we were all through early. I sewed some on Nette's Lone Star quilt in p.m. we had a big rain in afternoon. rained most of p.m. then some during the night.

9/12/33 Cloudy and cool. rained early this a.m. we heard it had rained 3.35 of an inch. we ironed, and made sandwich spread. I started to bind Ruby's quilt. Clara here few minutes in evening.

9/13/33 Pleasant, went to hear the gospel singers, then come home and finished binding Ruby's quilt. went up to Mrs Swaney's few minutes to see her and Mrs Doty. in p.m. fixed collar on Nette dress. several were in, this p.m. Clara here in even-

9/14/33 Cloudy and cool. helped with the work. Lena Smith come to see us in a.m. was here for dinner, then I went with her up to see Cady about middle of p.m. we took ride with Mrs Kelley and girls after super. went over to see the lake.

9/15/33 Pleasant, this a.m. about two thirty Mira, Jesse, John and Doris got here in thier auto. all tired out. they left home about eight o'clock thurs a.m. we visited a while, then got settled for little sleep. dident do much but visit, eat and wash dishes.

9/16/33 Pleasant but warm. just done what we had to, visited, was late with dinner, Thorne, Mary and girls got here about three o'clock. we visited back and forth the rest of the day and evening. we all went to the show. Mira and I went together. Nette, Jesse Mrs Kelley and Mc. John & Mary, the Kelley girls, Doris and Mary's girls.

9/17/33 Sunday. Pleasant. I went to S.S. and church. Nette, Jesse, Mary and John went to church. we had picnic dinner at Ruby's 27 in all. Mrs Kelley and three girls, Thorne Mary and two girls, Lon, Ruby, Patrice her boy friend, Patty, Elaine's baby, Mrs Nickols, Mrs Hayden and Irvin, Mira Jesse, John and Doris, Mr Henderson, Nette and I. had fine time and good eats.

9/18/33 Pleasant, Nette washed some with Mrs Koskie we dident do much else. visit eat and wash dishes. Thorne and family started home last night, little after seven. we had picnic lunch on Mrs Kelley's porch. four of Mira's, Mrs Kelley and girls, Nette and I. we had ice cream. had nice visit.

9/19/33 Pleasant, we looked over things found some things for Mira to take home. gave her some dishes, I went over to Mrs Dominy's few minutes. Eva ate dinner with us Saturday. Lulu was in Sat. p.m. and Mon a.m. Mira and I went down on street to see and hear the band. some of the folks went up to high school, and to the temple.

9/20/33 Wednesday. Pleasant in a.m. but windy and dusty in afternoon. we got up at five o'clock. got breakfast for the folks, they got started for home at seven o'clock. was a long, lonesome day. we dident do very much. straightened around and put back things. Nette went to Mrs C. Brown's in evening pot luck supper. I went to Mrs Dominy's. she went with me to see Lucy.

9/21/33 Pleasant in a.m. but some windy in afternoon again. I went to hear gospel singers. Nette made fried cakes. I went to see Patrice. Nette called in a.m. and p.m. then we went to see Mrs Reeves and Orpha in evening. I started to make slip out of my old black silk dress skirt. Mrs Swaney was here.

9/22/33 Pleasant, Nette went and got a per-

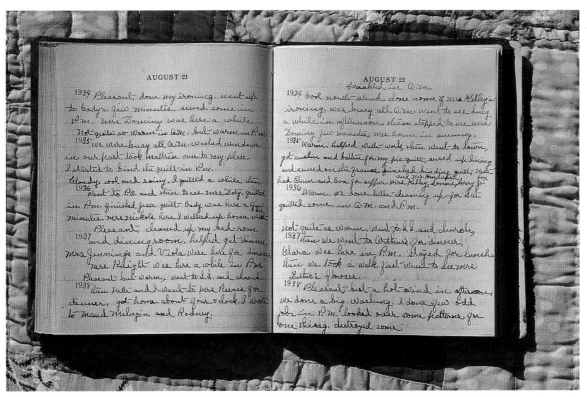

manent. I done little washing. Nette went calling in p.m. I pieced some. went to see Mrs Franklin. Mrs Hayden and Nette made ice cream we went over to Mrs Kelley's to eat it. Mrs Hayden, Irvin, Mrs Kelley, Mary E. Ruth, Nette and I. cream was fine
9/23/33 Pleasant, we done up our work. Nette made apple pie. we were busy all a.m. Eva and Lulu here in p.m. Nette went to see Mrs Elmer Mullen in evening. Clara come to see me. we took little walk.
9/24/33 Sunday. Pleasant. went to S.S. and church. Nette and I went with Mrs Kelley and her girls and three other girls out in country to eat our dinner. had nice time and good dinner, fried chicken and roasting ears, besides other good things. got back at five o'clock. we went to church in evening.
9/25/33 Pleasant, got up little early. Mrs Kelley took Nette to McCook in a.m. left here about eleven. was a long day to me. for all was busy. Clara was over while in evening. I sewed some on Nette's Star quilt little cool
9/26/33 Partly cloudy all day, and quite cool. I went to see about a hat, went to see Lucy. stopped at Mrs Dominy's a minute. sewed on my black slip. went over to stay with the Kelley girls a while in evening. Clara come a while.
9/27/33 Pleasant. wrote to John, then done little cleaning, and straighten up. finished my black slip. went up to Mrs Swaney's while in p.m. pieced on star quilt. was home in evening. wrote to Nette
9/28/33 Fine a.m. I went over to hear gospel singers. then Mrs Dominy come home with me to cut out some pieces. after she left, I went and mailed a letter to Nette, then to court house to see about my taxes. was home all p.m. sewed on star quilt.
9/29/33 Warm. done up work. then helped Mrs Berry fix some string beans. went over to Mrs Giles few minutes. went to Ray Bennett funeral in p.m. sewed on star quilt when got home. Ruby was over, went for little ride with Mrs Kelley after supper. then Clara come, we took a walk.

9/30/33 Cold north wind, dident do much work, but was busy all a.m. shelled some butter beans, that took quite a while. got few carrots for dinner. finished Nette's Lone Star about two o'clock, after that pieced few of my yellow and white nine patches. Lulu and Eva here in p.m. Clara come over, we walked down to Mrs Doty's a few minutes.
10/1/33 Sunday. Pleasant. done up work. then went to S.S. no preaching. Mrs Doty come home with me for dinner, we rested a while then went up to Mrs Swaney's stayed for supper, then we three went to the Nazarene church. was late when got home
10/2/33 Cool. I washed with Mrs Berry. Lulu and Frank were in a few minutes. Mrs Doty come and helped me put in Mrs Paulson quilt. then we quilted some before and after supper. Mrs Doty went home about eight o'clock.
10/3/33 Cloudy, cool and rainy in p.m. wasent bad in a.m. just little cloudy. I quilted a while then went to see Mrs Plantz, then Dr Dowler. come home got dinner, Mrs Doty come in a.m. we dident get very much quilted in p.m. was so dark.
10/4/33 Pleasant. done up the work then quilted some in a.m. Mrs Doty come in morning. we went to our S.S. class meeting in p.m. at Mrs Dominy's had nice time. a good number out. 14
10/5/33 a wonderful day. made pie to take to the pot luck dinner at Mrs Brown's the Aid met there. we quilted on Aid quilt. had election of officers. Mrs Frye president, Mrs Plantz first vice Pres Clara Bump second vice Pres, Mrs Elmer Mullen Sec and Treasurer.
10/6/33 Pleasant but little cool. I ironed in a.m. Mrs Doty come in a.m. went home about eight thirty. we quilted pretty steady in p.m. we both quilted some in a.m. Clara come over in evening, we walked home with Mrs Doty.
10/7/33 Pleasant, but cool north wind. cleaned up house some. done few odd things. quilted some in a.m. then till four in p.m. Lulu and Eva were here few minutes,

Clara come over in evening we took little walk. I done some trading. they had the water shut off working on one of the mains.
10/8/33 Pleasant but quite cool. warmed up some in p.m. I went to S.S. and church, went home with Mrs Doty for dinner. come home about three, rested a while then wrote to Nette. went to church in evening.
10/9/33 Cool in a.m. but fine in afternoon. I dident do much in a.m. but little work, then quilted some. Mrs Doty come in a.m. we quilted in p.m. I went piece with Mrs Doty after supper. when she went home.
10/10/33 A peach of a day. Fine a.m. done up part of my work, then went to hear the gospel singers. Mrs Doty was here when I got back. I quilted in a.m. until time to get dinner, then after I rested went down to Mrs Preders to see about a hat. then from there went up to Clara Walts. she sent for me. said she was sick. I come home about five. went over to Mrs Kelley's while in evening, to stay with girls
10/11/33 Some cloudy, cool wind. done up work, went over to Ruby's few minutes, then to Mrs Haydens to get some Jennica seeds. quilted in a.m. and p.m. Mrs Doty went home about seven thirty.
10/12/33 Pleasant. done part of my work. then went to hear the gospel singers. washed out a few pieces when come home. then quilted some in a.m. and p.m. then went with Mrs Dominy to see Mrs Reeves. then from there I stopped to see Lucy. when got home Mrs Doty was here quilting. we quilted some after supper, then I went a piece with her.
10/13/33 Pleasant, I done up work. Mrs Doty come about eight. we quilted in a.m. and p.m. Mrs Doty went home about four o'clock. Mrs Swaney, Mrs Doty and I went to the Seth Parker programme.
10/14/33 Pleasant, I done up part of my a.m. work then went to town. went to see Mr Birrer, paid him some on my lumber bill. Mrs Doty come little after eight. I took Nette letter to P.O. went to George McDougal's

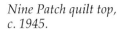
Nine Patch quilt top, c. 1945.

funeral in p.m. Clara was over in evening went down town with her.

10/15/33 Pleasant in a.m. but got windy in p.m. disagreeable. Mrs Doty come in p.m. we went to band concert. I went to S.S. had no church Dr Plantz was sick. Mrs Doty and I went to the Nazarene church. I come home after dinner rested a while then wrote some. about four o'clock Mrs Doty come and we went to band concert.

10/16/33 Pleasant, quilted some in a.m. and p.m. Mrs Doty come in morning. I washed with Mrs Berry. Lulu and Eva here few minutes. Ruby in a while.

10/17/33 Partly cloudy, little cooler. Mrs Doty come in a.m. we both quilted in a.m. and p.m. then while after supper. finished the quilt and took it out of the frames about seven thirty. I went over to Mrs Dominy's few minutes in a.m.

10/18/33 Cool, windy and dusty. I done odd jobs. sewed some in p.m. pieced on little nine patch. stayed with Ruth and Lonnie while Mary Elizabeth went to practice. I made fried cakes in a.m.

10/19/33 Cool, ironed, Mrs Dominy come over to tell that Mrs Doty's brother in law had passed away. we had little party for Mrs Gerald and Mrs Swaney, for thier birthday's at Mrs Dominy's, had nice time. Mrs Doty come by to go up to Mrs Swaney's. I went with her

10/20/33 Windy and cool I cleaned the bedroom and washed bath-room window on in side, also the west window. got Mira's letter ready and took to P.O. Mrs Doty was in few minutes. I went to see Lucy, then stopped at Mrs Dominy's a few minutes. Clara was over in evening we took a walk.

10/21/33 Cool all day. I cleaned up the room some, then went to town on few errands. went over to Mrs Dominy's about eleven to hear a programme. Eva and Lulu were in p.m. Mrs Paulson come and got her quilt. she seemed well pleased. Clara come over in evening. we went to town, done little trading, then walked up to Mrs Swaney, and stopped at Cady's

10/22/33 Still cool, went to S.S. and church.

come home got dinner, then rested a while, wrote some. looked through some of my Christmas cards. Mrs Swaney was in a while. Clara come in evening, we took a walk. went to see Mrs Reeves and Orpha.

10/23/33 Cool, done up work, went over to Ruby's a while, brought her quilt over. Mrs Doty come up in p.m. we put quilt in the frames. Ruby was over in p.m. and evening. we quilted some after got it in the frames. Mrs Doty went home about nine o'clock. Mr Berry had an operation at hospital

10/24/33 Cool all day. I washed with Mrs Berry. got through little after ten. I quilted some, then got dinner. Mrs Doty come little after eight, we quilted in p.m. and after supper. getting along fine.

10/25/33 Cold in a.m. warmed up in p.m. done up work. quilted some, then went to Mrs Doty's. we had a pot luck dinner with her. Mrs Reeves, Orpha, Mrs Swaney Clara and I. we had a nice time and good dinner. come home about four. Mrs Doty come. we quilted a while after supper. she went home about eight. I went a piece with her.

10/26/33 Pleasant, not so cold. done up work then quilted some. Mrs Doty come about eight. we went to Ladies Aid in p.m. at Mrs Plantz. fifteen there. Mrs Doty and I quilted some after supper.

10/27/33 Pleasant. done up work. quilted some. Mrs Dominy over a few minutes. went over to the church in p.m. to help with Halloween supper. Mrs Doty helped

10/28/33 Cool in a.m. but warmed up nice by noon. Mrs Doty come in a.m. to quilt. I quilted some in a.m. and p.m. started to make some mince meat for Ruby. in evening went down to the grade school, to

thier carnival.

10/29/33 Pleasant. quite warm in p.m. I went to S.S. and church in a.m. to Maggie Palmer's funeral in p.m. and back to church in evening. went over to see Mrs Kelley's folks from Beaver City, just before they started home. went to church in even

10/30/33 Pleasant. a peach of a day. real warm in the sun. I washed with Mrs Berry. dident have much, but she had a big one. Mrs Doty come this a.m. to quilt. Lulu come about ten she quilted, then Eva come. I got dinner, Frank come about the time I had dinner started, they all ate dinner with us. Frank

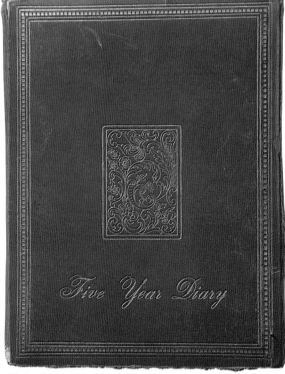

Ida's diary, 1934-1938.

was in looking for some one to husk corn. they started home about four o'clock.

10/31/33 Pleasant, warm like summer. went to hear the gospel singers. then quilted a while got dinner, then quilted again and some after supper. Mrs Doty come in a.m. was here until about eight in evening. moon light and nice.

11/1/33 warm and nice in early a.m. then the wind raised and was cold and disagreeable rest of the day. Mrs Doty come in a.m. we quilted some in a.m. a little after dinner, then went to Mrs Crist's to S.S. class meeting., had nice time, Mrs Doty went home about eight I went a piece with her, then went to Mrs Dominy's a few minutes.

11/2/33 Cooler. Mrs Doty come in a.m. we both quilted. we finished the quilt at about eleven o'clock. I got dinner then we went to see Mrs Reeves. invited her and Orpha to take dinner with us. we then went to the store done little trading. I come home, got busy and cleaned up the house. was real tired when got through.

11/3/33 Pleasant but cool. was busy all a.m. getting my part of the dinner Mrs Doty made pie and cooked sweet potatoes at her place. we had a real nice time. Mrs Charlie Harper called in p.m. had good visit with her.

11/4/33 Cloudy, rained first then turned to snow, quite cold. I dident have much to do. took Ruby's quilt over to her. went to the P.O. then got dinner, then done my little ironing. rested a few minutes, then washed my dishes. went to the P.O. again. then went over to Mrs Dominy's a while.

11/5/33 Sunday. Quite cold. went to S.S. and church. rested a while after dinner, then wrote to Oledine. went for little ride with Mrs Kelley and girls. Clara come by in evening, and we went to church. visited with Mrs Berry while after come home.

11/6/33 Pleasant, not as cold. washed with Mrs Berry. Hung some of the clothes out. mended some in p.m. Mrs Doty here a while.

11/7/33 Pleasant, done up work then went to town different errands. got coal in p.m. took my piecing and went over to Lucy's a while, stopped at Mrs Dominy's few minutes on way home.

11/8/33 Pleasant, after got my work done up went to town again in a.m. cut out pajamas for Nette in p.m.

11/9/33 Snowed a little in a.m. was cloudy a while, then cleared off and was a peach of a day. made fried cakes in a.m. then got ready and went to the all day Aid meeting at Mrs Frye's pot luck dinner, had nice time good dinner, and quilted quite a lot. Clara over after supper, we took a walk went up to Mrs Swaney's.

11/10/33 Fine. done up part of my work, then went over to hear the gospel singers, then helped Mrs Dominy make little krout. went to see Lucy few minutes. come home done my little ironing, then got dinner. Mrs Preder was over a little while. then Ruby come over. we watched the band practice in front of our house. I cleaned up the little room some.

11/11/33 Armistice Day. Fine. sure glad a nice day. done up work then went to hear the bands. stopped at Mrs Allens. visited with Letha a while. was over at court house yard until nearly two o'clock. had a visit with Mr Noble. had some of the barbecue beef. every thing went off fine. Clara and I walked around town in evening. Thorne, Mary and girls come about noon.

11/12/33 Windy, and blustry. acted like storm. went to S.S. and church. ate dinner at Mrs Kelley's eleven of us. Mrs K. and girls Thorne and family, Mr Henderson, Mr McIntosh and myself. Clara come by and we went to church.

11/13/33 Pleasant, done up work. then done few odd jobs. in p.m. went over to Mrs Dominy's a while, worked on white and yellow nine patch. was home in evening.

11/14/33 A fine day. done up work. washed out a few things. was busy all a.m. worked on nine patch in p.m. Trese Snyder Kincade brought a quilt to be quilted. got package and paper ready to send Nette was home in evening.

11/15/33 Pleasant but cool all day. we washed, I only had a few pieces. helped Mrs Berry some. went to Mrs Reeves in p.m. to a birthday party for Mrs Dominy and Mrs Littell. had a nice time.

11/16/33 Cool, some windy and dusty. done up work. then went to the church at nine o'clock to help with Lion's dinner, got home at two thirty. got along fine. rested a while, then worked on yellow and white nine patch.

11/17/33 Pleasant, done up work then went to town on several errand. it was a little cool in forenoon. went to see Mullen to give her money for Nette's Star dues. finished up Mira letter in p.m. and took to P.O. worked on nine patch. Ruby over little while in evening.

11/18/33 Pleasant. cleaned up the house some then went over to Lucy's few minutes. got dinner, rested a little, then worked on nine patch. Lulu and Eva were here in p.m. Frank put up the storm door.

11/19/33 Sunday Pleasant. went to S.S. and church. come home got dinner, then rested a while. wrote to Mrs Roberts. was alone all p.m. went to church in evening. Mary Gerald brought me home

11/20/33 Fine. done up work. washed out a few pieces. went over to Ruby's a while. sewed some on nine patch in p.m. finished joining it, went over to Mrs Kelley's few minutes after supper.

11/21/33 Mira's birthday. Pleasant in a.m. but clouded up and looked real stormy in afternoon. went to hear the gospel singers. then to P.O. to mail Nette a letter. cleaned part of the kitchen cabinet. cut out some pieces for my pie quilt. went up to Cady's a while in p.m. at home in evening.

11/22/33 Pleasant in a.m. but little windy in afternoon. done up work, then went over to Ruby's little while. worked on pie quilt. in p.m. went over to Mrs Giles a while Clara and Ruby in evening.

11/23/33 Some windy in a.m. quite bad a while in afternoon. I done up work then went to town on a errand. went up to Mrs Swaney's, and stopped at Ruby's on way home. went to Aid in p.m. at Mrs Frye's. wind and dust terrible while there.

11/24/33 Pleasant, little cool in a.m. I cleaned out little dust. went over to see Ella and her father. he is quite poorly. worked on pie qilt in p.m. took Mira's letter to P.O. Mrs Dominy was in few minutes in p.m. I was alone in evening.

11/25/33 Cooler. little windy in a.m. then got worse for a while. I finished cleaning up the house, just as the wind & dust was bad again. I worked on pie quilt. went after a few eats, just before dark. Clara and Mrs Swaney here in even a while. Mrs Doty here in forenoon.

11/26/33 Cool, but pleasant. went to S.S. and church. brought Mrs Doty home with me for dinner. I rested a while after she left. then wrote some went to church in evening.

11/27/33 Pleasant. done up my work, then washed with Mrs Berry. Mrs Doty come about eleven. she was here for dinner. after she left I went to see Lucy. when come home washed dinner dishes. went to see Mrs Doty while in evening. Clara come later to come home with me.

11/28/33 Cool but pleasant. about nine o'clock I went to register, then went to court house to work on relief for women. Mrs Doty come home with me for dinner. Mrs Swaney and I got off little before six.

11/29/33 Pleasant, but little cool. got up early done up my work, then went to the court house about eight, worked until twelve, went back at one worked until five. done little trading come home. Ruby was over few minutes. Clara was here. I went with her to P.O.

11/30/33 Thanksgiving Pleasant but little cool all day. went to the union services at Christian church at seven thirty. Dr Plantz preached was alone for dinner. Ruby sent me over nice dinner. was alone until about four thirty when Clara come over, we took little walk. I cooked part of my chicken, Clara stayed ate lunch with me. she went home little after eight.

12/1/33 Cloudy, raining and quite cool when got up this a.m. rained quite a lot during the day. done up work then went to court house, worked until noon. Mrs Doty and Mrs Swaney come over with me to eat dinner, they brought some eats with them. we worked only two hours this p.m.

12/2/33 Cloudy and dark. done up my little work. made a mince pie. after dinner went to county house to get my check. then went to farmers bank and got it cashed. $8.80 then went to Mrs Frye's and helped finish the Aid quilt. brought it home with me Clara going to bind it. Clara come in even we took little walk. went to see Mrs Doty.

12/3/33 A regular spring morning. nice all day, not very cold. went to S.S. and church. had communion. after dinner, I rested a while. wrote some to Nette. went to church in evening. Clara and I walked home together.

12/4/33 Pleasant, done up my work, then went to court house to work. Mrs Doty, Mrs Swaney and I hurried over home, ate our dinner, went back to work at One o'clock. quit at five. I went with Mrs Doty to look for a dress. I got one at Millers, Ruby over while in evening.

12/5/33 Pleasant, done up work, was little late getting up this p.m. went over to the court house to work. we hurried over home to get our dinner, and hurried back. quit at five. I went to see Dr Parker, to have my glasses adjusted.

12/6/33 Pleasant, done up work, then went to court house to work, hurried home at noon for lunch. Mrs Swaney and Mrs Doty come with me. we worked again in p.m. went for mail, then after crackers and bread, then hurried home. Ruby was over while in evening.

12/7/33 Pleasant. worked four hours at court house in a.m. and two in afternoon. Mrs Swaney, Mrs Doty and I then got ready and went over to Lucy's, to the class party and birthday party combined. four birthdays. Mrs Dempster Scott, Mrs Plantz, Cady Briney and Lucy Wallace. had a nice time. I went to town, when left there to pay some bills.

12/8/33 Pleasant, done part of my Saturday's cleaning. went over to Ruby's a few minutes. fixed front of dress got at Millers. Mrs Gaines was in few minutes in p.m. Clara over in evening. I went with her down to Paul Brown's

12/9/33 Pleasant. done up work then went and got my check, then went to bank, got it cashed, then went and paid my coal bill, come home done little more cleaning. Lulu, Frank and Eva were here for dinner. I made fried cakes right after got dinner dishes washed. mended a dress for Mrs Kelley, done little other sewing. Clara over in evening. we went to town.

12/10/33 Pleasant in a.m. sometime in afternoon turned quite cold. I went to S.S. & church. went home with Mrs Doty for dinner. come home about two thirty. wrote to Nette, Clara over little while. I went to church in evening.

12/11/33 Still cold. Mrs Berry and I washed. she had a big one. the clothes froze. Clara come over tied up box with Nette's spread in to send to Cora. she over in p.m. went with me to P.O. Mrs Doty here few minutes in a.m.

12/12/33 Cold. done my ironing in a.m. then mended some in p.m. went over to Mrs Dominy's little while. wrote some to Nette after supper. Clara come over a while. she went out to her brothers with her nephew.

12/13/33 Pleasant, not as cold. I done up my work. went over to Ruby's a few minutes, then to town. done little more mending. then went over to Lucy's a while. little cooler this evening again.

12/14/33 Pleasant this a.m. then toward evening the wind and dirt come up, and rained some. I done up work, went over to Ruby's few minutes, dident do any extra work. went over to Mrs Kelley's in p.m. to stay with Ruth, she has been sick, but better Mrs Dominy come to see me.

12/15/33 Pleasant, done up work, went to P.O. got ready and went out to Anna Reeves the Aid had a pot luck dinner, about twenty four there. had a nice time and lots of good things to eat. I rode out with Mrs John Roberts.

12/16/33 Pleasant but cool. done up work then went to town on few errands. stopped to see Lucy, and Mrs Dominy. done little mending in p.m. and worked some on my pie quilt. Clara come over in evening. we went to town, done some window shopping.

12/17/33 Sunday. Pleasant but quite cold. I went to S.S. and church. come home got dinner, rested a while then wrote some. went over to Mrs Kelley's about six, we had a neighborhood picnic for Mr Haydens folks. I come home about eight thirty. Clara stopped on her way home from church.

12/18/33 Pleasant, little cool in a.m. warmer in p.m. and evening. I went to the court house to work again. went to P.O. when quit work. Clara walked home with me.

12/19/33 Another fine day. done up work, then went to court house to work. hurried home ate my dinner and went back again. got home little after five. wrote letters and Christmas cards after supper.

12/20/33 Pleasant. done up work then went to the court house to work. at ten o'clock seven of us were called to go fill sack, down at Byrle Tillett's office. we got back to court house about three. worked till five. was real tired when got home. I ate dinner with Mrs Doty.

12/21/33 Pleasant, went to court house at eight again to work. I took some letters to P.O. we got out at three o'clock. I done little shopping. then went down to Mrs Dominy's little while. just real tired when got home. Mrs Doty ate dinner with me. Toots and boys come in here to eat lunch.

12/22/33 Like spring. made fruit cake, cleaned up the house some. got some mail ready and took to P.O. sent John some of my cake. Clara come over in evening. we took a walk, went down to Mrs Reeves a little while.

12/23/33 Another spring day. went over to hear the gospel singer. then come home finished up my work. went over to Ruby's few minutes. got dinner over, rested some, then went to P.O. Clara was over in evening, we went to town.

12/24/33 Pleasant but real cold. I went to S.S. and church. after dinner rested a while. Edith Walts Smith asked me to go with her out to see Eva. we got back in time to go to the Christmas pageant. it was good. one of the best I have ever seen.

12/25/33 Cold and mostly cloudy. I made a nut bread. cooked squash for dinner. we roasted Mrs Kelley's turkey in the range. The Berry's were away for dinner. I ate dinner over to Mrs Kelley's. Thorne's folks and Bill's were there, had a nice time, and good dinner. was there for lunch.

12/26/33 Cloudy and real cold. hurried around after got my breakfast. went to the court house to work. ate lunch over at Mrs Kelley's. Thorne took me back to work. sure felt lomesome & homesick when come home that evening.

12/27/33 Some warmer. little cloudy. was little late getting up. had to hurry, went to court house to work. work 4 hours in a.m. and p.m. Clara over little while in evening.

12/28/33 Pleasant, not as cold. went to work at eight o'clock. come home ate dinner, then hurried back again. after we got through work, I went to see Dr Dowler, then went to Cashman's drug store for a calander. then stopped at the store for few things.

12/29/33 Cloudy, stormy looking in a.m. sun come out about eleven o'clock. I hurried around, done up my work. then went to court house. hurried home for dinner and back again. we got through at three o'clock, Mrs Doty and I went and paid our coal bill. after supper, went by after Clara, we went to Mrs Reeves a while.

12/30/33 Cool in a.m. but pleasant. warmed up later. I cleaned up my rooms some went over to Ruby's few minutes in a.m. made nut bread. Ada Gaunt was here in p.m. Lulu and Cady were in few minutes. Clara come over in even-we went to town.

12/31/33 Pleasant, fine for this time of the year. went to S.S. and church. brought Clara home with me for dinner. we went to Mrs Mary Mason's funeral in p.m. at Christian church, Dr Plantz preached. we went over to Mrs Dominy's little while, then Mrs Doty, Clara and I went to see Mrs Short. then Clara come home with me we had lunch, then went to church. I feel little tired.

January 1, 1934 Pleasant but quite cool. done up my work. went over to Ruby's a few minutes, I done little mending, ironed out few pieces. Eva [Lambach] passed away this a.m.

1/2/34 Cloudy, cold and stormy looking all day. worked at court house in a.m. and p.m. dident do very much after come home. Mrs Berry was in little while.

1/3/34 Cloudy and still stormy looking. done up my work. went to court house in a.m. & p.m. several were in after I come home I was little tired. Wrote some to Nette and Mira.

1/4/34 Still cloudy and stormy looking, did rain a little in forenoon. I worked at court house in a.m. went out to Lulu's with Dr Plantz right after dinner. then come back in to Eva's funeral.

1/5/34 Pleasant, cleared off, was nice in p.m. I worked four hours in a.m. and 2 in p.m. went out home with Lulu and Ida little late in p.m. went with them over to Webb's for supper.

1/6/34 Cloudy and frosty in a.m. started to snow about middle of forenoon. Jim and Inez [Walters] finished their packing and started over to his folks then we hurried and got lunch then come right to town.

1/7/34 Cold north west wind. went to S.S. and church. after dinner rested a while, then started a letter to Irma and Rodney. Clara [Bump] come over, we went to see Mrs Reeves, I went to church in even.

1/8/34 Pleasant but cool. went to work at court house in a.m. hurried home got lunch then went back to work again. feel real tired.

1/9/34 Some cloudy, but not as cold. worked at court house this a.m. and p.m. we sewed on pants cloth to make comfortor tops. have enough for three nearly made.

1/10/34 Pleasant. went to court house to work. worked four hours in a.m. & p.m. was quite tired when got ready to sit down after supper.

1/11/34 Some cloudy. worked at court house in forenoon and afternoon both. not very cold. Clara over a while in evening. Clara was over last night, instead of tonight.

1/12/34 A bad blustry day. wind & dirt from the north I went and paid Nette's taxes and some of mine, mailed Mira a letter. then went to see Lucy little while. Cady was here in p.m.

1/13/34 Pleasant. I was busy all a.m. cleaning up my rooms. went over to Ruby's after dinner to hang up some clothes for her. mailed letter to Nette. Lulu was here. Clara here in evening. I was real tired

1/14/34 A spring day. went to S.S. and church. Clara come home with me for dinner. about two thirty we went up to Mrs Swaneys. then from there we took a walk. Clara ate lunch with me, then we went to church

1/15/34 Real cloudy in a.m. started to snow after dinner. worked at court house in a.m. and p.m. ground was white with snow when come home, but not very cold.

1/16/34 Pleasant. Looked like Christmas morning. Went to court house to work. worked both a.m. and p.m. not very cold.

1/17/34 Pleasant but some cloudy. worked at court house in a.m. and p.m. both. got in fuel when first come home, then went to see Ruby [Nichols] she was some better.

1/18/34 Pleasant, like a spring day. worked four hours this a.m. and two in p.m. come home then went over to Mrs Dominy's little while.

1/19/34 Pleasant. Mr Luther come and fixed the burners to oil stove. I went to see Ruby a few minutes. then to see Mrs Preder. wrote to Mira took to P.O. in p.m. went to 1-2-1 store

1/20/34 Pleasant in a.m. like spring. cleaned up the house some made fried cakes. I cut out a few pieces. Clara was here while in p.m. I went over to see Ruby. went to see Mrs Reeves in even-

1/21/34 Pleasant, went to S.S. and church. come home got dinner rested, then wrote to Hazel [Gaunt] went by to see Mrs Doty on my way to church in even-

1/22/34 Pleasant. worked at court house in a.m. and p.m. we had a pot luck dinner. had nice time and good dinner. Clara over few minutes in evening.

1/23/34 Pleasant. I worked again in a.m. and p.m. We only worked 15 hours yesterday and today. Ruby was over in evening.

and Clara was here few minutes.

1/24/34 Cloudy in a.m. sun shone out a while about noon, then in p.m. it clouded up, and blew real cold. I went over to Ruby's in a.m. Went to aid in p.m. at Mrs Gerald's.

1/25/34 Cool in a.m. warmed up some. I washed had nice surprise in p.m. Myrle [Chambers] come to see me. she went with me to Junior Aid. was lonesome after she left.

1/26/34 Pleasant but cool. I ironed in a.m. went over to Ruby's few minutes. then helped Mrs Berry quilt. Ruby was over in p.m. Clara come, she quilted. I went to see Mrs Doty after supper. Clara came later.

1/27/34 Pleasant, like spring. done up my work, then went to Mrs Reeves for dinner, stayed until about 3 o'clock. went to see Ella Greason. Joe Pinegar real bad. went to see Mrs Franklin few minutes. Lulu was there. Clara and I went to town in evening. My birthday.

1/28/34 Some cloudy. colder in p.m. wind in north east. went to S.S. and church. come home ate dinner alone. wrote to Jesse Gaunt. went to church in evening. Mrs Matheson come to go with me.

1/29/34 Pleasant. worked at court house seven and one half hours. stopped at store on way home.

1/30/34 Cool in a.m. fine in afternoon. worked seven hours again today. went over to Mrs Gaines while in evening. cool but nice and moonlight out.

1/31/34 Pleasant in a.m. but wind raised, and dust blew. I washed a few pieces in with Mrs Berry. went to see Ruby few minutes, then to town Mrs Doty come and helped me put in Mrs Kincaid quilt. Clara was over in p.m.

2/1/34 A spring day Ruby was over. I wrote to Nette, then went to see Mrs Allen about getting dress made. then to P.O. then to Mrs Kelley's office. went with her to dinner, at Air line cafe. Mrs D. and I quilted in p.m.

2/2/34 Ground hog day. An ideal spring day, from start to finish I went over to Ruby's a few minutes. then to town got meat for dinner. Mrs Doty was here for dinner. we quilted some in a.m. and p.m. Clara here in even-

2/3/34 Pleasant in a.m. little windy and dusty middle of day. I cleaned up some then went over to Lucy's few minutes. Mrs Doty here quilting when I got back. we quilted in p.m.

2/4/34 Pleasant but little cooler. I went to S.S. and church. come home got my dinner, rested a while then wrote to John and Cora. went to church in evening. little cooler.

2/5/34 Pleasant, but some cloudy. worked at court house in a.m. and p.m. got letter from Mira and Doris.

2/6/34 A spring day. worked at court house in a.m. and p.m. was quite tired when had supper. Ruby was over a while in evening. I wrote to Thorne and Mary.

2/7/34 Another nice day, was a little cloudy in a.m. Mrs Doty come in a.m. to quilt, I had to go to town. we went to our S.S. class party at Cady's, had some thing special for Mrs Morton's, Clara Bump's and my birthday's. we sure had a nice time, good lunch.

2/8/34 Pleasant. I helped with Lions dinner. then went to parsonage to aid. Mrs Doty come home with me. she only staid few minutes. I was awful tired.

2/9/34 Cloudy and stormy acting all day. colder. Mrs Doty come in a.m. we quilted in p.m. a while she went home about three o'clock. didn't feel good. we went and got our checks.

2/10/34 Cloudy. some snow on the ground when got up, then started to snow about nine, and kept it up most of day. but not very cold. I went to town on few errands in a.m. quilted some in p.m. Ruby over in p.m.

2/11/34 Pleasant but cool. went to S.S. and church. come home, after dinner rested a while then wrote to Carl. went for little ride with Mrs Kelley and girls. went to church in evening.

2/12/34 Pleasant, another spring day. worked at court house in a.m. and p.m. went to see Clara few minutes when first come home. was real tired.

2/13/34 Another spring day. worked at court house again today. real tired when supper was over. Mrs Dominy, Clara, Mrs Doty and I went to the show, Little Women, it was good.

2/14/34 Pleasant. cleaned up the house a little, was busy all a.m. got real tired. Mrs Doty come soon after dinner. we both quilted all p.m. and while after supper. she went home about eight.

2/15/34 Pleasant, but little cool. I washed out a few pieces. Mrs Doty come in a.m. she quilted before and after dinner. I quilted in p.m. till about five or after. went after mail. Mrs Doty went home about 5:30

2/16/34 Pleasant, still felt tired, done little ironing, then quilted some. Mrs Doty come in a.m. we both quilted in p.m. until most five. I got supper. then went home with Mrs D rested, then stopped to see Mrs Reeves and Orpha.

2/17/34 Cloudy and rainy. I was busy most of a.m. didn't feel good laid down after dinner. Nette come in and suprised me. we visited most of p.m. I went to town about four thirty. rained all day. snowed during the night.

2/18/34 Pleasant, but quite cold. went to S.S. and church. Thorne's folks come. Mary and girls went to S.S. Nette and I ate dinner over to Mrs Kelley's with the folks. they started home little after seven. There was eleven of us for dinner.

2/19/34 Still cold. I went to work at court house. We had pot luck dinner. had nice time. was tired when got home. Nette went with Mrs Kelley to C.C. banquet.

2/20/34 Some cloudy but pleasant. work at court house in a.m. and p.m. both. was real tired when got home. Mrs Doty helped me bring the horses and clamps home so could have them to use.

2/21/34 Snowing when got up. and snowed most all day. dident do much, house work in a.m. fixed Mrs Kelley's apron in p.m. marked off some pattern for tea towels. Mrs Dominy over in evening.

2/22/34 Pleasant but little cool. we washed out a few pieces. wrote letter. went over to Mrs Dominy for Aid in p.m. then went to see Mrs Reeves and Orpha in evening.

2/23/34 Pleasant but cool. cleaned up a little, then brought out the quilt. I commenced to quilt about ten o'clock. Mrs Doty come about 12:30 we both quilted in p.m. I walked home with her.

2/24/34 Cloudy, snowed most all day. I helped with a.m. work. then quilted. Lulu [Lambach] was here a while in a.m. she and Inez here in p.m. I mended some. Nette and I were over to Mrs Kelley's a while in evening.

2/25/34 Snowed most all day. real cold. I went to S.S. and church. we ate dinner over at Mrs Kelley's 11 of us. Mrs Cox and four children, Mr Mc and a nephew. Ruby and Lon. had good dinner, and nice time.

2/26/34 Real cold. 8 below. worked at court house, took a lunch with me. warmed up

some toward nite. real tired when got home.

2/27/34 Pleasant, not as cold. worked at court house in forenoon and p.m. took my lunch. Nette washed. she went to Mrs Charlie Brown's in evening, and I went to see Lucy.

2/28/34 Warmer, the snow melted lots today. water run like after a rain. I helped with a.m. work. then quilted. Mrs Doty come in a.m. went home about 3:30 Ruby was over. Toots Henderson was here

3/1/34 Pleasant, snow about all gone. quilted in a.m. and p.m. Mrs Doty come while before noon. Went home about five o'clock. Nette, Mrs. Berry and I went to Junior Aid carnival in even.

3/2/34 Pleasant, like spring. quilted in a.m. and p.m. Clara come over in a.m. and quilted some, Mrs Doty come while we were eating dinner. We finished the quilt little after three. Lulu was here a while in p.m.

3/3/34 Not cold, but strong wind. We cleaned up the house some. Was busy all a.m. Mrs Doty here in p.m. We went after our checks. I sewed some in p.m. Lulu was here.

3/4/34 Pleasant but little windy. Went to S.S. and church. After dinner, rested a while then wrote to Rodney. Went to church in evening.

3/5/34 Cloudy all a.m. snowed a little, then sun shone out in p.m. I went and stayed with Mrs Collier in a.m. and p.m. come home for dinner.

3/6/34 A real spring day, until middle of p.m. wind come up from north was bad a while. I stayed with Mrs Collier again. Come home for dinner. went to see Mrs Reeves & Orpha in even.

3/7/34 Cloudy in a.m. started to snow middle of a.m. kept it up until some time in afternoon. not very cold. Nette worked at the temple. I done few odd jobs. Ruby was over.

3/8/34 Pleasant. not very cold. ironed some, then made holders, and cut out few pieces. Mrs Dominy was here little while in p.m. snow melted fast in p.m.

3/9/34 Cold, I washed out few pieces for us. Nette made fruit cake. I took some meat to Mrs Plantz, fixing new collar on dress Nette gave me. We went up to Cady's while in evening.

3/10/34 Some cloudy. cold wind. ironed, helped clean up the house. finished fixing my dress. Nette and I went to see Mrs Reeves and Orpha while in evening.

3/11/34 Fine. a spring day I went to S.S. and church. after dinner rested a while. Wrote some, Mrs Dominy come over few minutes. Went with her to Mrs Reeves. Nette and I went to church in even.

3/12/34 Pleasant. I went over to Mrs Collier's this a.m. Went to see Mrs Swaney in p.m. done little mending. Was alone in evening.

3/13/34 Windy, little cooler. stayed with Mrs Collier in a.m. and p.m. Clara was over in evening. Nette over to Ruby's.

3/14/34 Cold south wind. Went to town on few errands. Nette went with me to our S.S. class party at Mrs Frye's was her birthday. We had nice time. Went to Lucy's a while in evening.

3/15/34 Pleasant. Nette and I helped with Lions dinner. got home about two thirty. We rested a while, then I started to mend the lining to Nette's summer coat. Mrs Luther and mother were here in evening.

3/16/34 Cloudy and stormy acting, but real warm. I helped some with work. then worked on Nette's coat. I finished it about five o'clock. Nette went to the legion hall in p.m.

3/17/34 Turned cold in the night. Snowed some. quite cold all day. I went and stayed with Mrs Collier in a.m. and p.m. Ruby over in evening.

3/18/34 Cool. Went to S.S. and church. rode home with Mrs Kelley. Nette and I ate dinner with Cady and Jesse Briney. come home about three. Mrs Hayward come to see us. we went to church in even.

3/19/34 A peach of a day. I stayed with Mrs Collier in p.m. went to Mrs Dominy's few minutes in a.m. and over to Ruby's. was over to Mrs Kelley's while in evening. with Ruth and Lonnie.

3/20/34 Another nice day. stayed with Mrs Collier both forenoon and p.m. Nette went to see Mrs Mullen. Clara come over, wanted to know if didnt want to go to see Mrs Reeves & Orpha

3/21/34 Little cool, some cloudy. I stayed with Mrs Collier all day. quite tired.

3/22/34 Put in baby quilt for Elaine. Cool, helped do up the work, then went to Cady's few minutes. stopped at Ruby's in p.m. went to Aid at Mrs Frye's in evening Nette & I went to grade school house to play. Here comes Charlie.

3/23/34 Cloudy and cold. snowed some last night. snowed some during the day. didnt get much done in a.m. went to a tea in p.m. at Mrs Fred Snyder. she and Gladys Beamgard had it for Nette. In evening, Mrs Dominy and I went to see Mrs Reeves.

3/24/34 Cloudy and cold. helped do up the work. brought coal out of cellar. marked and quilted some. Paul was here this p.m. Frank and Lulu, Mrs Doty, Mrs Gaines come in few minutes.

3/25/34 Pleasant but cold. John and Cora come just as we finished breakfast. we visited a while then went for a ride. then took dinner at Air line Cafe then rode again. got back home about three. set them a lunch then they started home at 5:30

3/26/ 34 Some cloudy and still cold. went over to Mrs Dominy's in a.m. went over to the church to help get ready for pot-luck dinner, for darkie singers. went up to high school to hear them sing at eleven o'clock. Nette went to Mrs Dillons in evening.

3/27/34 Cloudy, windy and cool. quilted some on baby quilt, went with Nette over to Mrs Dominy's, Gertie Vincent, and Lucy's in p.m. then we went to Mrs Mullen's in evening. we washed some in a.m.

3/28/34 A peach of a day. We were both busy in a.m. I quilted some. Nette went to town. Mrs Kelley ate dinner with us. Mrs Doty here in p.m. Nette started back to Fairmont this p.m. Mary E. Kelley took her to depot.

3/29/34 A cold bad day. rained some about dark then sleeted and snowed a little. I quilted some went to church in p.m. to practice play. went again in evening. was a bad night.

3/30/34 Cloudy and cold in a.m. but cleared off and warmed up in p.m. I quilted some. went to P.O. then to Mrs Doty's she come up town with me. done little trading. Clara come over in evening. we went to Mrs Reeves.

3/31/34 Some cloudy. little windy and cold. I cleaned up some and quilted in A.M & p.m. went to town in p.m. Mary's folks come about four. they asked me over to eat supper with them. rained some after dark.

4/1/34 An ideal Easter day. 14 there A spring day. went to S.S. and church. ate dinner at Mrs Kelleys, Thorne's folks, Bill's folks, Mr McIntosh and myself were there. Thorne's started home at four. we went to the Easter Contata.

4/2/34 Cloudy, warm, I done few odd jobs, finished the quilt. went over to Mrs Dominy in p.m. a few minutes. went to P.O. Wrote to Nette in evening.

4/3/34 Cloudy and cool all day. went to mail Nette's letter. got piece of meat, went over to Ruby's few minutes, was busy all a.m. went over to Lucy's while in p.m. misted some during the day.

4/4/34 Was raining when I woke up this a.m. all cloudy, done up my work, wrote to John Gaunt. went to P.O. went over to see Mr Pinegar in a.m. went to our class party in p.m. at Mrs Bearley's. had a nice time.

4/5/34 Some cloudy, sprinkled some during the day. was busy all a.m. Mrs Swaney here in p.m. I quilted the pillow top for Burdette. Clara in few minutes in p.m. was alone in evening.

4/6/34 Pleasant, but little cool. I ironed, cleaned bathroom, and made a spice cake. took Mira's letter to P.O. Mrs Doty here in p.m. stayed for supper then I walked home with her. Ruby brought Mrs Missinger over with her. Cady and Mrs Dexter Lilly called.

4/7/34 Fine, cleaned up house some. Ruby was over. done little mending for Mary Elizabeth. Mrs Doty and Mrs Swaney here in p.m. Lulu was here.

4/8/34 Another fine a.m. went to S.S. and church. after dinner rested a while. then wrote some. Mrs Dominy come over to go to band concert. we sit in car with Fessie Hale. went to church in even.

4/9/34 Another nice day. was busy all a.m. Made banana bread for Mrs Berry. went to see Mrs Gaines a while in p.m. Cut some pieces went over to Mrs Dominy's in evening.

4/10/34 A warm pleasant day. done up work. put away some bedding in big box. went over to Ruby's, up to Cady's and Mrs Lillies in a.m. then to see Mother Moore in P.m. Mrs Reeves and Mrs Doty in evening.

4/11/34 Little cool and windy, done up work, then went to town, got material to cover a comfortor for Mr. Smith. put it in the frames after dinner. Lulu come in, she helped me tie it. was a big help. Toots was here.

4/12/34 Pleasant, but cool. I finished comfortor around edge. went to see Mrs Franklin in a.m. went to Mrs Reeves in p.m. they put on or rather had the play again. for a few that couldn't go the night at church. took little ride with Mrs Kelley.

4/13/34 Pleasant. I washed some with Mrs Berry. went over to Mrs Dominy's while in p.m. to see how Clara was. Mrs Doty was here while I was gone. I went down to her place a while in evening.

4/14/34 Cool, windy and dusty. cleaned up the house some. made few fried cakes. Lulu was here, also Mrs Swaney and Doty in p.m. Anna Lillie here a while in evening. I went to the store after supper.

4/15/34 Rained and then snowed in a.m. quite cool. I went to S.S. and church. after dinner rested a while, then wrote to cousin Idie. went to church in evening.

4/16/34 Cool all day. done up work, then went over to Ruby's a while, sewed mended and pieced some. got load or rather part of a load of cobs. Joe Pinegar passed away at 8:40 p.m.

4/17/34 Some cloudy all day. done up work, went over to see Ella. Ruby was here in a.m. I sent letter to Nette. worked on my pie quilt in p.m. took little ride with Mrs Kelley after supper. Clara was here.

4/18/34 Pleasant, I ironed few pieces for Mrs Kelley in a.m. in p.m. went to Joe Pinegar's funeral. they had it at the house.

went to see Mrs Reeves and Orpha few minutes after supper.

4/19/34 Pleasant but little cool. ironed few more pieces for Mrs Kelley. then went over to Ruby's a few minutes. worked on my quilt in p.m. went over to Mrs Dominy's in even.

4/20/34 Pleasant, but little cool. finished Mrs Kelley's ironing, and done what little I had. went up to Cady's and made her a ginger bread. I cut out some pieces in p.m. helped Ruth put out onion sets after supper.

4/21/34 Pleasant, cleaned up the house some. worked some on pie quilt. washed some in p.m. then helped Ruth plant some radishes. Clare here few minutes in p.m. went with me to P.O.

4/22/34 Some cloudy all day. went to S.S. and church ate dinner and supper at Mrs Kelley's went for little ride with Mrs Kelley, went to church in evening. We looked for Thorne's folks, but dident come.

4/23/34 Still cloudy and air full of dust. I wrote to Nette in a.m. went to P.O. in p.m. went to see Mrs Gaines in p.m. and to Mrs Dominy in evening.

4/24/34 Cloudy, little cool. ironed some for Mrs Kelley. Was home in p.m. went to market in a.m. Mrs Swaney here a while in afternoon. I worked on my quilt. Ruby here in evening.

4/25/34 Still cloudy, windy and dusty. ironed some for Mrs Kelley. went over to Ruby's a few minutes. worked on my quilt. went over to Mrs Dominy's in evening.

4/26/34 Still cloudy and cool. I made a banana bread. we had an all day aid meeting at Mrs John Roberts had nice time, good dinner, pot luck. quilted on little star quilt for Newton home.

4/27/34 Pleasant. finished Mrs Kelley's ironing and done mine. went to see Ella a few minutes. washed with Mrs Matheson in p.m. in evening had a clean up time in back yard. with a picnic.

4/48/34 Some cloudy, cleaned up my house some. Mrs Doty here in p.m. done little mending. then worked on quilt. Lulu was here. I went to P.O.

4/29/34 Cloudy and cool in a.m. warm and sunshiny when church was out. Clara come over about seven, we took a walk then went to church.

4/30/34 Real warm, an ideal a.m. I went to see Mrs Allen about my dress in a.m. done my ironing in p.m. Mrs Dominy in a few minutes.

5/1/34 Some cloudy in a.m. got bad in p.m. windy and dusty. air full of dust. I dident do much in a.m. took some flowers over and set them out at Ruby's. worked on my pie quilt in p.m. Burdette's birthday. Ruby over in evening.

5/2/34 Pleasant. went over to Mrs Dominy's few minutes in p.m. then went to P.O. our S.S. class met with Millie Huston in p.m. in honor of Mrs Mather's birthday. had a nice time.

5/3/34 Some cloudy. ironed some in a.m. went to Mrs Colliers funeral in p.m. at the house. was awful tired after supper. Mrs Doty was here in afternoon.

5/4/34 Pleasant. ironed for Mrs Kelley. rained some last night and this a.m. Mrs Lily brought me some asparagus. went over to Mrs Dominy's in evening.

5/5/34 Pleasant. done up some of my work, then went to Daddy Dunn's funeral at ten o'clock. mended and sewed some in p.m. Ada Gaunt was here in p.m. went to town in evening with Mrs Doty.

5/6/34 Very warm went to S.S. and church. ate dinner with Cady and Jesse. we went to high school in p.m. to a musical programme. Cady, Mrs Doty and I went up to Mrs Swaney's after that. Myrle was here in p.m. I dident see her.

5/7/34 Another warm day. Ruby was in, also Cady and Mrs Doty. done little dusting and cleaning around. Helped Ruthie put out some garden in p.m. after she come from school.

5/8/34 Windy, dusty day. I dident feel good in a.m. ate little breakfast then went back to bed. was in bed most of the day. several were in.

5/9/34 Some cloudy, wind in north today. not quite so warm. feeling some better, but in bed most of the day. Mrs Berry, Ruby, Mrs Kelley, Clara, Mrs Dominy and Mrs Walt were in today.

5/10/34 Pleasant, feeling some better. done little work. then pieced some. Clara here twice. Ruby brought me over my dinner. was here while in p.m. had her piecing. The aid met with Mrs Berry.

5/11/34 Some cloudy, windy. done little work in a.m. read, rested and pieced some in p.m. Ruby was in few minutes in a.m. was a long day.

5/12/34 Little windy from the north. cleaned up the house a little. dident feel very good. Ruby was over few minutes. Mrs Doty here in p.m. Lulu done some trading for me. Clara over in evening.

5/13/34 Mother's Day. Cloudy and quite cool. wasent able to go to church. was rather a long day, or a.m. rather. Clara was here in p.m. Mrs Plantz here a while. Frank and Lulu here a while. Clara here in evening. started to rain about dark.

5/14/34 Little cool in a.m. I dident do any extra work. got some mail ready to send P.O. Clara come over and took to office. worked with my pieces in p.m. feeling some better. Mrs Doty here in even.

5/15/34 Pleasant. done my little washing with Mrs Matheson. Mrs Dominy and Mrs Frye here in p.m. Alex called. I helped the Kelley girl after supper Ruby over few minutes.

5/16/34 Warm and windy. feeling some better but dident do much work. Clara Walts was in a few minutes. then Clara Bump come. I was alone all evening. felt worse after supper. so weak.

5/17/34 Pleasant. real warm in p.m. done my ironing. was busy all a.m. Mrs Walker Lily brought me some asparagus. Mrs E. Mullen come to see me. I went to see Mrs Franklin in p.m.

5/18/34 Warm. done part of my cleaning. was busy all a.m. worked on my quilt in p.m. was real tired. Mrs Doty and Clara here in evening. Mrs Berry operated on this a.m.

5/19/34 Real warm. done little more cleaning. was busy all a.m. Nette come home on p.m. train. it was little late. Mrs Kelley took us little ride after supper, around the lake. Nette went to the show.

5/20/34 Another warm day. I went to S.S. but was no church on account of speaking at high school. went over to music shell in p.m. to programme. then up to high school to Baccalaureate sermon. they dedicated the Legion Memorial home.

5/21/34 Windy, dusty day. I washed a few pieces with Mrs Matheson. Nette didn't feel good. had a headache. Mrs Doty here a few minutes. took little ride with Mary Elizabeth.

5/22/34 Pleasant, not so warm. dident do much of any thing in a.m. but the regular work. Clara Walts was in few minutes. I went over to Mrs Dominy's while in p.m. Nette went to hospital to see Mrs Berry.

5/23/34 Pleasant. Helped with work. sewed on my quilt. in evening we went up to the graduating exercises. turned cool while at high school.

5/24/34 Cloudy and cool. rained some. helped with a.m. work then went to the church to Aid, but wasent any. went to Mrs Frye's few minutes, then come by to see Lucy. was home in evening. Clara was over.

5/25/34 Cool. Nette walked up to see Mrs Berry in a.m. in p.m. we went to school meeting. Nette worked at temple

5/26/34 Pleasant. Nette done some odd jobs out side. I cleaned up the house fixed some pie plant and strawberries for sauce. we went up to the cemetery with Frank and Lulu in p.m.

5/27/34 Pleasant. went to S.S. and church. Thorne's folks were here. we had a nice time. Thorne's started home about eight. Elizabeth Ann stayed.

5/28/34 Pleasant, but real warm in p.m. Nette done our little washing with Mrs Matheson. I dident do much in a.m. Nette and I went to see Mrs Rhoda Robinson in p.m. she wasent at home.

5/29/34 Warm. went to cemetery to services for Mr Niel. was home in p.m. worked on quilt. was over to Mrs Kelley's in evening to eat ice cream. Mrs Rhoda Robinson was there.

5/30/34 Warm, some cloudy. went to cemetery 3 times, in a.m. p.m. and evening. Lulu M. folks were here for dinner, also Erma Treadwell and Mrs Kelley, her father, Ruth, Lonnie, and Lucille Carlson had 3 little showers after supper.

5/31/34 Pleasant, and warm. Nette done little washing I dident do much of any thing in a.m. in p.m. went to the church to quilt.

6/1/34 Some cloudy, and windy. Nette ironed. I went to court house on little business in a.m. pieced some in p.m. we went to the lake for picnic. Mrs Kelley's family, Ruby, Lon, Nette and I.

6/2/34 Pleasant, little windy. helped with a.m. work then went over to Mrs Dominy's few minutes. pieced some in p.m. Lulu and Frank were in p.m.

6/3/34 Pleasant in a.m. went to S.S. and church. warm in afternoon. windy in p.m. real windy at church time sprinkled some. to stormy to go to church in evening.

6/4/34 Pleasant in a.m. not quite as warm. Nette washed. I hung up the clothes. was busy in a.m. went to see Mrs Doty in p.m. Mrs Doty, Mrs Swaney, Beulah, and Clare here in even.

6/5/34 Warm and windy. Nette helped with Mrs Berry's washing. I done our ironing, then went to town on errand. was home in evening Mrs Dominy was over a while after supper.

6/6/34 A windy bad day. and warm. ironed some for Mrs Kelley. went to our class party at Mrs Reeves in p.m. Clara was here in evening. Nette went to McDonald with the Mullens.

6/7/34 not quite so windy, little cooler. had nice rain about nine o'clock. we finished Mrs Kelley's ironing in a.m. I went down town on errand in a.m. was home in afternoon. worked with pieces.

6/8/34 Windy, cleaned the bedroom, swept and dusted. went to see Mrs Franklin a while in p.m. was alone in evening. Nette went on a picnic for Mrs Jenning last evening Mrs Doty and Clara here in evening. I wasent alone.

6/9/34 Pleasant. we were busy in forenoon. was over to Ruby's a while in a.m. cut out pieces in p.m. went over to see Mrs Giles a

while. rode down town in evening with Mrs Kelley.

6/10/34 Childrens Day. Pleasant. went to S.S. had a splendid programme for children's day. rested and wrote in p.m. went to church in evening.

6/11/34 Pleasant but little warm. we washed by ourselves. put in a quilt in p.m. for Mrs Fred Snyder. Nette got dinner over to Mrs Kelley's. we ate over there.

6/12/34 Windy and warm. Nette helped Mrs Berry's girl wash. I ironed some for Mrs Kelley. was busy all a.m. quilted some in p.m. Had a bad wind and dust storm about 5 o'clock.

6/13/34 Some cloudy, finished Mrs Kelley's ironing in a.m. then quilted some in p.m. I went over to Mrs Dominy's few minutes in a.m. threatened rain toward night, but dident.

6/14/34 Some cloudy. we done our ironing in a.m. I quilted some in a.m. went to aid at the church in afternoon. Nette helped at Temple in p.m. and evening. Clara here in evening. had good rain about nine in evening.

6/15/34 Cloudy and cool. I quilted some in a.m. and p.m. had another good rain in evening. Nette went to see Mrs Mullen, in evening. I was home alone.

6/16/34 Some cloudy, pleasant. we cleaned up the house some. I quilted little in a.m. we both quilted in afternoon. Lulu was in. blew up in evening, rained some.

6/17/34 Cool, I went to S.S. and church. rested some after dinner then wrote letter to Audry. we went to church in evening.

6/18/34 Pleasant. Nette washed over with Ruby. I hung up the clothes, then quilted some. we both quilted in p.m. I worked out side a while after supper.

6/19/34 Some windy. real warm in p.m. we done our ironing in a.m. then quilted some. I picked a few cherries over at Ruby's. we quilted in p.m. Mrs Doty come and quilted.

6/20/34 Pleasant, not so warm. quilted some in a.m. went over to Mrs Dominy's few minutes. we quilted in p.m. Mrs Doty come. I went to see Mrs Reeves in evening.

6/21/34 Some windy and warm. we ironed some for Mrs Kelley, and quilted. Mrs Doty come in a.m. and p.m. we quilted in p.m. Nette called on Mrs Mullen's sister in law. Nette and I went to see Mrs Reeves in evening. had good rain.

6/22/34 Warm Nette made a cake, we finished Mrs Kelley's ironing. Mrs Doty come and quilted some in a.m. we quilted some in p.m. had Mrs Berry, her mother and Ruby in for coffee and cake. I went to see Lucy in even.

6/23/34 Warm. we quilted some in a.m. and p.m. then put the quilt up. Mrs Doty, I went with her up to Mr and Mrs Madsen's Golden Wedding. Mrs Dominy over few minutes. I walked home with her.

6/24/34 Warm and windy. went to S.S. was no preaching. Nette went over to Christian church they had Children's programme. Sadie Jones, husband and little girl stopped few minutes on way to Minden.

6/25/34 Warm. we washed in a.m. quilted some then finished it a little after two. I cut out some pieces and pieced on my wedding ring. Mrs Dominy over in evening. I walked home with her.

6/26/34 Warm and windy. we done little cleaning. then I went to town on few errands. Mrs Doty stopped on her way up to Mrs Swaney's

6/27/34 Warm. we ironed some for Mrs Kelley in a.m. went to Mr Heatons funeral in

p.m. Mrs Dominy was here in evening.
6/28/34 Warm and windy. finished Mrs K. ironing after dinner. Lulu Minney come in and we went home with her. acted like rain in evening, but only sprinkled.
6/29/34 Warm. helped some with the work. we went down to John Minney's for dinner. had a nice time and good dinner. I pieced some on my wedding ring.
6/30/34 Fine early in a.m. but warm later. helped some with the work. we come home in p.m. with Lulu. in evening rode some with Mrs Kelley.
7/1/34 Pleasant early, but real warm later in the day. went to S.S. and church. was a long afternoon. went to church in even.
7/2/34 Monday Real warm. we washed by ourselves. we went to Mr. Brownings funeral in p.m. the last old soldier in the county. Pleasant, we done quite a big washing.
7/3/34 Another warm day. we done our ironing in a.m. I went over to Ruby's a few minutes. Clara over in evening. we took a little walk. warmest day yet.
7/4/34 Not quite so warm. we done some of Mrs Kelley's ironing in a.m. Thorne, Mary and girls come and suprised us about two thirty. we had picnic supper on Mrs Kelley's porch. Thorne went back that evening. Mary and girls staying till Sun.
7/5/34 not so warm. Nette chairman of Lions dinner I went down and helped. got along fine. got home about three. had a bad dust storm little later. not much rain. I went to see Mrs Doty in even. stoped at Mrs Dominy's & Mrs Reeves.
7/6/34 Wind in north, quite cool. cleaned up the house some in a.m. then finished Mrs Kelley's ironing after dinner. Mrs Dominy and I went to see Mrs Franklin in even.
7/7/34 Pleasant. finished cleaning up, then got dinner. had Mary and girls eat with us. Lulu was here in evening. Nette went to show with Lonnie.
7/8/34 Sunday A very warm day. went to S.S. and church. Nette and I ate dinner with Mrs Kelley, Ruth, Lonnie, Mary and girls. in p.m. went Bebe Walker's funeral. went to church in even.
7/9/34 Another warm day. Nette and I done Mrs Berry's washing, done ours also. dident do much the rest of the day.
7/10/34 Warm. we done our ironing. in p.m. tied the silk slumber robe Aunt Nancy made. Clara was over in evening, we went to see Mrs Doty.
7/11/34 Warm. ironed some for Mrs Kelley in a.m. I went to class party in p.m. at Mrs Mortons. Nette and I went with Mrs Kelley to the lake. nice little ride.
7/12/34 Real warm again. finished Mrs K. ironing. I went to town to get muslin and pink and green print to join wedding ring. Clara was over. Nette and I went to see Mrs Reeves.
7/13/34 Another very warm day. we cleaned up the house some, I went to town about ten. a meeting about paving. worked some on wedding ring in p.m. to warm to do any thing.
7/14/34 Another warm day. we cleaned up the house some. dident do much. Lulu was here in p.m. Mrs Doty here in evening.
7/15/34 Sunday Another very warm day. Harry, Ann, John and Cora got here about eight o'clock. Harry and Ann stopped at Glenn's. Nette and I took John and Cora to the Air Line Cafe for dinner. to warm to cook. they started home about 8
7/16/34 Another warm day. we done Mrs Berry's washing and ours this a.m. Lucy Wallace and Manda Browning called to see

us about noon. Mrs Dominy over in evening.
7/17/34 Still warm. we done our ironing. I sewed some in a.m. went to see Lucy few minutes and stopped at Mrs Dominy's in forenoon. Clara over in evening. I worked on quilt. cut out some pieces.
7/18/34 A very warm day. I sewed some in a.m. went to see Lucy few minutes and stopped at Mrs Dominy's in forenoon. Clara over in evening. I worked on quilt. cut out some pieces.
7/19/34 Another very warm day. I done some of Mrs Kelley's ironing. Nette helped at the church, Lions dinner. dident do much in p.m. the heat about got me. Mrs Gulzow visited with us in evening.
7/20/34 Another hot day. we finished Mrs Kelley's ironing. I soure in p.m. Mrs Dominy was over in evening. I went home with her, then Clara and I went to see Mrs Reeves. Nette went to show.
7/21/34 Still very warm. we cleaned up the house Nette made an angel food cake. I finished the slumber robe in p.m. Nette and I went to the show in evening with Mrs Berry and her mother.
7/22/34 Sunday. A very warm day I went to S.S. but was no church, Dr Plantz away. the heat just about got me today. we were home all p.m. and evening. looked like rain, but only sprinkled.
7/23/34 Not quite so warm. we done Mrs Berry's washing and ours this a.m. I went to a meeting to see about paving. mended some stockings in p.m. had lots of company after supper. Mrs Earl Howard was in to see us.
7/24/34 Not quite so warm. we ironed some. I had to go to my office building. think have rented it. went to office building again after supper.
7/25/34 Not quite so warm. dident do much in a.m. Clara was over, I went home with her a while. in p.m. Nette and I started to work on Cora's quilt. I cut out the pieces to fill in.
7/26/34 Cloudy, quite pleasant. Mrs Doty come to help on Cora's quilt. Was here all day. Clara over in evening. she and Nette went to social. Mrs Hauptman here in evening.
7/27/34 Cloudy, rained a little. Pleasant in a.m. Mrs Doty come in a.m. helped me with the quilt. we worked a while in p.m. then we went up to town on little business. got back just noon. dident do much in p.m. Lulu was in . I went over to Ruby's before supper.
7/28/34 Pleasant in a.m. then got warm, helped with work, then went to town on little business. got back just noon. dident do much in p.m. Lulu was in. I went over to Ruby's before supper.
7/29/34 Sunday Cool in a.m. early, but very warm in p.m. I went to S.S. then come home went to Christian church. I was home all p.m. and evening. Nette went for a walk.
7/30/34 Another warm day. we done Mrs Berry's washing and ours. Clara was over in p.m. and evening. she cut some pieces in p.m. and evening. I done a few odd jobs.
7/31/34 A very warm day. we done our ironing. I went up to Cady's few minutes in a.m. home all p.m. done little sewing. went over to Mrs Dominy's while in evening.
8/1/34 Pleasant in a.m. warm in p.m. we done few odd jobs in a.m. in p.m. we had our S.S. class party at Mrs Dominy's. she asked me over for dinner. Mrs Reeves was there for dinner. Henry, Clara, Claud and Glenn Martin come to see us in p.m. we had lunch together with Mrs Kelley, M.E. and Ruth on Mrs Kelley porch. had nice time.
8/2/34 Nice early. but warm later. I went to town on few errands in a.m. then went to see

Lucy. worked some on Cora's quilt. Mrs Morton, Mrs Dominy, and Mrs Nickols here in p.m.
8/3/34 Another warm day. we done Mrs Kelley's ironing in a.m. I finished getting Cora's quilt together in p.m. Mrs Dominy, and Clara come over in evening, we went to hear band concert.
8/4/34 Warm, we cleaned up the house. then I went over to see Ruby. she is down in bed. worked some on wedding ring in p.m. Clara over in a.m. and evening. Nette and Mrs Berry went to show.
8/5/34 Sunday. Another warm day. went to S.S. and church. rested in p.m. wrote to Bro John. went to hear the male quartette from Salina in evening, at our church.
8/6/34 Still warm. we washed. I went to see Ruby a few minutes. Clara over a while in a.m. I went to see Mrs Franklin in evening.
8/7/34 Primary. Warm. we ironed. I went to court house to vote. Nette on the board. she went about twelve. I went over to Ruby's a while in p.m. Clara was over. Mrs Berry and I went to band concert.
8/8/34 Warm. I dident do much in a.m. Nette was late getting home. dident get up early. Clara was over in p.m. I dident go any place all day.
8/9/34 Warm. Nette helped with Lions dinner I ironed some of Mrs Kelley's clothes. went over to Mrs Dominy's few minutes, and over to Ruby's. Nette and I went to see Mrs Reeves and Orpha in even.
8/10/34 Not quite as warm. we finished Mrs Kelley's ironing in a.m. Nette went to town to see Dr Seisure, and I went to see Ruby. We were home in afternoon, Clara was over in evening. I walked home with her.
8/11/34 Not quite so warm. we cleaned up the house. Nette went to town. we were busy most of a.m. had an early dinner. I sewed on quilt in p.m. had Frank and Lulu here in p.m.
8/12/34 Pleasant in a.m. plenty warm by noon. I went to S.S. and church. heard a good sermon. had a big dust storm in p.m. sprinkled a little. went to church in evening. sprinkled just after got home.
8/13/34 warm. we washed. dident do much in p.m. Mrs Dominy here few minutes in afternoon. I was home all day and evening. good rain about 9 p.m.
8/14/34 Warm. we done our ironing. I went to court house to see about my taxes. dident do much in p.m. Nette packing and getting read to go to Fairmont. we went over to Mrs Dominy in even had another good rain.
8/15/34 Not quite so warm. Nette made 2 apple pies, dident do any extra work. we ate dinner over to Mrs Kelley's. Thorne, Mary and girls come about noon. Thorne went back that p.m. Mary and girls stayed. Nette started this p.m. for Fairmont.
8/16/34 Pleasant. had little more rain last night. I done part of Mrs Kelley's ironing. ate dinner at Mrs Kelley's. Ruby was over few minutes in p.m. Clara and I took little walk in evening.
8/17/34 Warm. finished Mrs Kelley's ironing. then went over to Ruby's few minutes to see Patrice. Mrs Dominy come over in p.m. to cut few pieces. rained some last night.
8/18/34 Pleasant. I done some of my work then helped Mary with dinner over to Mrs Kelley's. Henry and Clara Martin and two oldest boys were there for dinner. I went down town with Mary in even— Mrs Nickols come in to see me.
8/19/34 Cool. went to S.S. and church. Mrs Kelley and girls. Mary and girl went out Bill's. then from there on home. Thorne come

after them. I went to church in evening. Mrs Swaney was here.

8/20/34 Warm. some windy. we washed. I went over to see Mrs Franklin while in p.m. pieced some on quilt. went over to Mrs Dominy's after supper.

8/21/34 Pleasant. done my ironing. went up to Cady's few minutes. sewed some in p.m. Mrs Dominy was here a while.

8/22/34 Cool north wind. done some of Mrs Kelley's ironing. was busy all a.m. went to see Lucy a while in afternoon, then stopped to see Mrs Dominy few minutes. was home in evening. sprinkled in a.m.

8/23/34 Cool north wind. done some more ironing for Mrs Kelley. in p.m. went over to Mrs Allen's to have my dress fitted. then went to Lucy's and Mrs Gaines, neither one at home. went to Mrs Frye's in evening, to aid meeting.

8/24/34 Real cool all a.m. and part of afternoon. finished Mrs Kelley's ironing. went to town done little trading. was home in p.m. worked on quilt. home in even.

8/25/34 Pleasant. done up my Sat work. then went and mailed letter and paper to Nette. sewed some in p.m. went for a ride with Mr and Mrs Barry. then stopped down town with Mrs B. Ada Gaunt was here in p.m.

8/26/34 Pleasant. quite warm in p.m. went to S.S. and church. rested after dinner. Mrs Dominy was here a while. I went with her to see Mrs Nickols. went to church in evening.

8/27/34 Pleasant. I washed. Mrs Nickols was here a few minutes. I worked on quilt in p.m. went after mail. got letter from Mira went to see Mrs Giles in evening.

8/28/34 Pleasant. done my little ironing. went over to see Ruby a few minutes they got home last nite. then went to town to get some meat. Mrs Dominy here few minutes in p.m.

8/29/34 Warm, windy and dusty. Ruby over in a.m. a while. I went to town on few errands. ironed some for Mrs Kelley in p.m. Mrs Berry was in a while. I went to see Mrs Franklin in evening.

8/30/34 Pleasant, but warm. I ironed some more for Mrs Kelley. went to see Ruby little while. mended some in p.m. Mrs Berry and I went to band concert in evening.

8/31/34 Warm during the day. I finished Mrs Kelley's ironing. Ruby was over. I wrote to Mira in p.m. we had a good rain in p.m. was cooler after rain.

9/1/34 Pleasant. done little cleaning. went to town in a.m. sewed on quilt in afternoon. Frank and Lulu were here. Clara come over after supper. she Mrs Berry and I went to town.

9/2/34 Cloudy and cool. went to S.S. and church. sprinkled as went to church. rained when come home. Clara come over in a.m. we had nice visit. ate lunch together. then went to church. was cool

9/3/34 Cloudy and cool in a.m. warmed up later sun come out. we washed. I brought Mrs Berry's clothes in and folded. went to P.O. worked some on quilt. went to see Mrs Reeves and Orpha in evening.

9/4/34 Pleasant. A fine day. made six quarts of dill pickles. went to town twice. made 2 peach pies, got dinner for Mrs Kelley. ate dinner with them, then washed the dishes. worked on my quilt.

9/5/34 Cool and windy. ironed some in a.m. went to town in a.m. got dinner for Mrs K. rested a while then got ready and went to S.S. class party at Mrs Littell's. had nice time. Clara over in evening.

9/6/34 Cool. went to town on little business, paid some bills. got dinner for Mrs Kelley. ironed some in p.m. Mrs Dominy over a while in p.m. Clara here in evening. I went to see Mrs Franklin after supper.

9/7/34 Pleasant, I finshed Mrs Kelley's ironing then got dinner for her. come home to take a rest, and Nette come. so we visited some. then I went with Clara over to Ruby's to get some pieces.

9/8/34 Some cloudy, wind come up in a.m. blew quite bad all p.m. we cleaned up the house. Nette made a cake. worked on quilt in p.m. was home in evening. Nette went to the show. I had four callers in evening.

9/9/34 Cloudy, cool and rainy. went to S.S. & church. had pot luck dinner and programme in p.m. got home about four thirty, was no evening service. Mrs Berry visited with us in evening. A big day at the church. every member Sun.

9/10/34 Pleasant. we washed. I made pepper hash. Nette went to Quinter with Mary Gerald in p.m. I went over to Mrs Dominy's a while in p.m. Clara come over in evening, we went to see Mrs Reeves. got dinner for Mrs Kelley.

9/11/34 I got dinner for Mrs Kelley. worked some on quilt in p.m. had picnic in back yard for Nette birthday. Mrs Kelley and family. The Berry family, Nette and I. had nice time. Clara & I took a walk. An ideal day. Nette cleaned oil stove.

9/12/34 Another fine day. Nette ironed some in a.m. I got dinner for Mrs Kelley. was real tired when got through. laid down part of p.m. was alone in evening. sewed a while went to bed early.

9/13/34 We ironed some in a.m. then started to put Cora's quilt in the frames. I got dinner for Mrs Kelley. we finished putting quilt in frames in p.m. brought it home from Mrs Kelley's. Nette went to aid at Mrs Bastians. Real warm in p.m.

9/14/34 Pleasant in a.m. clouded up about noon, and got real cool. we finished the ironing. John and Cora come while we were eating dinner. we just visited in p.m. went to see Glenn & Lucille Jones few minutes after supper. then come home and visited some more.

9/15/34 Real cool. John and Cora started home about 7:30 we done up the work. I made some fried cakes. was busy all a.m. worked on quilt in p.m. we were both home in evening. Clara was over a while.

9/16/34 Cool in a.m. warmed up in p.m. I went to S.S. and church. after dinner rested a while, then wrote to Oledine. went to church in evening. Nette went out to Daisy Guy's.

9/17/34 Pleasant a while in a.m. then wind raised. Nette washed. I dident do much in a.m. got dinner for Mrs Kelley. in p.m. finished my wedding ring quilt. Nette went to Oberlin in evening. I went to see Lucy a while.

9/18/34 Pleasant, warmed up. Clara here in a.m. we got the quilt down. quilted some in a.m. Nette helped me with Mrs Kelley's dinner. in p.m. we went to see Bertie McIrvin, then quilted some when got back. Mrs Dominy was here.

9/19/34 Pleasant, warm in a.m. clouded up in p.m. little cooler. we ironed some. I got dinner for Mrs Kelley. washed my hair in p.m. Clara and Mrs Dominy were both here in p.m. quilted some.

9/20/34 Cold north wind. finished the ironing. quilted some in p.m. I got dinner for Mrs K. Nette went to help dress chickens. I sewed some in p.m. our S.S. class had surprise on Mrs Scott and new husband. had nice time.

9/21/34 Cool in a.m. but warmed up. we finished Mrs Kelley's ironing in a.m. quilted some in p.m. I went to hear Governor Sandon speak in p.m. Nette helped at Temple. got dinner for Mrs Kelley.

9/22/34 Pleasant. done up our Sat's work, then I made some Chille Sauce. Thorne and family come about eleven thirty. quilted some in p.m. had quite a little company.

9/23/34 Warm, but cloudy and gloomy most all day. went to S.S. and church. we ate dinner at Mrs Kelley's in p.m. Mrs K, Mary, Nette, Mary E.K. and I went over to C.C.C. camp. went to church in even.

9/24/34 We washed, Mrs Berry's and ours. I got dinner for Mrs Kelley. quilted some in p.m. Some cloudy and windy. but a fair wash day.

9/25/34 Cloudy, cold and gloomy. I quilted some in p.m. Nette done our ironing. I quilted in a.m. then got dinner for Mrs Kelley. was home in evening. Nette went to see Mrs Mullen.

9/26/34 Cool but pleasant. frosted last night. I quilted some in p.m. ironed in a.m. got dinner for Mrs Kelley. went to see Mrs Franklin in p.m. and went to see Clara & Allie.

9/27/34 Cool but pleasant. we cleaned our bedroom. I got dinner for Mrs Kelley. quilted some in p.m. Nette and I went to see Mrs Reeves and Orpha in evening.

9/28/34 Cloudy and cool in a.m. but was fine in p.m. we finished Mrs Kelley's ironing in a.m. I got dinner for her. mended some in p.m. and quilted. went to see Mrs Gaines after supper.

9/29/34 Pleasant. done up work. then took things out of big box. I got dinner for Mrs Kelley. was busy all a.m. we quilted in p.m. Ann Jones was here. Clara and I went to see Mrs Mullen.

9/30/34 An ideal day from start to finish. Clara and I went with Mrs Frye & Marion to Colby to hear Bishop Mead. got back at one 30 rested and wrote some in p.m. & evening.

10/1/34 Another nice day. we washed. I got dinner for Mrs Kelley. quilted some in p.m. Nette went to see Mrs Mullen in evening. I went to see Mrs Nickols.

10/2/34 Not quite as nice as yesterday. we done our ironing. Nette helped me with dinner for Mrs Kelley. we quilted in p.m. Clara was over. Mrs Berry, Nette and I went to the show.

10/3/34 A disagreeable day. windy and dusty. done part of Mrs Kelley's ironing. Mrs Jennings and Ruby was here in a.m. I got dinner for Mrs Kelley. Nette went with me to S.S. class party at Mrs Reeves.

10/4/34 Pleasant, we finished Mrs Kelley's ironing Nette helped me get dinner for Mrs K. we quilted in p.m. Mirth Heaten and little girl were here in p.m.

10/5/34 Another nice day. was little windy in p.m. I made fruit cake we got dinner for Mrs K. Lulu was in. we quilted in a.m. and p.m. I went up to Cady's few minutes in evening.

10/6/34 Fine in a.m. some wind a little later. Nette made 3 pumpkin pies for Ruby. we done up our work then went on little picnic. Clara, Mrs Swaney, Mrs Berry, Nette and I out south on the rocks. quilted some in p.m. Lulu was in.

10/7/34 Pleasant, went to S.S. and church. after dinner rested a while, then wrote to cousin Idie. Nette went riding with the Mullens. we went to church in evening. she got back just in time.

10/8/34 Pleasant in a.m. but wind raised, was dusty and bad. we washed. I got dinner for Mrs Kelley. we quilted in p.m. Clara was over in evening a while.

10/9/34 Windy and bad all day. we done our ironing. in a.m. I quilted some. got dinner for Mrs Kelley. we both quilted in p.m. and while in evening.

10/10/34 Pleasant. we done some of Mrs K. ironing. I quilted some in a.m. went to town on an errand, stopped at Mrs Dominy's. quilted some in a.m. then all p.m. Mrs C Brown come and quilted in p.m.

10/11/34 Pleasant, finished Mrs Kelley's ironing. got dinner for Mrs Kelley, quilted some in p.m. we went to see Mrs Reeves and Orpha in evening.

10/12/34 Pleasant in a.m. then wind raised. quilted some in a.m. then got dinner for Mrs Kelley. put in a long p.m. quilting. we quilted some after supper.

10/13/34 Pleasant, but little windy. we finished Cora's quilt about ten twenty in a.m. then cleaned up the house. Nette made a cake and made some soap. I done little mending in p.m. Frank and Lulu were here.

10/14/34 Cloudy and rainy looking. did sprinkle. went to S.S. and church. Jesse and Cady Briney ate dinner with us. rested and wrote some. went to church in evening.

10/15/34 A bad day. windy and dusty. we washed. was bad to hang up the clothes. Nette helped at Temple in p.m. and evening. I wrote some to Mrs Roberts in p.m.

10/16/34 Pleasant, little cool. we done our ironing, I went over to Mrs Dominy's few minutes in a.m. I got dinner for Mrs Kelley.

10/17/34 Cloudy and stormy acting. we done all of Mrs Kelley's ironing in a.m. Ada Gaunt was here in p.m. had other company. Nette and I went to Mrs Reeves for supper.

10/18/34 Cloudy and misty. the ladies aid went out to Mrs B.M. Sawer's for all day meeting. Pot luck dinner. had business meeting and election of officers.

10/19/34 Pleasant. we dident do much but regular work. I got dinner for Mrs Kelley. felt quite tired. Mrs Doty was here in p.m. I sewed binding on Cora's quilt. I went to see Mrs Nickols in evening.

10/20/34 Real windy and dusty in a.m. we cleaned up the house some. got the heater set up. Lulu & Frank here in p.m. I got dinner for Mrs Kelley. sewed some on Cora's quilt.

10/21/34 A peach of a day. went to S.S. and church rested a while after dinner. had company all p.m. Mrs Nickols come, then Mrs Allen, then Mrs Dominy. we went to church in evening.

10/22/34 Pleasant. we washed, was nice to dry the clothes. I got dinner for Mrs Kelley. we put Ruby's wedding ring quilt in the frames in p.m. the Kelley's, Berry's, Nette and I had picnic in evening.

10/23/34 Windy and dusty. we done our ironing I went over to Mrs Dominy's few minutes. I got dinner for Mrs Kelley. we quilted in p.m. Clara was in few minutes. Nette and I went to see Lucy.

10/24/34 Nice in a.m. then wind raised. we ironed some for Mrs Kelley. I got dinner for her. then we quilted in p.m. Ruby come over and quilted some. finished Cora's quilt.

10/25/34 Pleasant, little windy. we finished Mrs Kelley's ironing. I got dinner for her. we quilted in p.m. Ruby and Christine come over in p.m. and quilted. Nette and I went to Mrs Reeves in evening.

10/26/34 Pleasant. I done little mending, then quilted some in a.m. and p.m. got dinner for Mrs Kelley. Clara over in evening, we took little walk. Jesse Gaunt 27 years old today.

10/27/34 Pleasant, helped clean up the house. quilted about an hour. got dinner for Mrs Kelley. rested a while, then quilted till

after five o'clock. was real tired, after supper. wrote letter to Aunt Elda.

10/28/34 Cool in a.m. but pleasant, warmed up. I went to S.S. and church. when got home John and Cora were here. they took us to Air Line for dinner. They started home just before five.

10/29/34 Cool in a.m. but warmed up. we washed I got dinner for Mrs Kelley. Mrs Nickols here a while in p.m. I quilted some in p.m. and evening. Nette was gone all evening.

10/30/34 Pleasant. we done our ironing. I got dinner for Mrs Kelley. rested a while then quilted till about five, then went out and raked leaves. Nette gone again this evening.

10/31/34 Pleasant, we done our ironing yesterday. part of Mrs Kelley's today. I got dinner for Mrs K then quilted some in p.m. and evening. Clara and I went up to bond fire last night.

11 /1/34 A bad day, windy, dusty and cool. we quilted some in a.m. finished Mrs K. ironing in p.m. then put comfortor in frames for Mr. McIntosh. quilted some. I went to see Mrs Reeves and Orpha.

11/2/34 Cool, windy and dusty. we finished tieing that comfortor and tied another one. Ruby helped us some. I fixed one around the edge in the evening.

11/3/34 Cool and windy today. I helped clean up the house, then fixed the other comfortor around the edge. cleaned up some over to Mrs Kelley's in p.m. then sewed some.

11/4/34 Pleasant in early a.m. then about noon, wind and dust was terrible for a while. went down toward night. I went to S.S. and church in a.m. then to church again in evening.

11/5/34 Cloudy and cool in a.m. then cleared off toward noon, was real nice. we washed, had an early dinner, rested, then quilted in p.m.

11/6/34 Election. Pleasant, sun real warm in middle of day. Nette done our ironing. I quilted some in a.m. got dinner for Mrs Kelley, quilted in p.m. Ruby was over. went to court house in evening. Nette & I come home at 9:30.

11/7/34 Pleasant most of day. quilted in a.m. got dinner for Mrs Kelley. went to S.S. class party in p.m. at Mrs Morton's had a nice time. quilted some after supper.

11/8/34 Cool in a.m. but warmed up fine by p.m. we quilted some in a.m. then went to ladies aid in p.m. at Mrs Frye's. Nette and I served the lunch. I took some over to Lucy.

11/9/34 Cool but pleasant. we done Mrs Kelley's ironing this a.m. I got dinner for Mrs K. Nette helped me. I went to see Mrs Giles and Mrs. Franklin in p.m. quilted some in p.m. and evening.

11/10/34 Pleasant. helped clean up the house, then quilted some in p.m. Nette had some wood chopped. we put some in cellar and coal house.

11/11/34 Pleasant, went to S.S. and church. after dinner rested a while. went to church in evening.

11/12/34 Cold in a.m. but warmed up by noon. we washed, then quilted in p.m. Clara come over about three, she quilted some. Nette, Clara and I went to Mrs Doty's for supper, Clara treated with oysters and trimmings.

11/13/34 Cool in a.m. then warmed up. we ironed, then quilted some in a.m. and p.m. Nette went to help at the church supper for S.S. board. I went over about six to help with the dishes.

11/14/34 Pleasant. done part of Mrs Kelley's

ironing. then quilted some. Mrs Doty come in a.m. quilted until about five. Clara was here for dinner. she quilted some in p.m. Ruby was over and quilted.

11/15/34 Cool in a.m. warmed up later in day. ironed some more for Mrs Kelley. Frank and Lulu came in and papered the dining room. got through about six. Nette and I quilted in p.m. I went to Mrs Reeves in evening.

11/16/34 Cloudy part of the day. Nette ironed some more for Mrs Kelley. I quilted. we both quilted in p.m. we quilted some in even.

11/17/34 Cloudy part of the day. rained a nice shower toward night. we finished Ruby's quilt about ten o'clock. then cleaned up the house. I went to see Mrs Doty after supper.

11/18/34 Some cloudy. I went to S.S. and church. rested after dinner then went down to Mrs Doty, took her some S.S. papers. Mrs Dominy was over a while Clara come over and went to church with us. Thorne was here today.

11/19/34 Cool this a.m. but warmed up later. we washed clothes dried nice. I got an early dinner. rested a while. then went over to Mrs Dominy's, she went with me to see Madison Turner.

11/20/34 Cloudy and rainy. we done our ironing in a.m. then in p.m. put Mrs DeWort's quilt in the frames.

11/21/34 Mira Birthday. Cool and cloudy most all day. we ironed some for Mrs Kelley then in p.m. we commenced to quilt. Mary & girls and Ruby here in evening. we quilted.

11/22/34 Pleasant but cool. Nette helped with Lions dinner. I quilted in a.m. then went to Mrs Madsen's funeral in p.m. then went up to Mrs Jennings to Aid.

11/23/34 Pleasant but cool. we done some more ironing for Mrs Kelley. quilted some in a.m. and afternoon.

11/24/34 Foggy and cloudy most all day. quite cool. we cleaned up the house. then quilted some in a.m. and p.m. I went to see Mrs Doty after supper, she wasent home. so went to see Mrs Reeves.

11/25/34 Cloudy and cool this a.m. but cleared off about noon. went to S.S. and church. after dinner rested a while. Elmer and Mrs Mullen come and took Nette and I a ride.

11/26/34 Cool in a.m. but warmed up later in day. we washed, was noon when got through. we quilted in p.m. Mrs Doty was here a while. Clara was here in evening. was raining when went to bed.

11/27/34 Ground white with snow in a.m. not so very cold. we done our ironing quilted some in a.m. I got dinner for Mrs Kelley. we quilted in p.m. Nette and Mrs Berry went to the show.

11/28/34 Cloudy most of day. cool. we ironed some for Mrs Kelley. I quilted in p.m. & evening. I got dinner for Mrs Kelley.

11/29/34 Thanksgiving. Cloudy. snowed most all day. we went to the church at seven thirty a.m. for communion. Mrs Berry and children, Nette and I had our dinner together. had a very pleasant time.

11/30/34 Cool, sun shone most of day. we quilted in a.m. and p.m.

12/1/34 Pleasant but cool. we finished Mrs K ironing. cleaned up the house, then quilted some. put the quilt away early, then I done little other sewing.

12/2/34 Cloudy and snowing. went to S.S. and church. still snowing at four o'clock. I wrote to Hazel in p.m. we dident go to church in evening to cold and snowy.

12/3/34 Pleasant but cold. we washed. brought machine in kitchen. hung some of the clothes up in house. I got dinner for Mrs Kelley. we put baby quilt in frames for Ruby.

12/4/34 Pleasant, but cold. we done our ironing. I got dinner for Mrs Kelley. we quilted some in a.m. and p.m. I went over to Mrs Dominy's to see about quilt pattern. Ruby was over in evening.

12/5/34 Cloudy in a.m. but cleared off nice. quilted some in a.m. got dinner for Mrs K. we went to Madison Turner's funeral in p.m. Nette went to Mrs Dillon's in evening.

12/6/34 Some cloudy. snowed for a few minutes about noon. we ironed some for Mrs Kelley, and I got dinner for her. in p.m. I went to Mrs Frye's for our S.S. class party. turned colder toward night.

12/7/34 Pleasant but cool. finished Mrs Kelley's ironing. we quilted in p.m. after supper I went to see Mrs Doty. then come by and stopped to see Lucy. Nette went out to Della's to party.

12/8/34 Pleasant but cool. we finished the baby quilt about ten thirty. then cleaned up the house some. I sewed in p.m. made Mona little apron.

12/9/34 Cloudy part of the day. I went to S.S. and church. rested a while after dinner, then wrote some to cousin Idie. we went to church in evening. Clara was here few minutes.

12/10/34 Cloudy part of day. was nice in a.m. then got colder then warmer again in p.m. we washed. I got dinner for Mrs Kelley. we quilted in p.m. Mrs Dominy was over a few minutes after supper.

12/11/34 Pleasant, snow melted today. we done our ironing. I got dinner for Mrs Kelley. we both quilted in p.m. Nette went to the high school play.

12/12/34 A spring like day. we quilted in a.m. and done some ironing for Mrs Kelley in p.m. I went to see Mrs Reeves and Orpha after supper. Nette went to Chapter.

12/13/34 Another pleasant day. we both quilted in a.m. I went to Aid in afternoon. Nette went a little later. we met with Mrs Plantz. we quilted some when got home. Nette went to see Mrs Mullen in even.

12/14/34 Pleasant, we quilted in forenoon and afternoon. then again after supper. put the quilt up. and done other things, rest of evening.

12/15/34 Pleasant. cleaned up the house some was busy all a.m. then, I sewed some in p.m. we went to Junior Aid tea in p.m. had oysters in evening.

12/16/34 Some cloudy and stormy looking went to S.S. and church. we went up to Cady's for dinner. had nice time. went to church in the evening.

12/17/34 Cloudy most of the day. we washed. I hung out some of the clothes I got dinner for Mrs Kelley. quilted in p.m. just real tired. Mrs Dominy here in p.m. Mrs Nickols was in.

12/18/34 Pleasant. ground white with snow. we done our ironing. I got dinner for Mrs Kelley. we quilted in a.m. p.m. and after supper. snow about all gone by evening.

12/19/34 Some cloudy. we quilted in forenoon Nette took quilt out about noon. I got dinner for Mrs Kelley. Mrs Nickols here in p.m. Nette at Mrs Kelley to a card party in even.

12/20/34 Pleasant. we done Mrs Kelley's ironing. then I got dinner for Mrs Kelley. Nette went up to high school musical then to the Temple in evening. I wrote some cards and letter

12/21/34 Like a spring day. I washed my

dress out by hand that Rodney and Irma gave me. got dinner for Mrs Kelley. in p.m. went to see Flora Turner. then we went to Mrs Reeves in evening.

12/22/34 Fine in a.m. then had a bad wind and dust storm in p.m. we cleaned up the house in a.m. I got dinner for Mrs Kelley. dident do much in p.m. went down town in evening.

12/23/34 Pleasant, little cool. went to S.S. and church. brought Clara home with me for dinner. went over to Clara's about 5 o'clock. we went to church together. then, I stayed all night with her.

12/24/34 Pleasant, but cool. I come home about 8:30. helped with washing. we went to town in p.m. to see Santa. took Mona with us. we went to the church in evening. to Christmas programme.

DECEMBER 12/25/34
Fine morning. we got up at 5 o'clock, went to the church to help get breakfast for the Carol singers. we ate dinner at Mrs Kelleys, had a fine time and good dinner. there were 15 of us. Mr Henderson, Bill H. and family. Thorne and family, Mrs Kelley and girls Nette and myself. we all went to picture show in evening.

12/26/34 Cold, just real cold. we dident do much all day. Mrs Berry and Mary ate dinner with us. then Mary asked us over there for supper. Nette went to Chapter, and I went to the show again. with the folks.

12/27/34 Not quite as cold. Thorne's folks started out to Bill's about 10:30 in p.m. I went to see Mrs Dominy and Clara and Lucy. in evening Nette and I went down to Mrs Reeves for supper.

12/28/34 Pleasant but cool. we done Mrs Kelley's ironing. I went over to Ruby's a few minutes in a.m. Nette and I were invited over there for tea in p.m. had a nice time.

12/29/34 Pleasant but cool. we cleaned up the house. I went over to Mrs Giles few minutes in a.m. wrote to John Gaunt in p.m. in evening went up to see Mrs Nickols

12/30/34 Pleasant. went to S.S. and church. went to Mrs Hemming's funeral in p.m. it was at the house. Nette and I went to the cemetery. we went to church in evening.

12/31/34 Pleasant in a.m. but wind raised, was bad for a while, then pleasant again. I washed out a few pieces. Nette helped at the temple in p.m. and even—I went to see Mrs Franklin in p.m. went to town in a.m.

January 1, 1935 A pleasant day, the whole day through. Frank and Lulu ate dinner with us. had a nice time.

1/2/35 A wonderful day. I got dinner for Mrs Kelley. in p.m. went to my S.S. class party at Mrs Gerald's Nette went out to Della Mettlers in even. I went up to Cady's.

1/3/35 Pleasant. Nette helped with Lion's dinner for me. I ironed some in a.m. and p.m. for Mrs Kelley. worked on Elizabeth Ann's apron in evening.

1/4/35 Pleasant, little cool, some cloudy. we finished Mrs K. ironing in a.m. I got dinner for Mrs K. in p.m. done some mending. Clara was here.

1/5/35 Pleasant. we cleaned up the house some. Mrs Doty here a while in p.m. Frank and Lulu were in. Clara here few minutes in evening.

1/6/35 An Ideal day. went to S.S. and church. in p.m. Mrs Walker Lily come and asked Nette and I to take a ride with her and Mrs Dexter S. Mrs Kelley went. we went to church in evening.

1/7/35 Cloudy and cool in a.m. but cleared off fine. we washed. was nice to dry clothes. I

got dinner for Mrs Kelley. went to see Clara and Mrs Dominy in p.m.

1/8/35 Pleasant. we done our ironing in a.m. I got dinner for Mrs Kelley. in p.m. we went up to Mrs Lily's. Mrs Anna Lily asked several in. I went to see Mrs Doty in evening. Nette went over to Mrs Kelley's

1/9/35 Pleasant. done Mrs Kelley's ironing. I got dinner for her. put in a comfortor for Mrs Kelley. in p.m. went to the church in even. A prisoner at the Bar

1/10/35 Pleasant. tied some on comfortor. went out to Delle Mettlers about ten. had an all day Aid meeting. had good time, and lots to eat.

1/11/35 Some cloudy. I helped do up the work. got dinner for Mrs Kelley. in p.m. we put in comfortor for her. I went up to Mrs Nickols in even. Clara over in p.m.

1/12/35 Cloudy in a.m. cleared off by p.m. we finished tieing Mrs Kelley's comfortor in p.m. Frank & Lulu were here. we dident do much cleaning.

1/13/35 Pleasant but cold. went to S.S. and church. rested a while after dinner. wrote two letters in p.m. went to see Clara. we went to church in evening.

1/14/35 Cold in a.m. warmed up later in the day. we washed. fixed Mrs Kelley's comfortor around the edge in p.m. Ruby was over a while.

1/15/35 Real cold. we ironed in a.m. in p.m. went to Mrs Andrew's funeral. after that Nette and I went to Mrs Dominy's. then I went to Mrs Gaines.

1/16/35 Cloudy and dark most of forenoon. Nette and I wrote to Jesse Gaunt. in p.m. I made Patty Chambers apron. cut out some pieces. Lillian was over. Nette gone to party at Byrle Miller's.

1/17/35 Partly cloudy. I washed and dusted the dishes in my china closet in a.m. Nette went to town. done some sewing in p.m. was alone in evening. Nette went to see Eva

1/18/35 Some cloudy and damp. I cleaned our bed-room Nette cleaned the small room. I went to see Ruby. cut and sewed some pieces in p.m. went to see Mrs Nickols in even.

1/19/35 Cold. down to zero. I helped do up the work, then went over to Mrs Dominy's few minutes. made a holder. cut out and pieced some. Ruby was over in p.m.

1/20/35 Real cold. went to S.S. and church. snowed some during the night Clara was over a while in p.m. dident got to church in evening.

1/21/35 Still real cold. but warmed up quite a lot before night. I worked with my pieces, after helped do up the work. Clara here today.

1/22/35 Pleasant, warmed up nice. we washed. the clothes got dry nice. I went to Mrs Cullison's father's funeral in p.m. then went to see Lucy.

1/23/35 Colder than yesterday. we done our ironing this a.m. then put in a quilt for Mrs Roy Briney. Mrs Dominy here this p.m.

1/24/35 Pleasant, quilted some in a.m. then went to Gertie Vincent's to Aid in afternoon. had a nice time. Nette and I went to Mrs Reeves in even.

1/25/35 Another fine day. made me think of early spring. I quilted a while then went up to Mrs Swaney's quilted in p.m. went over to Ruby's a while and cut some pieces. we went to the pie festival in even.

1/26/35 Some cloudy and cool. we done up our little work then quilted some in a.m. and p.m. put the quilt up about five o'clock. I worked some on my baby quilt.

1/27/35 Pleasant but cooler. went to S.S. and

church. we ate dinner at Mrs Kelley's. about five o'clock Mrs Swaney, Mrs Doty, Mrs Dominy & Clara come with eats and surprised me. we had a nice time.

1/28/35 A springlike day. we washed, quilted some in p.m. Lulu asked Mrs Kelley and girls, Nette and I out there for supper. had a good supper and a fine time. Lulu made me a birthday cake.

1/29/35 Another fine day. was little cooler early. I quilted some in a.m. and p.m. went over to Ruby's and up to see Cady in a.m. Clara over in p.m. I went up to Mrs Nickols in even.

1/30/35 Pleasant, I done our ironing. Nette had to got to town. I quilted some in a.m. and p.m. went to see Mrs Morton in p.m. stopped at Mrs Dominy's went to see Mrs Doty little while in evening.

1/31/35 Another nice day. Nette went to McCook with Mrs Kelley. I done up a.m. work. then quilted. was home all day. quilted in p.m.

2/1/35 Pleasant. we quilted some in a.m. then went to the Legion home for dinner. Mrs Frye invited us to pot luck dinner Auxiliary ladies were having. had nice time good dinner.

2/2/35 Another fine day. we done up our work then quilted some in a.m. and p.m. I went up to see Mrs Nickols in evening.

2/3/35 Another nice day. went to S.S. and church after dinner rested then wrote to Aunt Elda. Mrs Nickols here while in p.m.

2/4/35 Another fine day. we washed. then quilted in p.m. I went to see Mrs Doty in evening. Sun shone most all day. but real cold. I was busy all a.m. straightened around some Mrs Kelley stopped to see me.

2/5/35 Cloudy and some cooler. we ironed this a.m. I quilted a while then went up to see Cady little while. quilted again in p.m. been cloudy all day. looks stormy.

2/6/35 Cloudy and damp. quilted some in a.m. went to S.S. class party in p.m. at Mrs Mullens. 21 were there. had a nice time.

2/7/35 Cloudy and cool. helped with a.m. work. Nette helped with Lion's dinner. I went over to Mrs Allen's in a.m. quilted

some in a.m. and p.m.

2/8/35 Still cloudy and damp. we quilted in a.m. then little after dinner. took the quilt out about two o'clock. I went over to Mrs Dominy's a few minutes in p.m.

2/9/35 Still cloudy and damp. snowed a little we done up Saturday work. was busy all a.m. I emb, a tea towel in p.m. went up to see Mrs Nickols in evening.

2/10/35 Clear and pleasant. went to S.S. and church. after dinner went to Mr Madsen's funeral. took a nice long ride with Mrs Kelley. went to church in evening.

2/11/35 Cool early, but warmed up later. was a fine day. we washed. I sewed binding on quilt went over to Mrs Dominy's few minutes in p.m. and to Mrs Doty's after supper.

2/12/35 Pleasant most of the day. wind blew for while. I done the ironing. Nette made a cake. we had little surprise on Clara Bump. was her birthday.

2/13/35 Cloudy and rainy. I went over to Mrs Allen's in a.m. sewed binding down on Mrs Moors quilt sewed border on Rodney's quilt. Mrs Dominy over in a.m.

2/14/35 Cleared off again. wind and dirt bad for a while sewed quilt lining on sides this a.m. we went to Aid this p.m. at the church. to see Mrs Reeves in even.

2/15/35 Cloudy, snowed some. we cleaned the pictures and wiped the upper part of the wall in living room. in p.m. put Rodney's quilt in frames. the Lone Star. in evening we went to see Mrs Luther & Mother.

2/16/35 Cleared off, but quite cold. we cleaned up in a.m. then quilted in p.m. Ruby was over. Frank and Lulu here. I went to see Mrs Nickols.

2/17/35 Pleasant. little cool. went to S.S. and church. rested a while after dinner. wrote to Oledine. Clara here a while in p.m. we went to church in even.

2/18/35 A spring like day. we washed. rested a while after dinner, then got the quilt out and quilted. I went over to Mrs Dominy's a few minutes. Mrs Doty was here.

2/19/35 Cloudy a while in a.m. then cleared off nice. we were busy all a.m. invited in a

few to quilt in p.m. Mrs Dominy, Clara, Bell Sawer, Mrs Berry, Mrs Doty, and Ruby. Nette had lunch. had nice time. I went up to Mrs Nickols in evening.

2/20/35 Pleasant, but cooler. we ironed, then took down stove pipe and cleaned it. quilted in p.m. Nette went to party in evening. I went to see Lucy.

2/21/35 A fine a.m. just like spring. wind raised about eleven, and by twelve was terrible. was bad all p.m. to dark to work. I went with Mrs Berry to the little folks programme at grade school in a.m.

2/22/35 Pleasant, Nette and I cleaned all forenoon we quilted some in p.m. Nette went to town two or three times. Nette and Ruby had little party.

2/23/35 Pleasant, but some cloudy. Nette busy all a.m. I helped with a.m. work, then quilted some. Nette started for Fairmont on p.m. train.

2/24/35 Blowing and snowing when I got up. I went to S.S. and church. dident have either. not enough out. has been a regular blizzard all p.m.

2/25/35 Cloudy a while then the sun come out, cleared off. I was busy all a.m. doing odd jobs. had to get coal up out of basement. got quilt out and quilted some in p.m. Ruby over while in p.m.

2/26/35 I done up my work, then quilted some, rested few minutes after dinner, then quilted. Ruby come over and quilted a while. I went after the mail. warmed up some.

2/27/35 Pleasant. done up my work, then quilted some in a.m. and p.m. Ruby & Clara come and quilted in p.m. Clara stayed for supper, then we went to see Mrs Reeves and Orpha.

2/28/35 Another grand day. lots of snow disappeared. done up work. then went up to Mrs John Roberts to an all day aid meeting. pot luck dinner. had a nice time.

2/29/35 Pleasant, like spring. I done my little ironing then cleaned up the house some. busy all a.m. and part of p.m. sure tired. Clara over in p.m. and quilted. Clara and I took little walk in evening. she stayed all nite.

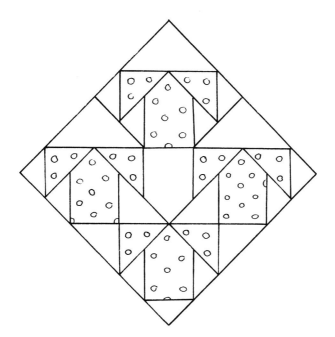

Notes

[1] Craig Miner, West of Wichita: *Settling the High Plains of Kansas, 1865–1890* (Lawrence, Kans.: University Press of Kansas, 1986), p. 134.

[2] Betty J. Savage Mills, *Calico Chronicle: Texas Women and Their Fashions 1830–1910.* (Lubbock, Texas: Texas Tech Press, 1985), p. 92.

[3] Ivy Morton Yoos, *This Is My Life* (Atwood, Kans., 1970), p. 19.

[4] Merikay Waldvogel, *Soft Covers for Hard Times: Quiltmaking & the Great Depression* (Nashville, Tenn.: Rutledge Hill Press, 1990), p. 58.

[5] Marilyn Holt, Bobbie Pray, and Dot E. Taylor, *Textile Diaries: Quilts as Cultural Markers* (Kansas State Historical Society, 1990), p. 58.

[6] Nancyann Johanson Twelker, *Women and Their Quilts: A Washington State Centennial Tribute* (Bothell, Wash.: That Patchwork Place, 1988), p. 64.

[7] Gladys Beamgard was a friend of Ida's, a member of the "M.E. Church," who as a young wife and mother spent many hours with Ida seated around a quilting frame in the church basement. A strong, erect woman, Gladys firmly and proudly stated that she had raised four "ordinary" children. Of course, Gladys would have considered herself an ordinary woman also, but when we met in 1991, in an Atwood nursing home, her pride and upright carriage revealed a unique and courageous character. In her nineties at that time, Gladys had not let blindness keep her over the years from her beloved quilting. Each morning before she had moved into the rest home, one of her boys came by her house to thread a pin cushion full of needles. With a supply of threaded needles, Gladys could stitch by touch a fine, even line.

Bibliography

Brackman, Barbara. *Clues in the Calico: A Guide to Identifying and Dating Antique Quilts.* EPM Publications, Inc., 1989.

Crews, Patricia Cox, and Ronald C. Naugle. *Nebraska Quilts and Quiltmakers.* Lincoln, Nebr.: University of Nebraska Press, 1991.

Dick, Everett. *The Sod-House Frontier: 1854–1890.* Lincoln, Nebr.: University of Nebraska Press, 1979.

Ferrero, Pat, Elaine Hedges, and Julie Silber. *Hearts and Hands: The Influence of Women & Quilts on American Society.* San Francisco: The Quilt Digest Press, 1987.

Goldman, Marilyn, and Marguerite Wiebusch. *Quilts of Indiana: Crossroads of Memories.* Bloomington, Ind.: Indiana University Press, 1991.

Hayden, Ruth Kelley. *The Time That Was.* Colby, Kans.: Colby Community College, 1973.

Holt, Marilyn, Bobbie Pray, and Dot E. Taylor. *Textile Diaries: Quilts as Cultural Markers.* Kansas State Historical Society, 1990.

Khin, Yvonne M. *The Collector's Dictionary of Quilt Names & Patterns.* Washington, D.C.: Acropolis Books Ltd., 1980.

Mills, Betty J. Savage. *Calico Chronicle: Texas Women and Their Fashions 1830–1910.* Lubbock, Texas: Texas Tech Press, 1985.

Miner, Craig. *West of Wichita: Settling the High Plains of Kansas, 1865–1890.* Lawrence, Kans.: University Press of Kansas, 1986.

Oringderff, Barbara. *True Sod.* North Newton, Kans.: Mennonite Press, Inc., 1976.

Stratton, Joanna L. *Pioneer Women: Voices from the Kansas Frontier.* New York: Simon and Schuster, 1981.

Twelker, Nancyann Johanson. *Women and Their Quilts: A Washington State Centennial Tribute.* Bothell, Wash.: That Patchwork Place, 1988.

Waldvogel, Merikay. *Soft Covers for Hard Times: Quiltmaking & The Great Depression.* Nashville, Tenn.: Rutledge Hill Press, 1990.

Woodard, Thomas K., and Blanche Greenstein. *Twentieth-Century Quilts* 1900-1950. New York: E.P. Dutton, 1988.

Yoos, Ivy Morton. *This Is My Life.* Atwood, Kans.: 1970.

Quilt Patterns

The quilts of Ida Melugin demonstrate how dynamic even the simplest of patterns can be in the hands of a talented quilter. The basic Four Patch and Nine Patch blocks become part of an interlocking, diagonal design through the use of blocks as part of the sashing. The size of sashing is given with the patterns so you can recreate this effect for yourself.

When making the blocks, start with the smallest units first. For example, in the Double Nine Patch, the small squares are joined into three rows, then the rows are sewn to form a Nine Patch. These small blocks are sewn to the plain squares in rows, then joined to form the Double Nine Patch.

When Ida Melugin "worked with pieces," she was stitching by hand. Since all the blocks feature straight edge pieces, the sewing machine could also be used. The Kansas Dugout variation of the Friendship quilt should be hand pieced since it has some inset pieces. Prepare templates by tracing the patterns directly onto translucent plastic (available at quilt shops) or by tracing onto paper and pasting to poster board.

Hand Piecing–Trace the outside line of the patterns. Cut carefully, then place the template on the wrong side of the fabric following the grainlines. Mark around the templates, using a sharp pencil. Several layers can be pinned and cut together. The 1/4 inch seam can either be estimated or marked.

A more careful method is making the templates without the seam allowance. While marking, allow at least 1/2 inch between the shapes. Cut 1/4 inch away from the lines. Join the pieces, sewing on the line.

Use a single strand of thread and a small needle and sew with small, even stitches. Begin and end the stitching 1/4 inch from the edges. Do not sew over seams; simply move them away from the line of stitching. Press the seams to one side.

Machine Piecing - Include the seam allowance on the templates. Following the grainlines, mark around the shapes on the wrong side of the fabrics. Cut several layers together, pinning first.

Sew the pieces with a 1/4 inch seam allowance, either judging by eye or marking the surface of the sewing machine. Begin and end the stitching at the edge of the pieces. It is not necessary to backstitch. When crossing other seams, place them in opposite directions. This will reduce bulk and insure a better match. Press the seams to one side. For complete instructions on making quilts, check your local fabric or quilt shop or library for current books on the subject.

Four Patch

9" block

3" x 9" sashing

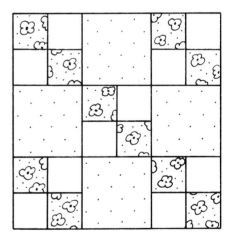

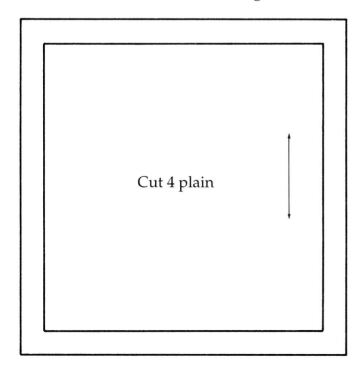

Cut 4 plain

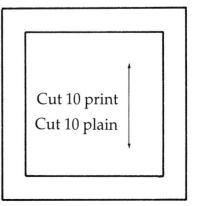

Cut 10 print
Cut 10 plain

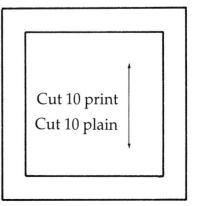

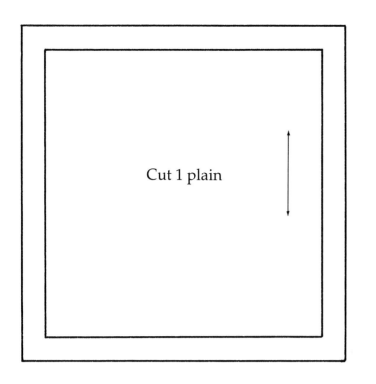

Cut 1 plain

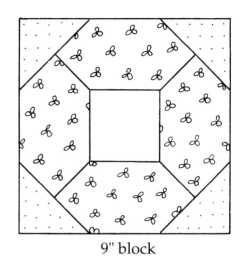

9" block

Kansas Dugout
Friendship Block

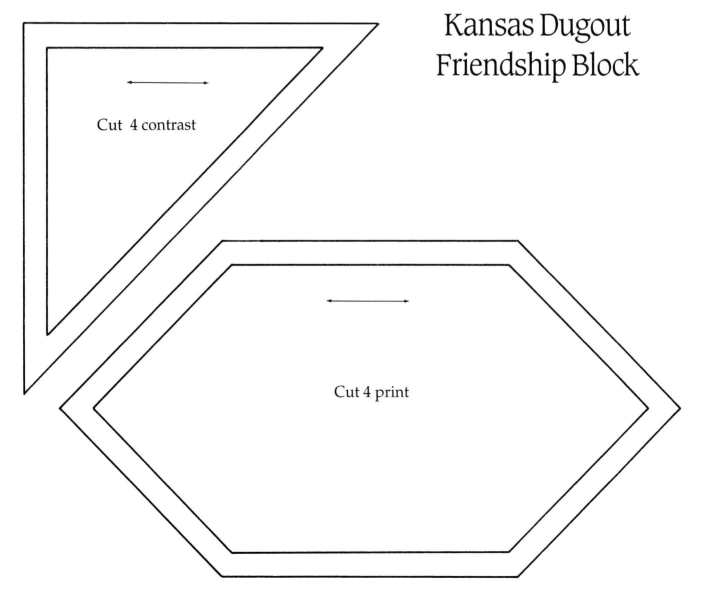

Cut 4 contrast

Cut 4 print

Puss in the Corner

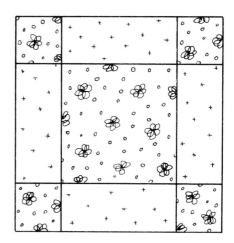

8" block

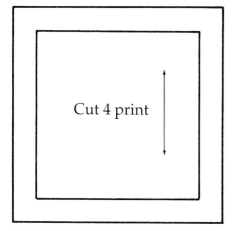

Cut 4 print

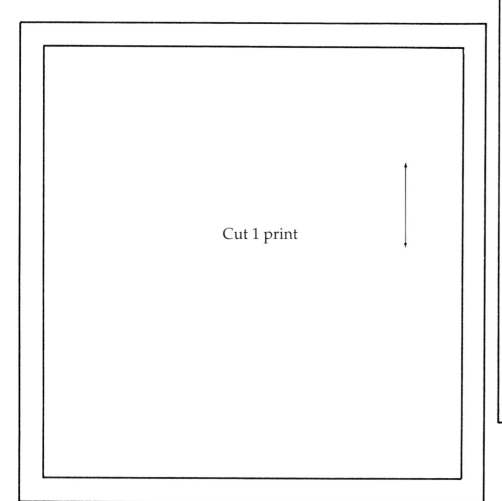

Cut 1 print

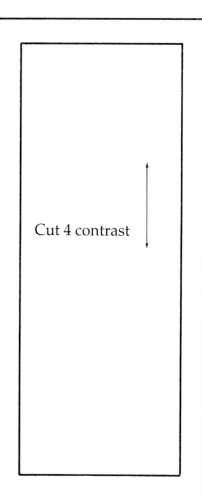

Cut 4 contrast

Friendship Block

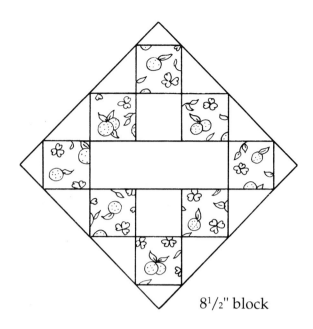

8½" block

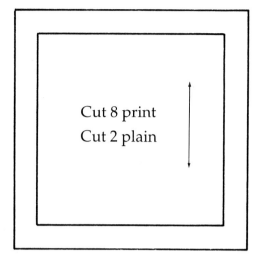

Cut 8 print
Cut 2 plain

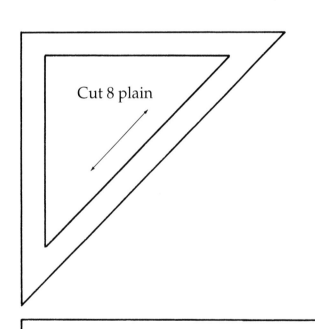

Cut 8 plain

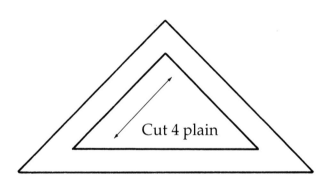

Cut 4 plain

Cut 1 plain

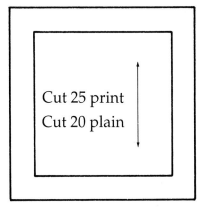

Double Nine Patch

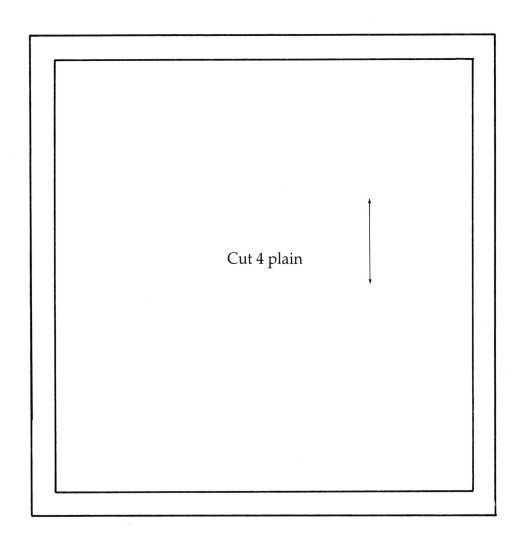

13¹/₂" block

4¹/₂ x 13¹/₂" sashing (add seams)

Cut 25 print
Cut 20 plain

Cut 4 plain

Also by Carolyn O'Bagy Davis…

Pioneer Quiltmaker

The story of Dorinda Moody Slade 1808–1895
by Carolyn O'Bagy Davis

PIONEER QUILTMAKER is the biography of a remarkable 19th-Century woman living on the isolated frontiers of Texas and Utah. Although a mother and stepmother to sixteen children, Dorinda Slade still found the time for quiltmaking, her first creative love. Many of her stunning quilts were created from cotton that she had grown, spun, woven and dyed. Dorinda's quilts and the story of her life is portrayed in *Pioneer Quiltmaker,* in over 40 color plates, illustrations and more than 25 vintage photos. Foreword contributed by Helen Young Frost, nationally known quilting teacher and author. Also included are patterns for piecing and quilting Dorinda's favorite quilts. 8 1/2" x 11"; 80 pages $17.95 plus $3.00 shipping.

Sanpete Publications • P.O. Box 85216 • Tucson, AZ 85754-5216 • (602) 622-6007